MW00563931

סדר
הגדה
של פסח
באותיות אמשטרדם

JPS Commentary on the Haggadah

To our parents,

Jean and Michael Best

and

Rachel ז״ל *and Allan Zukerman,*

who imbued us with the centrality of Torah,

importance of Israel, and

a love of the Jewish people; and to our children,

Jacob, Noah, and Ari,

to whom we strive to pass on these values.

Jane and Edward Best

JPS Commentary on the Haggadah

Historical Introduction, Translation, and Commentary

Joseph Tabory

Foreword by David Stern

The Jewish Publication Society
Philadelphia
2008 • 5768

JPS is a nonprofit educational association and the oldest and foremost publisher of Judaica in English in North America. The mission of JPS is to enhance Jewish culture by promoting the dissemination of religious and secular works, in the United States and abroad, to all individuals and institutions interested in past and contemporary Jewish life.

The Jewish Publication Society
2100 Arch Street, 2nd floor
Philadelphia, PA 19103

Design and Composition by El Ot, Israel

08 09 10 11 12 10 9 8 7 6 5 4 3 2

Library of Congress Cataloging-in-Publication Data:

JPS commentary on the Haggadah : historical introduction, translation, and commentary / Joseph Tabory ; foreword by David Stern. – 1st ed.
p. cm.
Includes the text of the Haggadah in English and Hebrew.
Includes bibliographical references.
ISBN 978-0-8276-0858-0
1. Haggadah. 2. Haggadot–Texts. 3. Sefer–Liturgy–Texts. 4. Judaism–Liturgy–Texts. I. Tabory, Joseph. II. Jewish Publication Society. III. Haggadah. English & Hebrew. IV. Title: Jewish Publication Society commentary on the Haggadah.
BM674.79J69 2008
296.4'5371–dc22

2007038589

To my siblings,

Ita, Judy, Binyamin, and Ephraim.

The Passover seder represents our shared past

and our hopes for the future.

Contents

Foreword

Aside from the Bible, the Passover haggadah is probably the Jewish book most familiar to Jews. It is also, arguably, the single-most beloved Jewish text. As both script for the seder and its main subject, the haggadah has earned an unrivaled place in Jewish culture, both religious and secular. Of all the classic Jewish texts—the Talmud, the Jewish Bible, and the prayer book—the haggadah is the one most "alive" today. Jews continue to rewrite, revise, and add to its text, recasting it so as to maintain the haggadah's relevance to their lives.

That proclivity for contemporizing the haggadah can be traced back to the haggadah text itself. In one of its most famous passages, it instructs its reader, the participant in the seder, "to see him or herself as though they had gone out of Egypt." Historically, Jews have fulfilled this instruction in different ways, sometimes even acting out the Exodus by marching around the seder table! Since the early Middle Ages, however, probably the most typical way Jews have made the haggadah speak to their contemporary concerns and needs has been through the act of composing commentaries on it and then drawing on their elaborations and interpretations at the seder. These commentaries have been of every conceivable type—midrashic, legalistic, homiletical, ethical, philosophical, and mystical. And each has added a different and additional layer of meaning to the ritual.

The most recent type of commentary is the scholarly, critical commentary that traces the historical development of the seder and the haggadah through the ages. This type of commentary is itself a product of history; it was born out of the rise of the modern historical study of Jewish culture that began at the end of the nineteenth century and has since produced the rich body of scholarship known popularly today as Jewish studies. The first such modern attempts at a critical-historical study of the haggadah were made nearly a century ago, and until now the definitive historical commentary on the haggadah has been the edition published by the eminent German-born Israeli scholar E. D. Goldschmidt in 1960. In its time, Goldschmidt's haggadah set a new standard in modern Jewish scholarship. In the years since then, however, there have been many advances, both substantive and methodological, in the study of Jewish classical texts in general and of the haggadah in particular, and these new findings have created a need for a new historical commentary. The present volume by Professor Joseph Tabory, one of the world's leading authorities on the history of the haggadah, is a worthy successor to Goldschmidt's work. Although it is in the very nature of all scholarship to eventually be superseded by new discoveries and insights, Tabory's commentary will certainly remain the definitive work on the haggadah for many years to come.

Probably more than any other classical Jewish text, the haggadah lends itself to historical commentary. For one thing, it virtually wears its history on its sleeve (or napkin), as it were. Biblical verses, Rabbinic interpretations, medieval hymns, and still more recent passages all mingle in the text. Virtually every historical period and geographical center of Jewish culture is represented in its pages. But its historical character goes deeper than merely a listing of its sources. The haggadah is a book about remembering the past, and the vicissitudes of history touch on virtually every moment in its own development, beginning with the invention of the seder itself.

Like most things in Judaism, the roots of the seder go back to the Bible, specifically to the account in the book of Exodus (12–13) of the Passover sacrifice that was offered and eaten on the night before the Israelites left Egypt. The Passover seder as we know it, however, actually originated in late antiquity, in Roman Palestine in the first centuries of the Common Era. That historical context is very important because both the very structure and format of the seder derive from the Greco-Roman banquet and its specific conventions. The haggadah text reflects not only those conventions but also the inevitable changes that occurred when Jews moved from Roman Palestine to other cultures in the Diaspora: first, Babylonia, and later, the European centers known as Ashkenaz and Sepharad—where, among other things, Jews ate and dined in the styles and fashions of their gentile hosts in each separate diasporic culture.

Let me give one brief example: The passage that we know as the Four Questions originally consisted of three, not four, questions, and each question directly addressed one of the three symbolic foods eaten at the seder—the *maror* (which are the bitter herbs customarily eaten with haroset), the matzah, and the Passover sacrifice. As it happens, each of these three foods also related to the three courses that were customarily eaten at a Greco-Roman banquet—the appetizer course, the main course (known as "the bread course"), and dessert.

The *maror* related to the appetizer course, typically included, among other delicacies, leafy greens, especially bitter lettuce, and it was eaten after being dipped into a sauce. At the seder, however, in addition to eating lettuce or another green at the appetizer course, the part of the seder known today as *karpas* (when participants dip a sprig of parsley or a scallion, sometimes a potato, into saltwater), lettuce was also eaten as *maror*. Accordingly, in early texts of the haggadah that reflect the original Palestinian custom, the question about *maror* reads: Why on all other nights do we dip once (that is, during the appetizer course), while on this night we dip twice (first during *karpas* and second as *maror*)? The matzah was, of course, the core of the bread course. As for the Passover sacrifice, the Rabbis imagined that it was eaten at the end of that course, after everyone had filled up on other food, when dessert would have been eaten (but wasn't). A further connection between the haggadah and Greco-Roman custom can be drawn from the seder being conducted with participants in a reclining position, as it was only customary and expected at Roman banquets to dine and drink while reclining on couches or banquettes.

What happened, however, when Jews began to live in other cultures and ceased to banquet like Romans? As early as the late third century, the center of Jewish life in the ancient world gradually moved from Roman Palestine to Sassanian Babylonia, where banquets did not include an appetizer course with greens, so the original question (on "all other nights") made no sense since no one dipped even once. As a result, the question changed to "Why on all other nights do we not dip *once,* but on this night twice?" And still later, when the Jews had distanced themselves still further from Greco-Roman eating customs, the bewildered astonishment behind the question grew more intense in some versions: "Why on all other nights do we not dip *even* once, and this night twice!?" Similarly, once Jews stopped reclining like Romans at their festive meals, that practice also became a fit subject for inquiry, and the fourth question—about reclining—was added to the other three, while the practice itself (originally as routine as wearing a tuxedo to a black-tie affair) was ritualized and given religious meaning so as to symbolize the Jews' journey from slavery to freedom.

As even this brief account demonstrates, the history of the seder and the haggadah is not merely a history of a ritual's development over time or solely the account of the formation of a literary text. It is actually a story about the Jews themselves and the vicissitudes of their history, and how human invention and creativity created a religious tradition of lasting significance in response to the changing conditions and needs of historical moments.

The haggadah is the exemplary Jewish book about redemption: By remembering the redemption of the past, the Exodus from Egypt, it imagines the redemption to come. As Tabory's commentary repeatedly shows, however, the very development of the haggadah itself can be traced, virtually step by step, by following the movements of its authors, the Jewish people, deeper and deeper *into* exile, as they moved from one diasporic center to another, from Roman Palestine to Babylonia, from Babylonia to the European centers of Ashkenaz and Sepharad, and from those centers to all the later homes of Jews in North Africa, Arabia, eastern Europe, the Americas, and finally, to the State of Israel. It is this linked double movement—the imaging of redemption and the experience of exile—that most profoundly informs the haggadah's own history.

And so, reader, take this book and use it at your seder. Quote it, discuss it, and elaborate on it. And remember what the haggadah itself tells us: Whoever talks excessively, at too much length, about the Exodus from Egypt—now that is worthy of praise!

David Stern

Preface

The Passover eve ceremony, commonly known as the seder, is probably the most universally celebrated Jewish ritual. It is the founding ceremony of the Jewish people, a ceremony based on the centrality of the family as the basic Jewish institution. It is also a celebration of freedom of person and of nation.

Despite its honored history, the traditional observance of the ceremony has changed during the centuries. The present work is an attempt to portray the origins and evolution of the modern traditional seder, using a critical, historical, and philological approach. One of the challenges to this approach is the problem of dating the materials relating to the seder. Modern Jewish traditional life relies on both written sources and oral, living traditions. In antiquity, the reliance on oral sources was much greater. However, since some of the oral tradition is lost to us, we must rely on written sources. It is certain that many details of the ritual were in existence some time before they were first documented, but we have no way of knowing for how long. The scholarly assumption is that, usually, we are dealing with decades or less before the earliest documentation, rather than centuries earlier, but this assumption is not generally provable. With this caveat, let me proceed.

Before I do so, I must pay a debt to scholars who have worked in this field and whose works were greatly helpful in creating my presentation. The first scholar to attempt to collate the evidence about the text of the haggadah from manuscripts was Bruno Italiener (1881–1956) in his introduction to the facsimile edition of the illuminated haggadah manuscript found in Darmstadt, published in 1927.[1] Almost ten years later, in 1936, E. D. Goldschmidt, who had been trained in classical philology, published a haggadah in German with a scholarly introduction. After his immigration to *Eretz Yisra'el,* he published a Hebrew version of the haggadah in 1948. This was followed by his edition of 1960, which has become a classic—even though it is very outdated today.[2] An English version based on his work was published in 1979 by Nahum Glatzer.[3]

1. *Die Darmstädter Pessach-Haggadah: Codex Orientalis 8 der Landesbibliothek zu Darmstadt aus dem vierzehnten Jahrhundert, herausgegeben und erläutert von* Bruno Italiener, *unter Mitwirkung von* Aron Freimann, August L. Mayer, *und* Adolf Schmidt (Leipzig: Karl W. Hiersmann, 1927–1928), 71–165.
2. E. D. Goldschmidt, *The Passover Haggadah: Its Sources and History* [in Hebrew] (Jerusalem: Bialik Institute, 1960).
3. *The Passover Haggadah with English translation* [by Jacob Sloan], introduction and commentary based on the commentaries of E. D. Goldschmidt; edited by Nahum N. Glatzer, 3d rev. ed., including readings on the Holocaust, illustrated with woodcuts from the first illuminated Haggadah, Prague, 1526 (New York: Schocken, 1979).

An important contribution to the study of the haggadah was the work of Menahem Mendel Kasher, who received the Israel Prize in 1963, the first year this prize was given. Kasher published a haggadah with variant readings from manuscripts, both complete manuscripts and fragments from the Cairo Genizah. His first publication was in 1950, when he published two versions, one in Hebrew and another containing an English translation. This was followed by a more comprehensive Hebrew edition, called *Haggadah Shelemah* or *The Complete Passover Hagada,* published first in 1955. All of these works have been reprinted.[4]

I began work on the Passover ritual in 1970, writing a master's thesis and a doctoral dissertation, completed in 1978, on the history of the ritual. A revised and expanded version of this work was published in 1996, in Hebrew, and has been reprinted several times.[5]

A major work on the haggadah and its ritual is the Hebrew work titled *Haggadah of the Sages,* by Shmuel Safrai and Ze'ev Safrai, father and son, published in 1998.[6] The work seems to have been completed some years before publication for the bibliography does not list some important works that appeared several years before 1998. An important contribution of this work to the history of the haggadah is the presentation of the Palestinian or *Eretz Yisra'el* version of the haggadah, with an attempt to present the variant readings from all the *genizah* manuscripts. This was a great improvement on Goldschmidt's edition of 1960, in which he presented only a facsimile of the Dropsie manuscript of the *Eretz Yisra'el* version.[7] After the publication of the Safrais', the *Eretz Yisra'el* version of the haggadah has become better known through the publications of Ezra Fleischer and Jay Rovner.[8]

---

4. For publication of Kasher's haggadah, see Isaac Yudlov, *The Haggadah Thesaurus: Bibliography of Passover Haggadot from the Beginning of Hebrew Printing until 1960* [in Hebrew] (Jerusalem: The Magnes Press, 1997), numbers 4186, 4187, 4425, 4433, 4476, 4713.
5. *The Passover Ritual Throughout the Generations* [in Hebrew] (Tel Aviv: Hakkibutz Hameuchad, 1996). The present introduction is mostly based on this work and there will be no further references to it. For a survey of recent scholarship on this subject, see Josh Kulp, "The Origins of the Seder and Haggadah," *Currents in Biblical Research* 4:1 (2005): 109–134.
6. Shmuel Safrai and Ze'ev Safrai, *Haggadah of the Sages* [in Hebrew] (Jerusalem: Carta, 1998).
7. The Dropsie manuscript was one of the first *genizah* manuscripts of the *Eretz Yisra'el* version of the haggadah. At the time of its first publication, it was owned by David Werner Amram who presented it to Dropsie College. Dropsie College eventually became the Center for Advanced Jewish Studies affiliated with the University of Pennsylvania.
8. Jay Rovner, "An Early Passover Haggadah According to the Palestinian Rite," *Jewish Quarterly Review* [hereafter *JQR*] 90 (2000): 337–396; idem, "A New Version of the Eres Israel Haggadah Liturgy and the Evolution of the Eres Israel 'Miqra' Bikkurim' Midrash," *JQR* 92 (2002): 421–453; idem, "Two Early Witnesses to the Formation of the

Finally, mention must be made of the work of Heinrich Guggenheimer, *The Scholar's Haggadah.*[9] Guggenheimer presented three versions of the haggadah, Ashkenazic, Sephardic, and Oriental, in parallel columns (where necessary). He also provided an extensive commentary, presenting the sources for the texts and linguistic elucidations. Despite a fundamentalist approach to the history of the ritual and to the dating of texts, the work is indispensable for its sources and insights.

The nature of this type of work is that many of the discoveries and insights have long become part of the scholarly, and even popular, discourse. Documenting the discovery and history of each statement made here would make the footnotes overweigh the book. Therefore, I have presented this brief survey and its notes to give only general documentation. Statements made below that are not my own ideas may be found in one or more of the cited works. I leave it to the reader who is interested in the history of research to discover who was the first one to make any particular comment.

This survey is organized as an historical study. After a brief discussion of the sources, I present what little is known about the prehistorical seder, that is the celebration of the paschal meal from the Bible until the Mishnah, at which time the history of the seder begins. This history is divided into two sections. The first section gives an overview of the history, focusing on the general order of the evening ritual and its development throughout the generations. The second section describes the order of the evening, starting with the opening blessings over the wine and concluding with the final songs of the haggadah. We look at each rite and attempt to trace its history from earliest times to modern times. The Hebrew text of the haggadah is the Ashkenazic text in its eastern European version.

Miqra Bikurim Midrash and Their Implications for the Evolution of the Haggadah Text," *Hebrew Union College Annual,* 75 (2004): 75–120. One of the most complete texts of a *genizah* haggadah has been published by Ezra Fleischer, "An Early Siddur of the Erez Israel Rite" [in Hebrew], in *Me'ah She'arim: Studies in Medieval Jewish Spiritual Life in Memory of Isadore Twersky,* edited by Ezra Fleischer et al. (Jerusalem: Magnes, 2001), 21–59.

9. Heinrich Guggenheimer, *The Scholar's Haggadah* (Northvale, N.J.: Jacob Aronson, 1995), 1st softcover ed., 1998.

Acknowledgments

One of my earliest childhood memories is that of the Passover seder in my parent's home. The uniqueness of that evening has always inspired me with thoughts of our people's past and our future redemption. Thus it was more than a fortuitous accident that caused me to devote my doctoral studies to the history of the Passover eve ceremony. An article by S. Stein had recently appeared that focused attention on the relationship between festive meals among the Greeks and Romans, especially those meals that revolved around food and drink on the one hand and scholarly discussions on the other hand and on the Passover eve ritual. This inspired me to examine classical literature that describes those meals, in an attempt to discover how much the Greek and Roman culture had affected the development of the seder. My mentor, Professor I. D. Gilat (of blessed memory), encouraged me in this study, guiding and helping me in many ways, and I am always grateful to him. My dissertation was approved in 1978.

My involvement in the scholarly study of the history of this ceremony continued throughout the years, stimulated by the need to give annual public lectures about the subject while I served as rabbi of Kibbutz Be'erot Yitzchak and the Dati Leumi Synagogue of Har Nof in Jerusalem.

My research into this subject reached its peak with the publication of my book *Pesach Dorot* (*Passover Throughout the Generations*) in 1996. This is considered a successful book, and it is now in its fourth printing. Still, the book dealt with the history of the ritual, and very little of it was devoted to the history of the text of the haggadah. Thus I am very grateful to Dr. Ellen Frankel, CEO and editor-in-chief of the Jewish Publication Society, who asked me to write an introduction to the projected JPS Haggadah. This was eventually expanded into a translation of the text and a commentary. This gave me an opportunity both to present the results of my research to an English-speaking audience and to expand my research into wider issues of the history and development of the text itself. I am also grateful to the staff of JPS, Carol Hupping, Janet Liss, and Julia Oestreich for their great help in improving this work.

I wish to thank my friend George London; my brother, Rabbi Binyamin Tabory; and my nephew, Rabbi Noam Himelstein, who read early drafts of the introduction. Their comments have been helpful to me in presenting, I hope, an improved work. My grandchildren, Oshrit Rachel, Yedidyah Zvi, Netanel Aryeh, Hodayah Devorah, and Talyah, have instructed me about other aspects of the seder and the importance of these other aspects in the transmission of culture. Above all, my thanks to my wife, Judy, my partner both in studying the history of the seder and in performing it.

The Haggadah and Its Ritual

The Sources

The evening in which the paschal meal is eaten and the haggadah is recited is called the night of the "seder," meaning "order," because the various actions and recitations comprising it must be performed according to a prescribed sequence. The Passover haggadah is the text that is read during the evening, and it contains texts to be read during each part of the celebration and, usually, instructions for performance of the ritual. Thus the text should not be thought of as a separate entity but rather as the script of a play, which, like the script of a play, includes not only the words said but also the instructions for the performance of the drama. The necessity of ensuring that the detailed rite of the evening is conducted in the correct order brought about the composition of a number of mnemonic devices for the order. Kasher lists fourteen such devices.[1] The most famous of these is *kaddesh urechatz, karpas, yahatz, maggid, rahtzah, motzi matzah, maror, korekh, shulchan orekh, tzafun, barekh hallel, nirtzah*. This device is reputed to have been composed by Rashi or by Rabbi Samuel ben Solomon of Falaise, a French tosafist, and I will return to this device later, using it as a basis for our discussion.

The earliest sources that help us understand the modern seder are those found in talmudic literature. Although these sources were created during the period that stretched from sometime before the destruction of the Second Temple until the beginning of the sixth century, they were apparently not written down until the eighth century. These sources emphasize the ritual and present few details about the text. From the eighth century on, the sources generally present both aspects of the script: the text to be read and the instructions for its performance. However, some of the sources give more details about the text and skimp on the instructions, whereas others deal at length with the instructions and take the text for granted. The sources may be divided into two types: *haggadot*,[2] which give all the texts and some of the instructions, and rabbinical

1. See Menachem M. Kasher, *Hagadah Shelemah* [in Hebrew] (Jerusalem: Torah Shelema Institute, 1967), 77–82.
2. The haggadah is one of the most ubiquitous Jewish books; many Jewish homes have several. The haggadah is perhaps the most lavishly produced Jewish book, and many medieval manuscripts of the haggadah, which have been sumptuously illustrated and decorated, are now museum pieces. Ironically, the haggadah is also one of the most cheaply produced Jewish books, with some printed as appendices to newspapers and as advertisement handouts. For a bibliography of printed *haggadot* see Yudlov, *The Haggadah Thesaurus*.

literature, both rabbinic books of law, which give general instructions, and rabbinic responses, which deal with specific questions about the law.

The earliest extant *haggadot* are divided into two major versions: the Babylonian version and the *Eretz Yisra'el* version. The modern text is a direct descendant of the Babylonian version. The earliest complete Babylonian *haggadot* are found in the siddur of R. Amram Gaon and the siddur of R. Saadiah Gaon, although doubt has been raised about the authenticity of these texts, especially that of R. Amram Gaon. The *Eretz Yisra'el* version was completely forgotten some time after the Crusades and has only again become known relatively recently, through discoveries in the Cairo Genizah.[3] The identification of the *genizah haggadot* as *Eretz Yisra'el* tradition is based, mainly, on two factors: one negative and one positive. The negative factor is that a responsum of a Babylonian *Ga'on,* R. Natronai (853–858), vehemently rejects the type of haggadah found in the *genizah,* going so far as calling any one who uses this haggadah an apostate.[4] This would seem to show that this text was not prevalent in Babylon, and by process of elimination we are left with an *Eretz Yisra'el* provenance for this type of haggadah. The positive factor is the fact that some of the halakhic instructions about blessings over food found in these *haggadot* follow the *Eretz Yisra'el* tradition as known to us from the Jerusalem Talmud.[5] We may assume that elements common to both traditions reflect practice before *amoraic* times, before the division between *Eretz Yisra'el* and Babylon became so pronounced. It has been estimated that about 10 percent of the *haggadot* found in the Cairo Genizah represent the *Eretz Yisra'el* custom, whereas the rest follow the Babylonian tradition. Some of the *Eretz Yisra'el haggadot* show evidence of Babylonian influence. The text of the haggadah was part of the anti-Karaite polemic in gaonic times, and in their controversy with the Karaites, the *Ge'onim* attempted to stamp out any text or ritual that did not follow the Babylonian custom. In their zeal, the *Ge'onim* regarded those who used the *Eretz Yisra'el* haggadah as Jews who rejected the Oral Law and the gaonic tradition.[6] This was one of the major reasons that these *haggadot* fell out of use and became known again only after the discovery of the Cairo Genizah.

---

3. See pp. xiv–xv, n. 8.
4. For a further discussion of this, see Lawrence A. Hoffman, *The Canonization of the Synagogue Service* (Notre Dame, Ind.: University of Notre Dame, 1979), 7–23. Hoffman points out that the polemical tone of Natronai is due to the controversy with the Karaites.
5. For a fuller discussion of the Byzantine Haggadah, see my article "*Haggadat Ha-Pesach Ha-Eretz-yisraelit Ba-Tekufah Ha-Byzantit,*" in *Zechor Davar Le-Avdecha: Asufat Ma'amarim Lezecher Dov Rappel,* edited by Shemuel Glick (Jerusalem: Michlelet Lifshitz, 2007), 489–508.
6. See Hoffman, *Canonization of the Synagogue Service,* 10–23.

The post-talmudic Babylonian version spread throughout the Jewish world and split into various subversions: mainly Ashkenazic, Sephardic, and Yemenite. There are several personalities who have left indelible imprints on the haggadah. Besides Maimonides, whose instructions are almost precisely followed still today by the Yemenites of the Baladi rite, I must mention three other figures. The first is Rabbenu Tam, one of the greatest of the tosafists, the influential grandson of Rashi, whose decisions were accepted throughout almost all the Jewish world. The second figure is Rabbi Meir of Rothenburg (d. 1298), whose decisions were followed in western Germany. The third figure is Rabbi Isaac Luria (d. 1532), commonly known as the Ari, whose kabbalistic ideas and their implementation in the paschal ritual spread throughout the Jewish world. Finally, I must mention the *Shulchan Arukh* of Rabbi Joseph Caro, published with the glosses of Rabbi Moses Isserles. This work is the basis of modern traditional Judaism.

The three main versions noted above have, in turn, split into many branches and some of these branches have reunited. I will not go into the subbranches because there is relatively little difference in the basic text of the haggadah within the descendants of the Babylonian versions.[7]

From the Bible to the Mishnah

Our history of the paschal ritual begins at the end of the Second Temple period, some years before the destruction of the Temple and the cessation of the Temple-centered paschal sacrifice. We have very little information about how the ritual was celebrated until then, but we may assume that the rules prescribed by the Torah for this ritual were observed, as they were understood at those times. The only rule that the Torah gives for the consumption of the paschal sacrifice is: "This is how you shall eat it: your loins girded, your sandals on your feet, and your staff in your hand; and you shall eat it ḥurriedly: it is a passover offering to the Lord" (Exod. 12:11). The few surviving Samaritans consider this instruction applicable today, and they continue to eat the paschal lamb in this way. However, rabbinical sages considered this a onetime instruction for the first paschal meal, the "Egyptian Passover," and that rule would not apply to the Passover meal in following generations. In post-Exodic times, the Passover meal was presumably celebrated as a festive meal at which people were not hurried but rather took their time. The Torah itself prescribed no such distinction between two types of paschal meals; it distinguished only between the Passover sacrifice as celebrated before the establishment of God's central shrine

7. There were, at one time, more differences regarding the additions to the text that were inserted in various communities. However, many of these additions are no longer recited. The main differences between the versions today are in performance of the ritual, that is, whether they use two or three matzot, whether they hide the *afikoman,* and so on.

and the Passover sacrifices celebrated following this event. The Torah declared that once the People of Israel had settled in the Promised Land and God had selected a site for the temple, the Passover sacrifice could be offered only at that temple (Deut. 16:2). This directive meant a significant change in the nature of the ritual. The Egyptian Passover was a home ceremony, the entrance of the home being a quasi altar as the site of the sprinkling of the blood of the sacrifice. After God had selected the central shrine, the ritual became a Temple-oriented sacrifice.

As I have noted, the Torah does not prescribe exactly how the post-Exodic paschal meal should be eaten nor does it prescribe any ceremony connected with it. From what we know of patriarchal societies, it is hard to imagine that the meal in which the family sacrifice was consumed was not accompanied by some verbal elaboration on either the history of the celebration or its significance. This is especially true, as the Torah does prescribe, on several occasions, that the paschal sacrifice should be used as an opportunity to transmit historical traditions to the younger generations. In one case, this prescription appears as a response to a child's question "What do you mean by this rite?" The answer is "You shall say, 'It is the passover sacrifice to the LORD, because He passed over the houses of the Israelites in Egypt when He smote the Egyptians, but saved our houses'" (Exod. 12:26–27). In another instance, the Torah demands that the significance of the matzah festival be explained to the children "And you shall explain to your son on that day, 'It is because of what the LORD did for me when I went free from Egypt'" (Exod. 13:8). This latter command appears in the context of the seven-day feast of unleavened bread and the paschal lamb is not mentioned in this commandment. Nevertheless, specifying "that day" would seem to refer to the first day of the feast, which was the time that the paschal lamb was eaten. Although we have no idea what text was used, if any, for these purposes or how the story was combined with the meal, it is hard to imagine that a meal in memory of the Exodus would not be used by parents to transmit the story of the Exodus to the younger generation—even if there were no specific Torah mandate. Some scholars suggest that the original context of various psalms may have been the Passover evening. Among those mentioned in this connection we may count Psalms 77, 78, 105, and 106.[8] However, any suggestion about what form this took in the years before the construction of the Second Temple is pure speculation, as we have no sources.[9]

There are some sources from the Second Temple period that discuss the paschal sacrifice. Among these sources there is the book of Jubilees, written several centuries before the destruction of the Second Temple. This book follows the biblical pattern of giving us extended details about the sacrifice and very little information about its consumption at the meal. The book of Jubilees refers to the Jews eating the meal: "And all Israel was eating the flesh of the

8. See Tabory, *The Passover Ritual,* 350–351, and the literature referred to there in nn. 6–8.

9. Cf. Judith Hauptman, "How Old Is the Haggadah," *Judaism* 51:1 (winter 2002): 9.

paschal lamb, and drinking the wine, and was lauding and blessing, and giving thanks to the LORD God of their fathers, and was ready to go forth from under the yoke of Egypt, and from the evil bondage" (Jub. 49:9).[10] The presumption is that this is an anachronistic description and that it shows that, at the time of the composition of this book, drinking wine was an essential part of the evening and that there were texts associated with the meal.

Another apocryphal book, The Wisdom of Solomon, composed around the beginning of the first century C.E., portrays the Jews participating in the Egyptian paschal meal as "Singing the while the fathers' songs of praise" (Wis. of Sol. 18:9).[11] Philo, several decades later, reports that the content of the evening is "prayers and hymns"[12] and that "those who are to share in the feast come together not as they do at other symposiums, to gratify their bellies with wine and meat, but to fulfill their hereditary custom with prayer and songs of praise" (*De Specialibus Legibus* 2:148).[13] However, we have no idea what type of prayers or songs he had in mind.

Other writings of the Second Temple period, scrolls from Qumran, and Josephus provide interesting information about the paschal sacrifice but they add no details about the meal. Therefore, when I talk about the paschal ritual before the first century C.E., I cannot go beyond generalizations and there is no evidence that the texts used in the haggadah today antedate the end of the Second Temple period.[14]

---

10. The translation is that of R. H. Charles in R. H. Charles, ed., *Pseudepigrapha of the Old Testament* (Bellingham, Wash.: Logos Research Systems, 2004).
11. The translation is that of Samuel Holmes in Charles, ed., *Apocrypha of the Old Testament,* 1:564–565.
12. *Met' euxwn te kai hymnwn.*
13. *The Works of Philo: Complete and Unabridged,* translated by C. D. Yonge (Peabody, Mass.: Hendrickson, 1993).
14. Cf. Finkelstein's claims that some of the present Haggadah text existed in Hasmonean times (L. Finkelstein, "The Oldest Midrash," *Harvard Theological Review* [hereafter *HTR*] 31 [1938]: 291–317; idem, "Pre-Maccabean Documents in the Passover Haggadah," *HTR* 35 [1942]: 291–352; 36 [1943]: 1–38) have been soundly refuted by later scholars (see Goldschmidt, *Passover Haggadah,* 30–47; Hoffman, *Canonization of the Synagogue Service,* 90).

From the Mishnah Until the Modern Seder

An Overview of the Seder and Its History

This brings us to the earliest detailed description of the paschal meal, the description found in the tenth chapter of tractate *Pesachim* of the Mishnah, finally redacted by R. Judah the Prince at the beginning of the third century C.E., some 150 years after the destruction of the Temple and the cessation of the paschal sacrifice in Jerusalem. Scholars are divided on the value of this description for understanding how the meal was conducted during the Second Temple period. Many agree that some of it does represent practice during the Second Temple, but there is disagreement about the details.

Any attempt to present the Mishnah as a source for Second Temple practice must take into consideration the fact that there are details in the Mishnah's portrayal of the seder that were introduced after the destruction of the Temple. In the following presentation of the Mishnah, an attempt has been made to remove these details in order to get a clearer picture of the early practice. One of the methods used for identifying the details added later is syntactical analysis. Examination of the sentence structure in the Mishnah will enable us to discover the earliest layer of the Mishnah and thus find out what details were included in this layer. We find that the basic structure of the Mishnah consists of a series of sentences in which an action portrayed in the past tense is followed by an action portrayed in the present tense. Portraying the action in the past tense is meant not only to inform one that the action is done but also to present its completion as the time for doing the next action.[15] If we remove all the text that does not fit into this pattern, we find that what is left is the earliest detailed depiction of how the paschal lamb was eaten on Passover eve (the numbers are those in standard texts of the Mishnah):

2. They poured him the first cup . . . he recites the blessing for the day.
3. They brought him unleavened bread, lettuce, and *haroset* (fruit puree or relish) . . . they bring him the paschal lamb.
4. They poured him the second cup, he begins with the disgrace (or: lowly status) [of our ancestors], and concludes with glory and he expounds the biblical passage "my father was a fugitive Aramean" until the end of the section.
5. They poured him the third cup; he recites the grace after meals.
8. The fourth [cup], he recites the *Hallel,* and says over it the blessing of the song.

---

15. This pattern has been uncovered in other chapters of the Mishnah, which portray ceremonies and rituals conducted during the existence of the Second Temple. See J. Breuer, "Past Tense and Participle in Portrayals of Ceremonies in the Mishnah" [in Hebrew], *Tarbiz* 56 (1987): 299–326. Breuer did not find this method in our chapter because he did not strip away the later accretions to the chapter.

One of the most interesting observations based on this text is the interconnection between wine and texts. Here we have the evening organized around four cups of wine, and each cup of wine has a text attached to it. The texts of the first and third cup are ordinary texts, used on other days of the year. The text of the first cup, known as *Kiddush,* is customarily recited at the beginning of the meal on the eve of every *Shabbat* and every festival, whereas the text of the third cup, the grace after meals, is customary at the conclusion of every meal. Both of these texts are the subjects of disagreements between the Houses of Hillel and Shammai, who flourished during the last decades before the destruction of the Second Temple, and this fact is further evidence to the antiquity of this section of the Mishnah. The texts of the second cup, which embodies the story of the Exodus, and those of the fourth cup, *Hallel* or songs, are unique to this evening. Some of these texts belong to the tannaitic stratum of the haggadah, having been added between the destruction of the Second Temple (c. 70 C.E.) and the redaction of the Mishnah (c. 220 C.E.), while others were added even later.

Food at the Seder

What is presumably the major event of the evening—the meal—is unaccompanied, at least at this stage in history, by any texts. This is most remarkable when we realize that the paschal lamb was brought in whole. Bringing a whole animal before the participants must have been a dramatic event. Nevertheless, it is not marked by any text and the texts that we have are focused on the cups of wine. Modern scholarship has pointed out the resemblance of the way the paschal ritual was conducted to the way a symposium was conducted in late antiquity. Then, a symposium was a dinner at which people, usually scholars and intellectuals, gathered to share a meal and sophisticated discourse. The discourse was at least as important as the food. A large number of literary works that describe dinners eaten by a company of scholars who devoted time to discussions on various topics have survived from antiquity. The earliest literature portrays discussions that were conducted over wine after the conclusion of the meal. The most notable of these are the descriptions of symposiums in which Socrates participated, one composed by Plato and a very different one composed by Xenophon. Later sympotic literature portrays the discussions as arising during the meal—very often associated with foods brought to the table or to events that occurred during the meal.[16]

---

16. See Joseph Tabory, "Towards a History of the Paschal Meal," in *Passover and Easter: Origin and History to Modern Times,* edited by Paul F. Bradshaw and Lawrence A. Hoffman; Two Liturgical Traditions vol. 5 (Notre Dame, Ind.: University of Notre Dame Press, 1999), 62–80. Cf. Jonathan D. Brumberg-Kraus, "'Not by Bread Alone . . .'; The Ritualization of Food and Table Talk in the Passover 'Seder' and in the Last Supper," *Semeia* 86 (1999): 165–191.

Haroset

A further point that must be elucidated here is that the foods mentioned in the Mishnah, the paschal lamb, together with the matzah bread and the lettuce, were the meal in its entirety. These were the foods ordained in the Bible for the paschal meal. The presence of the nonmandatory *haroset* in the Passover meal is very significant. The Mishnah reports that R. Eleazar ben Zadok did maintain that *haroset* was mandatory (a mitzvah), but the significance of this statement is unclear. The opinion of the sages, that *haroset* was brought to the table even though it is not mandatory, was accepted. The Mishnah does not tell us what *haroset* was or when it was eaten. It is only in talmudic sources that we learn that it was a dip for the lettuce. The Babylonian Talmud tells us that *haroset* was a sort of antidote to lettuce, necessary to cancel the effect of something called *kappa* (BT *Pesachim* 115b). Early commentators disagree about the meaning of "*kappa.*" Although Rashi thinks that the *kappa* is the harmful juice of the lettuce, scholarly consensus accepts the opinion of Rabbenu Hananel that it is a type of worm that infests the lettuce. Of the composition of *haroset* we know, from the Babylonian Talmud, that it included apples—although an anonymous remark in the Babylonian Talmud (*Pesachim* 116a) seems to understand that it was tart or sour like apples but did not actually include them. Both Talmuds tell us that the *haroset* had the consistency of clay. However, another opinion found in the Jerusalem Talmud (JT *Pesachim* 10:3, 37d) maintains that the *haroset* was much more liquid like. The only other thing we know about the composition of the *haroset* is that it is mentioned in the Mishnah, together with mustard, as something that causes flour to ferment very rapidly (M. *Pesachim* 2:8). One of the main ingredients of *haroset* today is nuts and it has been pointed out that Greek literature tells us that nuts were eaten before a drinking bout to offset the side effects of the alcohol. However, we have no evidence from antiquity that the *haroset* contained nuts.

Haroset took on symbolic meaning already in *amoraic* times. The apple ingredient enabled it to be considered a reference to the verse "Under the apple tree I roused you; It was there your mother conceived you, There she who bore you conceived you" (Songs 8:5; BT *Pesachim* 115b). The significance of this verse was explained in a midrash that understood this verse as a reference to the way Jewish women had aroused their husbands to procreate under Egyptian rule. Its claylike consistency was considered to be a remembrance of the clay that the Jews used to build Pithom and Ramses. R. Yochanan adds that the spice that was included in the *haroset* was considered a remembrance of the straw that was part of the clay bricks (BT *Pesachim* 115b). Those who thought of it as having a more liquid consistency said it was a remembrance of blood but it is not clear which blood is meant here. It may have been thought to be a remembrance of persecution, the blood of Jewish children killed by Pharaoh, or a remembrance of the redemption, the blood either of the circumcision or the blood of the paschal lamb that was smeared on the doorposts. A compromise was accepted by R. Moses Isserles who said that one should make the *haroset* thick, in remembrance of the clay, and then add red wine or vinegar in memory of the blood.

We do not know exactly why *haroset* was part of the menu but its use seems to show that the meal was to be eaten according to the food customs prevalent at the time. The story told in talmudic times of the way Hillel ate a sandwich of matzah and *maror* (bitter herbs)[17] (possibly together with the flesh of the sacrifice) in the time of the Temple doesn't mention the use of *haroset* at all. In spite of the symbolism attached to the *haroset* in later sources, it seems more reasonable to assume that the *haroset* was not originally a symbolic food but was brought to the table as part of normal food patterns of the time. It is noteworthy that the main known ingredient of *haroset,* apple, was considered a typical dessert in Roman times. The phrase "from eggs to apples" (*ab ovo ad malum*) expressed a complete meal in the same way that its modern counterpart, "from soup to nuts," expresses this today.

The *Hagigah* Sacrifice

It is important to stress that *Pesach,* matzah, and *maror* made up the main course of the evening, in contradiction to later rabbinical theory, that maintained that these items, especially the paschal lamb, were not the main fare of the evening. According to the rabbinical understanding, these foods were eaten ceremoniously after the meal, which consisted of the meat of another sacrifice known as the *Hagigah.* The reason given by the rabbis for the need of another sacrifice was so that the paschal lamb should be eaten when one was no longer ravenous or hungry. Several reasons have been offered to explain why the paschal lamb should be eaten only when one was no longer hungry. One of these, suggested in the Jerusalem Talmud (JT *Pesachim* 6:4, 33c), involved the prohibition against breaking a bone of the paschal lamb. By eating the lamb when one was no longer hungry, there was less danger of breaking a bone by gnawing on it. However, according to the Babylonian Talmud, all sacrificial meat was to be eaten when one was not hungry, perhaps to show that the eating was done to fulfill a commandment of God and not in order to fill one's stomach (see Philo, *De Specialibus Legibus* 2:148). In spite of these rationales for the offering of the *Hagigah,* the sages admitted that there were a number of circumstances in which the *Hagigah* sacrifice would not be offered. It could not be offered when the fourteenth of Nisan fell on *Shabbat* or when the people who were to offer the sacrifice were ritually impure. The paschal sacrifice was offered in those circumstances, but the rabbis thought that this permission did not extend to the *Hagigah* sacrifice.

17. BT *Pesachim* 115a; JT *Hallah* 1:1 57b.

A more significant limitation of the *Hagigah* sacrifice was based on the number of participants in the paschal meal. If the paschal lamb supplied a sufficient quantity of meat for the participants, the *Hagigah* was not offered. In that case, serving the *Hagigah* sacrifice as the main meal would mean that some of the meat of the paschal lamb would not be consumed, whereas the Torah prescribed that no meat should be left over. Analysis of the size of lambs in the spring and the evidence that we have about the size of the group show that it would be a rare occurrence, if at all, when the lamb did not provide sufficient meat for everybody. Thus the theory about the *Hagigah* sacrifice seems to be more theoretical than practical, and there is no evidence that a *Hagigah* was ever eaten at the paschal meal. Nevertheless, this theory was an important one for it influenced the way that the seder was conducted in later times.

The Timing of the Meal

Another interesting point is based on that which the Mishnah leaves unsaid. It does not tell us at what point in the evening the meal was consumed. It must have been eaten after it had been brought to the table, as prescribed in Mishnah 3, and before the grace after meals, as prescribed in Mishnah 5. The question that the Mishnah leaves unresolved is whether the recital of the text, prescribed in Mishnah 4, took place before eating the food or after the meal. In later practice, the text was recited before the consumption of the meal, and this practice continues today. There is reason to assume, however, that in earlier times the meal was consumed before the recital of the text, giving the text the nature of an after-dinner speech. This was, indeed, the practice in the earlier classical symposiums, where speeches and discussions were conducted after the meal. It is even possible that the reason that the Mishnah gives us no clear indication of when the meal was consumed is that the redactor of the Mishnah knew that a change had taken place from meal-text to text-meal and, therefore, chose not to deal with this issue.

After the destruction of the Second Temple, it was no longer possible to continue the sacrificial tradition, but the problem of conducting a paschal meal without a sacrificial lamb was not a new one. Presumably, people who were not able to come to Jerusalem for the festival had some sort of festive meal wherever they were. However, we have no sources that deal with this issue and so we have no way of knowing whether the postdestruction practices were a continuation of the predestruction practice outside of Jerusalem. We do know that some people continued the paschal tradition, as much as possible, by serving a whole roast lamb at the table—even though it could not be considered a sacrificial lamb. This was actually frowned on by the sages who were afraid that people might mistake the symbol for reality and think that they were actually continuing the paschal sacrifice—without a Temple and outside of Jerusalem.

For those who did not try to retain the sacrificial tradition or some sort of surrogate, the cessation of the paschal sacrifice meant that the paschal meal was replaced by an ordinary meal, although of a festive nature. In these circumstances, the meal became of lesser religious importance, and the story of the Exodus became a more prominent feature of the evening. It is likely that one of the ways that this was shown was by postponing the meal until after the recital of the story of the Exodus.

The meal itself took on some of the aspects of festive meals according to the customs of the times. The most notable of these is the custom of "dipping" before all festive meals, described at length in the Tosefta (*Berachot* 8–9, p. 20). From it we learn that the function of this ritual at normative festal meals was much the same as the similar ritual of smorgasbord or buffet before a festive dinner, such as a wedding. The guests gathered together informally, partaking of light refreshments, while they waited for the arrival of all the other guests. Usual social custom, as derived from the Mishnah and classical sources, was for this gathering to take place in an anteroom where people sat upright on ordinary chairs. When the main meal was to begin, they entered the dining room, which was furnished with couches on which they reclined during the meal. A similar custom still prevails among some Yemenites, who regularly gather for *Kiddush* on *Shabbat* and eat a variety of nuts, cakes, and fruits before the main meal.

As we have noted, these hors d'oeuvres were ordinarily served in an anteroom where people sat on chairs before entering the dining room with its couches for reclining. This knowledge may help us understand a ruling about the necessity for reclining while drinking the wine during the seder. Conflicting reports about the ruling of R. Nachman, the third-generation Babylonian amora, in this matter were reconciled, in an anonymous passage, by declaring that reclining was necessary for only two cups, whereas the other two cups could be drunk while sitting up straight (BT *Pesachim* 108a). Based on the similarity to the Greco-Roman meal, it would seem that the first two cups were drunk while sitting up, and reclining was customary only for the last cups. However, the anonymous talmudic passage did not take this into consideration. Although it accepted the reconciliation of the two statements of R. Nachman—that reclining was necessary only for two cups—it could not decide if this referred to the first two cups or to the last cups. Due to this doubt, it was decided that one should not be lenient in this matter and that one should recline for all four cups. A lenient decision would have meant that it was not necessary to recline for any of the cups, and this ancient custom would have totally disappeared.

Matzah, *Maror,* and *Karpas*

A further distinction related to reclining is connected to the eating of *maror*. The Talmud rules that, while one is required to recline while eating matzah, one is not required to recline while eating *maror* (BT *Pesachim* 108a). One may suspect that the origin for this distinction is based on meal patterns. The vegetable eaten as hors d'oeuvres was ordinarily consumed in the anteroom, where people sat on chairs. It was only after entering the main dining room that people reclined. Thus *maror,* which was the vegetable used by many for both dippings in talmudic times, would not require one to recline while eating it. However, Rashi, in his commentary to the Talmud, explained that the difference between matzah and *maror* was conceptual. Reclining was an expression of freedom for only free men reclined. Matzah, which was a symbol of redemption, should be eaten while reclining; *maror* was a commemoration of slavery and, as such, did not have to be consumed while reclining.

A further limitation of the demand for reclining is related to the eating of *karpas*. Evidence has been brought from the Jerusalem Talmud that implies that one did not recline during the first dipping. *Shibbolei ha-Leket,* a thirteenth-century Italian halakhic work, states specifically that it is not necessary to recline while eating *karpas*. We may assume that this is a tradition based on the custom that the first dipping was not eaten in the dining room where the reclining couches were, but it is possible that this was just an expression of the unimportance of this dipping.

Although the first dipping is apparently based on the custom of eating hors d'oeuvres while seated in the anteroom, there is no evidence that the first part of the haggadah, as preserved in traditional sources, was ever conducted in a separate room. Indeed, the session in the anteroom on normal festive occasions was an informal session, whereas the first part of the haggadah has a very structured form. One must assume that the imitation of Greco-Roman customs was done selectively. Customs were copied that lent an atmosphere of festivity and a feeling of being in high society. But these customs had to take second place both to what was physically feasible and to what was spiritually necessary.

The cessation of the paschal sacrifice meant that the paschal meal was replaced by a normal festive meal, appropriate to any holiday. The instruction to serve a festive meal appears in talmudic sources as "they should bring him lettuce, *haroset,* and two dishes" (BT *Pesachim* 114b). The "two dishes" mentioned here are simply the minimum fare of a festive meal, as opposed to an ordinary meal in which only one dish was served. Babylonian *amoraim* gave examples of foods that were considered as two dishes, such as beets and rice. They understood the "two dishes" as being the fare of the evening. The two dishes were a minimum, and R. Saadiah suggests three or four dishes, among them something salty and eggs. In the process of time, the "two dishes" became part of the ceremony and were considered to be remembrances of the two sacrifices, the *Hagigah* and the paschal lamb, that had both been offered on this evening—at least theoretically.

The Food's Symbolic Significance

Another major change that occurred about the time of the destruction of the Second Temple was the introduction of texts relating to the foods that were eaten during the evening. The haggadah contains two texts of this type. The text most obviously connected with the foods is the statement of R. Gamliel: "Whoever did not recite [or, perhaps, explain] these three things at the paschal meal has not fulfilled his duty: *pesach, matzah,* and *merorim.*"[18] 1. *Pesach* (paschal lamb) because the *Makom* (an appellation for God) skipped over the houses of our ancestors in Egypt, 2. *merorim* (bitter herbs) because the Egyptians embittered the lives of our ancestors in Egypt, and 3. matzah (unleavened bread) because they were redeemed.[19]

R. Gamliel stressed that it was not enough to eat the foods—their significance had to be explained. The dating of R. Gamliel's statement is of great importance for understanding its context. It is generally assumed that the R. Gamliel of our Mishnah is the one who flourished somewhat after the destruction of the Second Temple. Thus his statement should either be considered as a postdestruction addition to the evening ritual or as a codification of a custom that had arisen some time before him—possibly even before the destruction of the Temple.

While we may find its parallel in the sympotic tradition discussed above, scholars have pointed out that there may be a connection between his explanations of the significance of these foods and the explanations of the significance of the bread and wine consumed at the last supper of Jesus, whether it was a paschal meal or not. Indeed, some scholars have thought that R. Gamliel's stress on the proper meaning of these foods was meant to oppose Christian explanations of the bread and wine used in their rituals.[20] However, there has never been an attempt to include in the text of the haggadah any explanation of the significance of the wine drunk during the evening. The earliest mention of any symbolic significance attached to the wine is found in the *Or Zaru'a* (whose author died in 1260), who mentions that the use of red wine is meant to signify blood—either the blood of suffering or the blood of redemption. The

18. *Merorim* is the generic term for all bitter herbs that may be used at the seder. The term *maror* originally referred to one of these herbs, but in later times it replaced the *merorim* as a generic term.

19. The translation follows Baruch Bokser, *The Origins of the Seder: The Passover Rite and Early Rabbinic Judaism* (Berkeley: University of California Press, 1984), 30.

20. For the most recent discussion of this issue, with references to earlier literature, see Israel J. Yuval, "Easter and Passover as Early Jewish Christian Dialogue," in *Passover and Easter: Origin and History to Modern Times,* edited by Paul F. Bradshaw and Lawrence A. Hoffman; Two Liturgical Traditions vol. 5 (Notre Dame, Ind.: University of Notre Dame Press, 1999), 106–107. Yuval expanded his ideas in *"Two Nations in Your Womb": Perceptions of Jews and Christians* [in Hebrew] (Tel Aviv: Am Oved, 2000).

blood of suffering referred to the blood of Jewish children shed by Pharaoh, whereas the blood of redemption referred to the blood of circumcision and the blood of the paschal lamb. The use of red wine was first mandated by Rabbi Jeremiah, a fourth-generation *Eretz Yisra'el* amora (JT *Pesachim* 10:1, 37c), but the reason given is that only red wine really looks like wine. In this context the Talmud quotes the verse "Do not ogle that red wine as it lends its color to the cup" (Prov. 23:31).

Less obviously connected with the foods eaten at the seder are the four questions that are asked by the child. These questions may be presented schematically as: Why do we eat matzah? Why do we eat *maror*? Why do we dip? Why do we eat while leaning? Traditional commentaries considered the text that follows these questions—"We were slaves in Egypt and God redeemed us from there"—as the answer to these questions. Some *haggadot* even have a subtitle immediately following these questions that states: "This is the answer." However, the text immediately following has no answer to these questions. "Leaning" is nowhere else referred to in the haggadah and even matzah and *maror* are mentioned in the following text only as a sidebar in the answer to the child who does not know what to ask. The verse quoted in this answer is "It is because of this that the LORD did for me when I went free from Egypt" (Exod. 13:8)[21] and "this" was explained by the sages as a reference to matzah and *maror*.

The lack of an answer to the questions is due to the fact that changes in the text of the questions have obscured the fact that the questions of the child refer to the same foods whose explanations are mandated by R. Gamliel. Examination of the best manuscripts of the Mishnah and early *haggadot* show that there were originally only three questions, which may be summarized as "Why do we eat only matzah? Why do we dip (referring to the dipping of the *maror*)? Why do we eat only roasted meat?" Thus it seems to be a reasonable assumption that R. Gamliel's explanations of the significance of *Pesach,* matzah, and *maror* are the answers to the three questions, although distanced from them in the haggadah. This type of discussion, that is, questions and answers about foods consumed during the meal and/or about events that occur during the meal, is characteristic of later sympotic literature. To cite one example, Athenaeus (flourished around the time of R. Judah the Prince, about one hundred years after R. Gamliel) writes that the bringing of fish to the table was the occasion for a lengthy discussion about fish that took up the better part of two volumes. A cynical participant in one of his symposiums complained that they spent more time talking about the food than actually eating it. If we accept the connection between the statement of R. Gamliel and the questions asked at the beginning of the evening, especially the question about dipping at the seder, this would support the postdestruction dating of R. Gamliel's statement as the dipping seems to be a feature of the seder that was added only after the destruction.

---

21. Author's translation.

The *Afikoman*

There was one aspect of the Greco-Roman festive meal that was specifically mentioned as being forbidden. The Mishnah declares that, after the paschal meal, one may not declare *afikoman*. This is to be understood as a reference to the revelry (*epikomos*) that was a common after-dinner feature at Greco-Roman meals.[22] The mishnaic term was explained by Rav, in a sense close to its original connotation, as meaning that one should not leave the paschal fellowship for another group. However, other sages reinterpreted this statement, in terms of meal customs of their times, as meaning that one should not eat dessert after the paschal meal. Although the original purpose of this ruling was probably to retain the solemn and serious nature of the evening, the reinterpretation brought about a new understanding of the reason. It was assumed, in late talmudic times, that the reason for the prohibition of dessert was to retain the taste of the paschal lamb in one's mouth. Although there was disagreement among the sages as to whether this ruling applied only to the flesh of the paschal lamb or also to the matzah, which was the most significant food eaten at the post-destruction meal, the consensus was that even if there was no paschal lamb one should not eat dessert in order to retain the taste of matzah in one's mouth. This, in turn, led to the custom of closing the meal with a piece of matzah, so that matzah would be the last taste in one's mouth. It was only in the thirteenth century that the piece of matzah that concluded the meal was first termed the *afikoman,* changing the term from something that was forbidden to something that was a positive requirement.

The children's game of looking for the *afikoman* is not documented in early sources. Putting aside the piece of matzah, which had been broken off from the whole for later consumption after the meal, is first documented in *Machzor Vitry,* compiled in France in the thirteenth century. According to this work, the broken piece should be placed under the tablecloth for use as *afikoman*. The reason for putting it under the tablecloth is not mentioned, but it seems that the main concern was that it should not be eaten by mistake, before the proper time. R. Eliezer ben Joel Ha-Levi of Bonn (1140–1225, commonly known as Ravyah), considers it sufficient to put the piece of matzah at the foot of the table. Nevertheless, in some places at least, the "hiding" of the matzah was considered a significant event as the *afikoman* is referred to in the mnemonic device *karpas, yahatz* . . . as *tzafun* (what is hidden). Perhaps connected with this is the fact that the tablecloth under which the matzah was hidden also began to take on symbolic significance. It was considered as a remembrance of the cloaks

22. In recent times, several scholars have attempted to revive the theory of David Daube that the word "*afikoman*" in the Mishnah is derived from a Greek word that means "he has arisen" (see Deborah Bleicher Carmichael, "David Daube on the Eucharist and the Passover Seder," *Journal for the Study of the New Testament* 42 [June 1991]: 45–67).

in which the kneading bowls had been wrapped at the time of the Exodus (Exod. 12:34). Based on this explanation, a custom developed of wrapping the *afikoman* in a napkin and walking around with it—to symbolize the Jews leaving Egypt with their bundles on their shoulders.

Structure and Symmetry

The structure of the seder took on a tripartite nature with the meal in the center. If we take an overview of the modern seder, we find that it presents an integrative whole that is constructed of three parts: (1) the story of the Exodus from Egypt, (2) a festive meal with special foods, and (3) songs that are meant both to praise God and to create a general feeling of festivity.[23] This introduction will focus on the ritual as a whole, demonstrating the interaction between the text and the ritual and showing the history of this interaction—based on examination of the sources. There is symmetry between the premeal rite and the postmeal rite as there are a number of details in the premeal rite that are repeated, with variations, in the postmeal rite. The basic order of the seder prescribes two cups of wine before the meal and two cups of wine after the meal. There were a series of texts to be read over the first two cups of wine that were drunk before the meal and a series of texts to be read over the second two cups of wine after the meal. Immediately before the meal, over the second cup, Hallel is recited and immediately after the meal, over the fourth cup, additional chapters of Hallel are recited. At the beginning of the seder, the wish is expressed, in Aramaic, that next year the seder will be celebrated in Jerusalem. The seder closes with the reiteration of this wish—this time in Hebrew. There are two Aramaic passages in the haggadah: one opens the evening (*ha lahma anya*) and one closes it (*Had Gadya*). Questions are asked twice during the seder: the four questions at the beginning and thirteen questions at the end (*Ehad Mi Yode'a*). There are two litanies in the haggadah: the *Dayenu* before the meal and *hodu* after the meal.

There is also symmetry in the central part of the evening—the meal itself. The opening ritual of the meal is mirrored in its closing ritual. The meal opens with a cup of wine, followed by washing of hands, followed by a symbolic eating of matzah. It closes with eating matzah, followed by washing of hands (no longer customary among all), followed by the cup of wine accompanying the grace after the meal.

23. Cf. Ruth Gruber Fredman, *The Passover Seder: Afikoman in Exile* (Philadelphia: University of Pennsylvania Press, 1981), 98. Fredman suggests that this division is structural: the first part deals with the past, the Exodus; the second part is the meal (the present); "the final part speaks mostly of hope of future deliverance." For a different analysis of the seder in its entirety see Tabory, *The Passover Ritual*, 378–384.

Beginning the meal	Ending the meal
1. wine (the second cup)	3. matzah (*afikoman*)
2. hand washing	2. hand washing
3. matzah	1. wine (the third cup)

More significant is the symmetric structure found in the first part of the evening, shown here:

Wine (first cup)		Wine (second cup)
Washing hands	Haggadah	Washing hands
Matzah (breaking but not eating)		Matzah
Vegetable (*karpas*)		Vegetable (*maror*)

The symmetry here is truly parallel. We find that the rituals performed at the beginning of the evening are repeated just before the meal. It is as if to say that the rituals performed at the beginning of the evening, before the reading of the haggadah, must be performed again after the recitation of the haggadah, but this time with increased significance and greater emphasis on the Exodus from Egypt. The blessing recited over the first cup is the ordinary *Kiddush,* recited on all festivals, whereas the blessing recited over the second cup is focused on the Exodus. The first washing of the hands is merely ceremonial, unaccompanied, in modern times, by any blessing, and in some communities it is not performed by all of the participants. The second washing is halakhically required of all the participants and is accompanied by a blessing. The matzah presented in the beginning is only presented and not eaten, but at the end it is eaten, accompanied by two blessings. Finally, the vegetable used for the first dipping has no halakhic significance, whereas the vegetable used in the second dipping fulfills the halakhic obligation of eating bitter herbs.

The Order of the Evening

Sanctifying the Day (*Kaddesh*)

The first instruction for the evening is *Kaddesh*—sanctify the day. This refers to the *Kiddush* blessing over the first cup of wine, as is customary on every *Shabbat* and festival. The minimal *Kiddush* consists of two blessings: the ordinary blessing over wine and a blessing that refers to the sanctity of the day. It is this latter blessing that gives the *Kiddush* its name. Although the *Kiddush* is a feature of every Sabbath eve and holiday eve meal, there are several aspects that need to be elucidated.

The blessing over wine was considered, in rabbinical terminology, a short blessing. It opened with the standard praise of God: "Blessed art Thou, O Lord our God, King of the Universe," followed immediately by the praise specific to the wine: "Creator of the fruit of the vine." In gaonic times we find that this blessing was expanded considerably, on special occasions, by the addition of a long praise of the beneficial aspects of wine. This expansion began "who has created sweet wine (*yayin asis*)" and it spoke of wine as causing one to rejoice, comforting mourners, healing the ill, and so on. This expansion changed it from a short blessing to a long blessing, requiring the addition of a closing formula, "Blessed art Thou, O Lord our God, the King who is exalted alone, the holy Lord, Creator of the fruit of the vine."[24] As far as we know, this expanded version was used only on Sabbaths and festivals. We know that *Ge'onim* objected to the use of this blessing, considering it a violation of the rules of blessings. Rav Saadiah Gaon mentioned the fact that people used this blessing and said that this was incorrect. It has effectively disappeared from the ritual, and the full text is known today only from the discovery of a manuscript in the Cairo Genizah. A scholarly assumption is that this expanded blessing belonged to the *Eretz Yisra'el* tradition, but there may be a reference to its use in Babylon in the Babylonian Talmud.

The main blessing of the *Kiddush,* the blessing of the sanctity of the day, was recited at the beginning of every *Shabbat* and festival. The standard *Kiddush* for Passover follows the normal pattern. It opens with the election of Israel, followed by the mention of the sanctity of the day. In some ancient texts of the *Kiddush* for Passover, the text of both of these ideas was expanded. The election of Israel was expanded by about one hundred words, and then, following the standard mention of the sanctity of the day, about seventy words were added, expanding on the uniqueness of the day of Passover. These two expansions, considered as one unit, are quoted in full in the siddur of Rav Saadiah Gaon, as an appendix to his instructions for the celebration of the evening. This expansion is considered by him as "permissible," and it is used even now by certain Yemenite communities.

The conclusion of the blessing of "the sanctity of the day" follows the pattern of the body of the blessing. It blesses God for sanctifying Israel and for sanctifying the day. However, there was a major difference between the closing formula and the body of the blessing. Although the body of the blessing used a formula that was common to all festivals, it also mentioned specifically the particular holiday on which the *Kiddush* was being said. The holiday was marked by its name and a designation of one of its major aspects. Passover, for instance, was referred to as the "festival of matzot, the time of our freedom." The closing formula, however, was generic—the same for all the festivals. One praised God in general, "sanctifier of Israel and the festivals (zemanim)" and this formula was used for all festivals. The most distinctive difference between this Babylonian tradition and the *Eretz Yisra'el* tradition was that the closing formula of the *Eretz Yisra'el* tradition was not generic but rather mentioned specifically the day on which the blessing was said. The closing formula was rather lengthy and included redundant terms: "Blessed art Thou, God, sanctifier of

24. For an almost complete translation and a discussion of the sources see Arnold A. Wieder, "Ben Sira and the Praises of Wine," *JQR* 61 (1970): 155–166.

Israel and the matzot festival and times of joy and times and pilgrimage festivals and holy assemblies" (*Baruch atah Adonai, mekaddesh yisrael vehag hamatzot umo'adei simhah vehazemanim veharegalim umikr'aei kodesh*).

Besides the two basic blessings of the *Kiddush,* wine and the sanctity of the day, it was customary also to recite the *Shehecheyanu* blessing as part of the *Kiddush*. This blessing is an expression of thanks for the joy felt at reaching this point in time and it is independent of the *Kiddush*. According to the sages, one could recite this blessing at any point of the day. However, it was customary to recite it when one was performing a specific act mandated by the holiday, such as reciting the *Kiddush*. On Hanukkah and Purim, when there was no *Kiddush* since the days were not sanctified, the blessing was said at the lighting of candles or before reading the Scroll of Esther. In later times, women used to say the blessing while lighting the candles.

The conjunction of *Shabbat* and Passover had its impact on the *Kiddush*. When Passover began on Friday night, mention of the incoming *Shabbat* was integrated into the blessing that dealt with the sanctification of Passover. This was a reasonable decision since the blessing already dealt with the sanctity of time. However, there was a basic difference about the closing formula between the *Eretz Yisra'el* tradition and that of Babylon on every *Shabbat*. According to the *Eretz Yisra'el* tradition, the closing formula for every *Shabbat* paralleled that of festivals: "sanctifier of Israel and *Shabbat,*" expressing both of the ideas that were included in the body of the blessing. But the Babylonians maintained that the sanctity of Israel should not be mentioned in the closing formula on *Shabbat* since the sanctity of *Shabbat* preceded the sanctity of Israel and was independent of it. The sanctity of Israel was relevant only to the festivals for these were dependent on Israel. Unless Israel declared the beginning of the month, there would be no festivals. This disagreement about the closing formula on *Shabbat* was reflected in the Passover *Kiddush* when Passover fell on *Shabbat*. The Babylonians mentioned the sanctity of *Shabbat* before the sanctity of Israel thus: "sanctifier of *Shabbat,* Israel, and the festivals." But the *Eretz Yisra'el* tradition just added the mention of *Shabbat* after the mention of the sanctity of Israel: "sanctifier of Israel, *Shabbat,* the matzah festival."

When Passover fell on Saturday night, it was necessary to add another blessing, *Havdalah,* which dealt with the separation or differentiation of the sanctified time of *Shabbat* from ordinary times or even of the differentiation of *Shabbat* from times of lesser sanctity. Although Passover itself is a sanctified time, its sanctity was considered less than that of *Shabbat* for it is permitted to do certain types of work on a festival that are forbidden on *Shabbat*. The standard blessing said when an ordinary day began at the close of *Shabbat* was "Blessed art Thou, O Lord our God, who separates holy from secular"; but when a festival followed the *Shabbat,* the closing formula was "who separates holy from holy." Although there was a tradition that this was the complete text of the *Havdalah* blessing, which would have been a short blessing, the Babylonian Talmud required one to lengthen the blessing by including from three to seven references to other separations (BT *Pesachim* 103b–104a). The text that became customary at the conclusion of *Shabbat* mentioned four separations: "between holy and secular, between light and darkness, between Israel and the nations, between *Shabbat* and workdays" and then concluded with the closing formula. When a festival began at the conclusion of the *Shabbat,* the body of the blessing was further expanded to include the following three phrases: "You have separated between the sanctity of *Shabbat* and the sanctity of festivals, and You have sanctified the seventh day from the six days of activity, You have separated and sanctified Your people, Israel, in Your Holiness." The first of the three was a necessary addition to reflect the special circumstances of the day. The two final clauses were rejected by some medieval authorities who felt that the first of the three, which expressed the idea of the closing formula, should be followed immediately by the closing formula. However, Rabbenu Tam justified the custom, explaining that the second and third clauses were not referring to separation of sanctity from secular but were referring to separation of various degrees of sanctity, just like the closing formula. He explained that the distinction between six days and the seventh was not referring to the ordinary six-day week but to the festival week, the intermediate days of which had some sanctity. Continuing this thought, he maintained that the separation of Israel was not referring to the division between Israel and the nations but to the internal division of Israel into different grades of sanctity—priests, Levites, and laymen.

The regular Saturday night *Havdalah* included a blessing over a candle and one for the smelling of spices. When Saturday night was the beginning of a festival, the blessing for the candle was retained although the blessing for spices was omitted. The blessing for the candle was retained because one of the major differences between *Shabbat* and festival was that one was permitted to light fires on a festival (with certain reservations). The omission of spices is somewhat complex, and it would seem to be closely connected with the reason for smelling spices during *Havdalah*. Scholars assume that the custom is connected to the Greco-Roman custom of burning incense at the end of the meal. This could, of course, not be done on *Shabbat* so it was done immediately after *Shabbat*. There was a disagreement about whether incense could be burned on festivals and the custom that developed was to refrain from it. So there could be no incense on Saturday night if it was the beginning of a festival, nor would one smell spices as a substitute for the incense. However, the original reason for the spices at *Havdalah* was reinterpreted as a support for the loss of the added spirit (*neshamah yeteirah*) that one had acquired on *Shabbat*. It was now necessary to give a new reason for the omission of the blessing of spices when Saturday night was the beginning of a festival. We find in *Machzor Vitry* two explanations for this. The first is that one receives sufficient fortification for the loss of the added spirit by the special foods that are served on festivals. The other reason is that it is actually forbidden to smell spices on festivals for fear that one might pluck them.

Due to the complexity of the integration of the *Kiddush* for festivals with the *Havdalah* rite on Saturday night—a total of five blessings—a mnemonic device to remember the blessings and their order appears in the Babylonian Talmud: *YaKNeHaZ* (*Yayin, Kiddush, Ner, Havdalah, Zeman*). It has often been suggested that the illustration of a hare hunt that appears in some Ashkenazic *haggadot* is meant to remind one of this device because *YaKNeHaZ* sounds similar to the German or Yiddish term for hare hunt: *yagen haz.*

Washing the Hands (*Urechatz*)

Washing one's hands before eating is a basic hygienic requirement, and it is customary, and even mandatory, in many societies. In Jewish tradition, hand washing took on a religious, halakhic aspect that determined exactly how one was to wash one's hands and what foods required washing of hands before eating them. In addition, washing of hands was also required before religious ceremonies, specifically before prayer. This aspect was a continuation of biblical tradition, which required the priests to wash their hands and feet before their service in the Temple (Exod. 29:4, 40:12). The outcome of this is that washing one's hands was required three times during the seder: once before the first dipping, the second time before the main meal, and the third time before reciting the grace after meals. In a tradition found in gaonic times, it was customary to make a separate blessing for each washing. The first blessing was *al netilat yadayim* (about pouring water over the hands; this is not an exact translation but the traditional translation for this blessing, "about washing the hands," is also not exact and, in this context, it is also misleading); the second *al rehitzat yadayim* (about washing the hands), and the third, *al shetifat yadayim* (which may be translated as "about laving the hands"). The existence of three distinct blessings, one for each washing, emphasizes the fact that each one of these washings had a slightly different rationale. The different rationales affected the way these washings were performed and the way that the custom was preserved at the seder. I shall, therefore, discuss the history of these lavings and their blessings separately, following the order in which they take place at the seder.

The first hand washing was considered a requirement for any food that had been dipped in liquid. The main social context of dipping solid foods in liquids was the prologue to the meal, the smorgasbord or buffet. From a rabbinical anecdote about R. Akiva we learn that, in the social context of this dipping, only one hand was washed. R. Akiva invited two students to his home to test their social skills. At the premeal part of the evening he served some sort of long food. One of the students took the food and, when he started pulling it, realized that he was unable to break it with one hand and that it would be uncouth to eat it in one piece. So he withdrew his hand from the plate. The second student used his other hand to break the food into a manageable size. R. Akiva remarked, sarcastically, that the student should have stepped on it to break it. The point of the remark was that only one hand had been washed and, therefore, touching food with the unwashed hand was just as objectionable as touching it with one's foot (*Massekhet Derekh Eretz* 7:2, pp. 215–217).

The rabbinical rationale for this washing was part of their general theory of impurity of liquids. Any liquid removed from its source that came into contact with any source of impurity received a high degree of impurity. If one should touch a liquid with hands that had not been washed, which were automatically presumed impure, the hands would defile the liquid, which would, in turn, defile the food. Since the rationale for this washing was clearly connected to a prohibition of eating impure foods, the custom fell into desuetude when people were no longer able to observe all the rules about impure foods—although some modern authorities thought that this washing was still mandated (see *Arukh ha-Shulchan, Orach Chayyim* 158:4). This washing has become a traditional feature of the seder ritual; and it is preserved by most traditional Jews, even those who do not ordinarily wash their hands to eat fruits and vegetables that have been in contact with liquid. The halakhic rationale for the custom of washing hands before *karpas* in modern times was the subject of much debate. Nevertheless, the custom continued to be observed at the seder because of the special nature of the Passover ceremony. On the one hand, it was meant to do things as they had been done in Temple times, and on the other hand, it was meant to do things as they would be done in future times, after the restoration of the sacrificial order. Besides these learned reasons, an important reason for preserving this tradition was because it was part of the traditional way of doing things. It has even been suggested that the purpose of this custom is to present the children with another oddity of the seder that is meant to arouse their curiosity.

A complication of this seder ritual appeared in Ashkenazic Jewry. Ashkenazic Jews developed a custom, on regular *Shabbatot* and holidays, of washing their hands for the bread before the *Kiddush*. This was probably done, originally, to avoid having to get up from the table to wash their hands after *Kiddush*. There was some deliberation about what they should do at the seder. A compromise was reached according to which everybody would wash their hands before *Kiddush,* but the master of ceremonies would wash his hands again after *Kiddush*. Eventually, it seems, most people refrained from washing before *Kiddush* at the seder, but many Jews of Ashkenazic origin retain the custom that only the master of ceremonies would wash before the eating of *karpas.*

The first washing was accompanied by a blessing, as noted above. This blessing was widespread. It is found in French, German, and Spanish communities; in Yemen; and in ancient China. Objection to the blessing over the first washing is first found in the writings of the students of Rabbi Meir of Rothenburg. Although the blessing is mentioned in the mnemonic device for the Passover order attributed to R. Meir, his students reported that he himself did not recite the blessing. The reason given for this is that the hand washing itself was obligatory only when people were careful about following the laws of food purity. Nevertheless, the blessing survived for many years. It is found in the haggadah printed in Prague in 1527 and in some later editions. In the early seventeenth century, Rabbi David ha-Levi, from Poland, called on people not to recite this blessing, even though it is printed in the *siddurim* (*Turei Zahav* on the *Shulchan Arukh* 473:7). Since then, it has disappeared, and even among Yemenite Jews it is no longer universally recited.

The second washing, before eating the matzah, is not unique to the seder evening for all traditional Jews wash their hands, with a blessing, before eating bread. There are no special traditions connected with Passover attached to it. The prevalent form for this blessing is *al netilat yadayim,* which does not follow the *Eretz Yisra'el* tradition.

The third hand washing, before reciting the grace after meals, also has a parallel in non-Jewish social customs, being simply comparable to the use of a finger bowl between courses and at the end of a meal, to remove grease and fat from one's fingers. This was especially necessary when people ate mostly with their fingers. The rabbis gave two rationales for this blessing: one theological and one hygienic. The theological rationale, which was supported by a biblical midrash, required washing one's hands before reciting grace as a way to reach the measure of sanctity required for reciting a blessing—much as hand washing was required before prayer. Perhaps it was thought that cleanliness is next to Godliness. The hygienic rationale was based on the fear the one might touch one's eyes with one's hands, which might have become contaminated during the meal. The rabbis even mentioned a specific substance, salt from the Dead Sea Valley, which was considered particularly dangerous to the eyes. These two reasons were the basis for discussions about the continuing necessity of washing hands before grace. We find strict constructionists, who insist that everyone must wash his or her hands before grace, and more limited opinions from those who say that only the one who says grace for a group of people must wash his hands. Many argued that the hygienic reason was the main reason, and in locales where this particular type of salt was not found, it was not necessary to wash before grace. Here too we find that a practice retained at the seder was originally an everyday custom that was abandoned. A student of Maharil, the fifteenth-century German rabbi, reports that his master did not ordinarily wash before grace but he did so at the seder (*Leket Yosher,* p. 36).

Dipping the Greens/Vegetable (*Karpas*)

The original custom of the first dipping, as evidenced in the Mishnah, was to dip some of the lettuce, which was later to be used for bitter herbs, into the *haroset.* The use of lettuce and *haroset* for the first dipping apparently evolved from the fact that these were what had traditionally been brought to the table at the time that the first dipping was instituted. Nevertheless, we should point out that lettuce was a standard appetizer in Roman times, so much so that one scholar, describing the festive Roman meal, writes that the appetizers served at the beginning of a meal included "vegetables and legumes of every kind—

especially the tart ones, raw or cooked, among which lettuce is almost indispensable."[25] Consumption of lettuce during the first dipping was apparently the most prevalent tradition, although a parallel source in the Tosefta implies that some meat from the internal organs of an animal was eaten then. In the *Eretz Yisra'el* tradition, as evidenced in *haggadot* found in the Cairo Genizah, this dipping evolved into a very elaborate course—including not only vegetables but eggs and fruits and even cakes—accompanied by an elaborate series of blessings both before and after the consumption of these items.

The custom of using lettuce for the first dipping presented a halakhic anomaly. The lettuce was to be used later in the evening, just before the meal, for fulfilling the commandment of eating bitter herbs, and then it was to be accompanied by a special blessing for this commandment. It seemed somewhat absurd to make a special blessing over the lettuce after one had already eaten lettuce. Therefore, a fourth-century Babylonian sage decided to substitute some other vegetable for the lettuce of the first dipping. The halakhic ruling, as later formulated, was that any vegetable could be used, as long as it was not one of the types of vegetables that could be used for bitter herbs. Rabbinical literature of gaonic times gives lists of various vegetables that are suitable for the rite. One of the most common vegetables used was *karpas,* which was apparently a generic name for a number of leafy vegetables such as parsley, and it was from this vegetable that the rite took its name. The use of this name for the ritual first appears in thirteenth-century France, but shortly thereafter, this name was homiletically explained as referring to the hard labor performed by the sixty myriads of Jewish slaves in Egypt (*k-r-p-s* = *s p-r-k* = 60 [myriads] hard work; the *s* [*samekh*] is the numerical equivalent of 60 and *p-r-k* is a Hebrew root meaning hard labor [*parekh*]). Since the *karpas* was one of the obligatory foods of the seder, early decisors ruled that one should eat a significant amount of it, at least the size of an olive (*Hilkhot Hametz u-Matzah* 8:2). However, the question of whether to recite a blessing after this dipping caused later decisors to rule that one should eat only a small quantity of the vegetable, less than the size of an olive, to obviate the necessity for a blessing after the *karpas.*

Haroset continued to be the relish of choice for the dipping. However, Rabbenu Tam and his brother, Rashbam, French sages of the twelfth century, thought that an analysis of the Mishnah showed that *haroset* had not been brought to the table before the meal. Therefore, it would have been impossible to use *haroset* for the first dip. In consequence, they ruled that one should not use *haroset* but some other liquid. They themselves used vinegar, but in later times, some used salt water. In Spain, the thirteenth-century rabbi David Abudarham knew that the great French sages were accustomed to use vinegar, but he remarked that most people followed the ancient custom of dipping the vegetable in *haroset.* Today, only some of the Yemenites still use *haroset* for the first dipping.

---

25. Doro Levi, *Antioch Mosaic Pavements* (Rome: L'Erma di Bretschneider, 1971), 132.

The Breaking of the Matzah (*Yahatz*)

After the first dipping, it is the custom of most Jewish communities to break the middle matzah of the three matzot into two pieces and put one aside to be eaten at the end of the meal. This custom, termed *yahatz* in the ancient mnemonic devices for the order of the evening, is not mentioned by Rav Saadiah Gaon, was unknown to Maimonides, and is not practiced by Yemenite communities that follow Maimonides.

There were two explanations for this custom. One explanation was that a broken matzah was considered more appropriate than a whole matzah as a broken one emphasized the idea that matzah was the "bread of distress" (Deut. 16:3). Distressed or poor people eat broken bread or half loaves rather than whole loaves. This idea is mentioned in the Babylonian Talmud in support of the ruling that on Pesach one is not required to prefer reciting the blessing over bread on a whole loaf (BT *Berachot* 39b). It is said that R. Hai Gaon understood the passage as meaning that there was no preference on Passover; one may recite the blessing over a whole loaf or over a broken one. He actually spoke against the custom of breaking the matzah before the blessing, thinking it unnecessary. Maimonides accepted the principle that the blessing over the matzah should be said over a broken loaf rather than a whole one, but he considered it sufficient to break one of the matzot later in the evening—just before reciting the blessing over bread. The blessing was then recited over two matzot, but one of them was broken. Maimonides gives no special instruction about what to do with the piece that had been broken off (*Hilkhot Hametz u-Matzah* 8:6). Traditional Yemenites follow the instructions of Maimonides but most communities now break the matzah at the beginning of the evening, apparently thinking that the haggadah itself should be recited over broken bread.

The other reason for breaking the matzah at this point is that this serves as an additional opportunity to arouse the curiosity of the children. Breaking the matzah would seem to mean that it was going to be distributed for eating. In other words, this would seem to be part of the pattern of a regular meal. However, instead of eating the matzah, one removes the seder plate and begins the story of the redemption. It may be that a somewhat obscure passage in the Tosefta refers to a custom of giving matzah to the children at this point in the seder.

The Story of the Redemption (*Maggid*)

The Structure

The heart of the haggadah is the section referred to as *maggid*. This section is a conglomerate of passages that have been added, and occasionally changed, throughout the generations. Nevertheless, we can discern a structure to this section, at least post facto.

The section begins with the four questions and concludes with the blessing over the second cup of wine. For this reason, the second cup is sometimes referred to as the cup of the haggadah. The connection between the second cup and *maggid* is illustrated by the instruction, already found in the Mishnah, to fill the second cup at the beginning of *maggid,* even though it will be drunk much later. The connection between the cup and the haggadah is further emphasized by the instruction of Maimonides to remove the table or tray (*Hilkhot Hametz u-Matzah* 8:2), which includes the matzah, before the questions. According to Maimonides, the tray or table is returned only at the presentation of matzah and *maror* (*Hilkhot Hametz u-Matzah* 8:4) just before the conclusion of the *maggid* section. Therefore, just the wine is left on the table during *maggid*.

However, rabbinical tradition connected the matzah with the story of the Exodus. Samuel expounded the biblical term "*lehem oni*" (bread of distress: Deut. 16:3) to mean "bread over which one recites many things" (BT *Pesachim* 36b). This is based on a play of words, reading "*oni*" as if derived from the root *o-n-h* (answer or recite). According to this theory, the matzah is the focus of the *maggid* section. This merged with yet another homiletic explanation of the term "*lehem oni,*" that the matzah of the seder should be broken bread, which was discussed above.

Using the bread as the focus of the *maggid* underlines the intrinsic difference between the first part of the *maggid* text and its final passages. The first part talks of the Exodus, expands on biblical passages connected to it, and explains its symbols. Matzah, which is a symbol both of slavery and of redemption, is a suitable focal point for this part of the *maggid.* The second part consists of songs of praise or *Hallel*—two chapters of Psalms (113, 114). The first of these psalms doesn't even have any specific mention of the Egypt or the Exodus. This difference between the two parts of *maggid* is first mentioned in twelfth-century French sources.[26] These sources state that one is to lift up the cup of wine just before the *Hallel* as song is connected to wine. Although this instruction is late, the distinction between the chapters of *Hallel* and the texts that precede it is clear and intrinsic.

There are two exceptions to the focus on matzah that are inherent in the performance of the seder. One is related to the passage *ve-hi she-amdah,* which refers to the covenant between God and Abraham. According to Rabbi Isaiah Horowitz (1565–1630), one should raise up the cup while reciting this passage, for unexplained kabbalistic reasons.[27] The corollary of this is that the matzah should be covered while holding the cup—because matzah, representing the staff of life, is more important than wine. Emphasizing the wine in the presence of matzah is considered disrespectful to the matzah.

The second exception to the focus on matzah comes when reciting the Ten Plagues. A custom arose of spilling out some wine at each of the plagues. This

26. H. L. Ehrenreich, ed., *Sefer Hapardes Le-Rashi Z"l* (Budapest, 1924), 51.

27. Isaiah Horowitz, *Shenei Luhot ha-Brit, Massekhet Pesachim, Ner Mitzvah* 31.

custom, first noted in Ashkenazic sources of the twelfth century,[28] is explained, in the earliest sources, as an expression of the idea that these plagues are not applicable to the participants but only to the enemies of Israel. Later sources explained that the reason for this was to express the idea that the participant's cup is not full when troubles befall others—even enemies. Later discussions of this custom refined this notion by stating that wine should not be spilled from the cup but should rather be sprinkled into a dish from a finger that had been dipped in the cup. These sources even defined which finger should be used to remove the wine from the cup, whereas other sources, perhaps more fastidious, thought that the wine should be spilled directly from the cup. A further modification was to remove drops from a surrogate cup, filled with vinegar. Modern scholars have noticed a similarity between the custom of spilling of wine into a cup and an ancient Sicilian game called *cottabos,* in which the participants flicked wine into a basin. However, there is no mention of this custom in ancient sources so one should rather look to medieval Germany for its origin.

Although these two exceptions give the appearance that the *maggid* section is not to be considered as a single unit focused on the matzah, the lateness of the connection of these two passages specifically with wine, rather than matzah, justifies our consideration of this whole unit as a single entity. This does not mean, of course, that all the passages included in this section were introduced at the same time or even at the same place. Nevertheless, it is not out of place to understand the whole unit as a structured unit. It opens with questions about the food and it closes with R. Gamliel's explanations of the foods. Between the opening and closing food statements, we find four main units: three versions of the Exodus story and a recapitulation of God's grace. Between the first and second stories of the Exodus we find passages that serve as transitions. A structured table of contents of the whole unit may help to clarify this.

A. The questions about the foods

1. First version of the Exodus story (*avadim hayyinu:* Deut. 6:21)
   The way the seder was conducted by the sages
   The way the message is to be explained to the four children
2. Second version of the Exodus story (*mitehilah ovdei avodah zarah:* Josh. 24:2)
   (mention of the covenant of Abraham)
3. The *bikkurim* story of the Exodus and its midrash (*arami oved avi:* Deut. 26:5)
4. A recapitulation of God's grace (*Dayenu* and *al ahat kamah vekhamah*)

B. R. Gamliel's explanation of the foods

---

28. Until recently, this was known only from later sources who attributed it to Rabbi Eleazar ben Judah of Worms, a German pietist who flourished at the end of the twelfth and beginning of the thirteenth centuries. It has recently been found in his writings; see Rabbi Elazar Vormsensis, *Oratio ad Pascam* [in Hebrew], edited by Simcha Emanuel (Jerusalem: Sumptibus Societatis Mekize Nirdamim, 2006), 101.

We notice that passage A is responded to in B, forming an envelope around the various stories of the Exodus. We may also discern an order in the way that the various stories of the Exodus are arranged. The first story, based on Deuteronomy 6:21, deals with the most immediate sense of the Exodus: we were slaves and now we are free. The second story, based on Joshua 24, expands on the spiritual meaning of the story: at first we were idol worshipers and now God has brought us into His service. The third, final story, based on the declaration of one who brings first fruits to the Temple in Deuteronomy 26, is open to interpretation—depending on how we translate the first verse. According to what we have assumed to be the earliest interpretation, this story tells of the ancestor of the Jewish people who was a homeless wanderer, and it ends with the settlement of the Jews in the Land of Israel. This, of course, broadens the story historically as the first story ends with physical freedom, achieved immediately at the Exodus; the second ends with spiritual freedom, reaching its peak at Mount Sinai; and the third ends with the settling of the Land of Israel, years later. However, as this story has been reinterpreted, its general message is one for the future: enemies have always risen against the Jewish people and God has always been there to save them from their enemies. This is followed by a recapitulation of the great things that God has done for the Jewish people, culminating in the building of the Temple, which, in this context, is clearly meant for the future.

Finally, the passages between the first and second story and the passage between the second and third story serve as transitions between the stories; their significance will be explained in context.

Questions and Answers—Paschal Foods

We have already noted the connection between the questions asked at the beginning of the evening and the declaration of R. Gamliel that comes shortly before the meal. This connection between the questions and the three main foods of the evening has become obscured due to the fact that the text of the questions in the haggadah has undergone a number of changes. As noted above, the earliest texts of the Mishnah have only three questions that relate to the three foods required to be eaten during the evening: Why matzah? Why dipping? Why roast meat? The questions relate to the superficial aspects of these foods, inquiring what the reason is for eating these foods and what their significance is. Despite the similarities between the questions, the everyday custom presumed by each is distinctly different.

The three foods that were required to be eaten were not special foods. In modern times, the matzah eaten at the seder is distinct from the foods usually served at the table. However, in talmudic times, unleavened bread, such as modern pita bread, may have been served frequently. It was easily prepared, as one did not have to go through the fermenting process, waiting for the dough to rise. Thus a question about this had to be formulated in a negative way: not

"Why do we eat matzah?" but "Why don't we eat any other kind of bread?" The same is true of the roast meat eaten at the meal. Meat is often eaten roasted. What was unique was that the menu consisted of only roasted meat, either the meat of the paschal lamb or roast meat eaten in commemoration of the paschal lamb. So the question took the form of "Why don't we eat meat prepared in any other way?" The preferred vegetable for *maror,* lettuce, was neither unique nor served in any special way. The only way to make the eating of lettuce distinctive was by serving or eating it in a different fashion from what was done regularly. Since everyday customs changed from place to place and from time to time, we find that early sources present us with different versions for the question of dipping.

What is probably the earliest version of the dipping question is found in the manuscripts of the Mishnah. The question was: "On all other nights we dip but once and tonight we dip twice." This version shows that the normal custom was to dip once. It is not clear exactly which dipping was the additional one but we might assume, based on Roman custom, that the dipping before the meal was usual, whereas the additional dipping was the one done at the beginning of the meal. The *Eretz Yisra'el* Talmud tells of the existence of another version of this question: "On all other nights we dip [or: eat] it with bread and tonight we dip it by itself." Babylonian sages also had to change the version of the question as it appeared in the Mishnah in order to make it appropriate for their customs. After several attempts at revising this question, the version finally accepted was that which appears in modern *haggadot:* "On all other nights we do not dip even once, tonight we dip twice."

A fourth question was added to the original three in *amoraic* times. This question is: "On all other nights we eat all kinds of vegetables, on this night *maror*." This is clearly a later question as it appears neither in the best manuscripts of the Mishnah nor in early manuscripts of the haggadah. The reason for adding this question was, apparently, the recognition that the questions should relate to the special foods of the evening, coupled with the difficulty of connecting the question of dipping vegetables specifically with bitter herbs. This latter difficulty was enhanced by the substitution of a vegetable other than lettuce for the first dipping, as noted above. The formulation of this question followed the pattern of the questions about matzah and roast meat—even though, at least in later times, it was no longer accurate: other vegetables were eaten at the seder and the first dipping itself was with an "other" vegetable.

The final change in these questions occurred in gaonic times. The campaign to eliminate roast meat from the meal succeeded and the question about roast meat was no longer relevant. It seems that by this time the number of four questions had become a canonic number, so the elimination of the question about roast meat required the addition of another question. The question added was: "On all other nights we eat either sitting or reclining, on this night we all recline." The custom of reclining at meals was no longer prevalent, and it was preserved only as a halakhic requirement at the seder. In earlier times it could not have been marked as a unique feature of the seder, but in gaonic times it was appropriate for an additional question. This question is not found in any text of the Mishnah or in early *haggadot*. The great majority of texts of any type have either the question about roast meat or the question about reclining, showing that "reclining" was a substitute for the question about roast meat. Nevertheless there are several *haggadot* from the Cairo Genizah that include both questions, such as TS H 152,[29] making a total of five questions for the evening.

R. Gamliel provides the answers to the questions: "Whoever did not say these three things on Passover has not fulfilled their obligation: *Pesach,* matzah, and *maror.*" It is unlikely that R. Gamliel meant that one just had to *say* these three words. The word "*amar,*" translated here as "say," might be better translated here as "explain," as it used in Aramaic. The explanations following this statement should also be attributed to R. Gamliel.[30] The version of these explanations found in the Mishnah differs from that found in the *haggadot* in a number of major points. I present the text of the explanations as it appears in the best manuscripts of the Mishnah:

> Passover—for the *Makom* passed over the home of our ancestors in Egypt; bitter herbs—for the Egyptians embittered the lives of our ancestors in Egypt; matzah—for they were redeemed.

The most significant difference between this text and the text preserved in the *haggadot* is the explanation of the matzah. The haggadah states that the reason for eating matzah is because "the dough of our ancestors had not risen before the King of Kings, the Holy one Blessed be He, appeared before them and redeemed them, as it is said: 'And they baked unleavened cakes of the dough that they had taken out of Egypt, for it was not leavened, since they had been driven out of Egypt and could not delay; nor had they prepared any provisions for themselves' (Exod. 12:39)." This explanation seems clear and reasonable, and Naomi Cohen has claimed to have found a parallel to this in the writings of Philo.[31]

The stark explanation given in the Mishnah, "for they were redeemed," is not clear. Some scholars have suggested that this explanation is based on a play on words—matzah sounds like *motzi* (brings out). The only justification for this interpretation of the explanation is that the explanations for Passover and bitter

29. A facsimile of this is found in Kasher, *Hagadah Shelemah,* 91.

30. G. Alon has suggested that the words "*Pesach, matzzah,* and *maror*" were not originally part of R. Gamliel's statement, which originally stressed the three explanations presented in the Mishnah.

31. Naomi G. Cohen, *Philo Judaeus: His Universe of Discourse* (Frankfurt am Main: Peter Lang, 1995), 308–309. For a discussion of the rabbinical sources see Tabory, *Pesach Dorot,* 51.

herbs are also based on wordplays. Indeed, the element of wordplay is most obvious in connection with the sacrifice for there is no other reason for calling this sacrifice "Passover" but for the fact that it celebrates the passing over. Nevertheless, the interpretation of the explanation for matzah is not satisfying, and no better explanation has been offered.

There are two major differences in the structure of the explanation between the Mishnah and the haggadah. The first is that the Mishnah gives direct explanations and is satisfied with that. The haggadah turns each explanation into the form of question and answer, that is: "For what reason do we eat this matzah? Because . . ." The second is that the haggadah is not satisfied with a simple answer but it supplies a biblical prooftext for each explanation. The formulation of the statements as questions and answers and the addition of biblical prooftexts in midrashic form give these statements the nature of other parts of the haggadah. There are some texts that retain the original explanation of the matzah with the prooftext: "And they baked unleavened cakes of the dough that they had taken out of Egypt, for it was not leavened, since they had been driven out of Egypt and could not delay; nor had they prepared any provisions for themselves" (Exod. 12:39).[32] This biblical prooftext is not really appropriate for there is no clear-cut relationship between the explanation, "for they were redeemed," and the biblical verse, which just points out that they had been driven out of Egypt before they managed to bake leavened bread. It was necessary to add a verse, since the other two foods also had verses attached to them. However, no more appropriate verse could be found. It is possible that its addition, necessary for structural reasons, was the cause of changing the explanation.

There are several other variants between the two texts that are of interest. One of the most significant is the actualization of the foods. In the Mishnah, the foods are discussed abstractly: *Pesach,* matzah, and *maror.* The haggadah, however, emphasizes that these foods are eaten by the participants. The question is not "For what reason is matzah?" but "For what reason do we eat this matzah?" In some manuscripts, this actualization appears only in connection with matzah and *maror*. The paschal lamb is not actualized for it could not be eaten after the destruction of the Second Temple. The traditional text presents a compromise: the paschal lamb is referred to as that "which our ancestors ate when the Temple existed." Perhaps connected with this is the substitution of "Holy One, Blessed be He" instead of the *ha-Makom*[33] as the appellation of God.

---

32. See the text of the Mishnah as preserved in the Valmadonna manuscript of the Babylonian tractate of *Pesachim*.

33. For the translation of this term see p. 86.

The Story: From Lowliness to Glory

The Mishnah prescribes that the story of the Exodus should present a contrast: beginning with disgrace or lowly status and ending with glory and pride. The Mishnah does not prescribe any specific text for this story, other than the midrashic explanation of Deuteronomy 26:1–5. Our first evidence for the first two stories of the Exodus in the traditional haggadah is from *amoraic* times. Rav is quoted as saying that one should recapitulate Jewish history as was done in the beginning[34] by Joshua, that is, "In olden times, your forefathers—Terah, father of Abraham and father of Nahor—lived beyond the Euphrates and worshiped other gods" (Josh. 24:2; JT *Pesachim* 10:5; 37d). The passage suggested by Rav appears in both the Babylonian and *Eretz Yisra'el* versions of the haggadah.

A somewhat different form of Rav's suggestion appears in the Babylonian Talmud (BT *Pesachim* 116a). Here we find a disagreement with Samuel over the definition of the mishnaic rubric for the haggadah that one "starts with disgrace." Rav states that one should begin "Originally, our forefathers were idol worshipers," which seems to be a paraphrase of the verse from Joshua quoted above. However, Samuel offered another suggestion—that one should use the recapitulation of Jewish history found in a Deuteronomic passage: "We were slaves to Pharaoh in Egypt" (Deut. 6:21). This passage is actually prescribed by the Torah as the beginning of a lesson to children who ask about the significance of the commandments. Samuel's suggestion was accepted in the traditional haggadah but it does not appear in the *Eretz Yisra'el* haggadah as defined by the *haggadot* found in the Cairo Genizah.

Apparently, neither Rav nor Samuel felt that the demand that the pattern of "shame and glory" should appear in the haggadah was fulfilled by expounding the above-mentioned Deuteronomic verses (or, perhaps, was no longer fulfilled by it; see below). Their alternatives described the shame but neglected to describe the glory with which one was to conclude. The traditional haggadah completes this pattern for Rav by noting that God has led us to His worship and, for Samuel, it notes that God has freed us from slavery. It is interesting to note that both biblical passages, that of Deuteronomy and that of Joshua, conclude the recapitulation of Jewish history with the gift of the Land of Israel to the Children of Israel. Traditional *haggadot* do not contain the complete biblical passages. This gives meaning to the statement of Rava, two generations after Samuel, that one must say "and us He freed from there" (Deut. 6:23). This is the final verse of the passage considered mandatory by Samuel. It would seem that people refrained from citing this verse as its conclusion—"that He might take us and give us the land that He had promised on oath to our fathers"—was not relevant to Diaspora Jewry. Therefore, Rava found it necessary to insist that at least the first part of this verse must be said.

34. This word, "*kit'chilah,*" was corrupted into "*mit'chilah,*" which was understood to mean "from the beginning" and was incorporated into the text of the haggadah.

The Midrash

The mishnaic description of the early paschal ritual tells us that "he begins with the disgrace (or: lowly status), and concludes with glory; and he expounds the biblical passage 'my father was a fugitive Aramean' until the end of the section." The specific passage denoted by the Mishnah to be part of the haggadah is the passage from Deuteronomy (26:5ff.), which was the declaration required by the Torah for one who brought first fruits to the Temple. The Mishnah marks the beginning of the passage by its opening phrase, but its definition of the end is not totally clear. All three clauses of the mishnaic prescription have been the subject of vast amounts of scholarly discussion. For purposes of clarity, I will deal with them in reverse order.

I will first deal with the interpretation of the closing phrase of the instructions: "until he concludes the portion." This phrase cannot be taken literally, in its present context,[35] for the portion concludes with the verse "Wherefore I now bring the first fruits of the soil which You, O Lord, have given me" (Deut. 26:10). This verse is obviously irrelevant and inappropriate for the seder evening. The question of the inclusion of the penultimate verse, "He brought us to this place and gave us this land, a land flowing with milk and honey" (Deut. 26:9), has been the subject of much scholarly discussion. This verse is not included, in rabbinical tradition, as part of the haggadah. However, it would have been appropriate for the people who ate the paschal lamb in Jerusalem, especially according to the rabbinical midrash that "this place" refers to the Temple (*Sifrei Devarim* 301, p. 319). Therefore, it has been suggested that this last verse was originally part of the haggadah of those who celebrated the Passover in Jerusalem, and possibly for all the residents of *Eretz Yisra'el*. This verse was eliminated from the haggadah after the destruction of the Second Temple, or perhaps even earlier—by people who conducted a paschal meal outside of Jerusalem and the Land of Israel.

We may now turn to an understanding of the correct translation of the opening biblical verse. The translation cited above, "My father was a fugitive Aramean" (Deut. 26:5), is the modern JPS translation. Rabbinical tradition, as preserved in the haggadah, translates this verse as "An Aramean (Laban) tried to destroy my father." Something of a compromise between these two understandings is found in the *Sifrei Devarim,* which expounds this verse as "this teaches us that Jacob went to Aram as a wanderer and the Torah considers Laban as if he had destroyed him" (*Sifrei Devarim* 301, p. 319). Some medieval commentators and many modern scholars have tended to accept the first translation as the correct meaning of this verse. Modern scholars have shown that this explanation was also known in antiquity, and scholars have tried to explain

35. This text appears also in the mishnah of *Bikkurim* 3:6, which tells of the reading of this passage in the context of bringing the first fruits. Scholars suspect that the passage in *Pesachim* was copied from *Bikkurim* in spite of the inappropriateness of the last phrase.

why the rabbis reinterpreted this passage.[36] It is possible that the two issues, the use of the penultimate verse and the understanding of the first verse, are related. While the Temple existed, people who included the penultimate verse of this portion in their haggadah understood the whole passage as truly representing their radical change in status. The people had started out as fugitives or wandering nomads, and now they stood in their permanent home, the land given to them by God. This interpretation fits in well with the Mishnah's description of the text as "beginning with disgrace and ending with praise." After the destruction of the Temple, the penultimate verse, no longer relevant, was omitted. It is possible that this verse was never part of the haggadah outside of Jerusalem. Without this verse, the portion closed with the salvation from Egyptian oppression. There was no longer any parallelism between the lowly beginning as nomads and their present status as people saved from persecution. Perhaps this was the reason that the first verse was reinterpreted to deal with oppression rather than with landlessness.[37] In this way, the rhetorical pattern was retained: we began as persecuted by Laban and now we have been saved from persecution and slavery.

Although the Mishnah demands the exposition of this biblical portion, it does not give any details about the nature of this exposition. We have three midrashim on this chapter: one found in the halakhic midrash to the book of Deuteronomy (*Sifrei Devarim* 301, p. 318), a second one found in the traditional *haggadot,* and a third in Cairo Genizah *haggadot*.[38] Although the *Sifrei Devarim* might be thought of as the earliest of the three, its great similarity to the version found in the traditional versions of the haggadah has suggested to scholars that it is an interpolation in the *Sifrei Devarim* from the haggadah. Be that as it may, the similarity between the two eliminates the necessity to deal separately with the version in *Sifrei Devarim.*

The two versions found in the *haggadot* apparently reflect differences between the Babylonian version of the haggadah, found in the traditional *haggadot,* and the *Eretz Yisra'el* version as found in the *genizah haggadot*. The *Eretz Yisra'el* version of this midrash has very little midrashic material. In fact, this midrash consists only of a few midrashic explanations of the opening verse and an expansion of the closing verse. There are only two comments that are

---

36. Tigay has suggested that the rabbis found it difficult to think of their ancestors as Arameans; see Jeffrey H. Tigay, *JPS Commentary on Deuteronomy* (Philadelphia: Jewish Publication Society, 1996), 243. The latest discussion of the history of the interpretation of this verse is Menahem I. Kahana, *Sifre Zuta on Deuteronomy: Citations from a New Tannaitic Midrash* [in Hebrew] (Jerusalem: Magnes, 2003), 415–417. See also Karin Zetterholm, *Portrait of a Villain: Laban the Aramean in Rabbinic Literature* (Leuven: Peeters, 2002).

37. For the possibility that the reinterpretation was influenced by Christian typology, see Yuval, "Easter and Passover as Early Christian Dialogue," 111–113.

38. See p. xiv, n. 8.

common to both traditions. The first is the opening comment that the meaning of this biblical passage is that Laban tried to destroy Jacob. The second is an expansion of the verse "And he went down to Egypt" (Deut. 26:5), explaining that Jacob did not do so by choice but rather that he was forced to do so by the word of God (see p. 90).

There is one other comment that seems to be common to both traditions and that is the midrashic expansion to the verse "The Lord freed us from Egypt by a mighty hand, by an outstretched arm and awesome power, and by signs and portents" (Deut. 26:8). The midrash took this to be a hint to the Ten Plagues. The first three terms ("mighty hand, by an outstretched arm and awesome power") refer to six plagues, as each term consists of two words, and the final two terms ("signs and portents") refer to four plagues as each of the two terms appears in plural form. Although this explanation appears in both traditions, in the Babylonian tradition it follows another, less fanciful explanation to this verse, and it is preceded by the words "another explanation" (*davar acher*). Thus this explanation may be an addition to the Babylonian tradition and an example of the influence of the *Eretz Yisra'el* tradition on that of Babylon.[39] The traditional haggadah, in turn, enhanced this explanation with the addition of an expanded numerical midrash counting the plagues, an explanation that was yet considered by R. Saadiah, in the tenth century, as a permissible option but not necessary.[40]

The midrash of the Deuteronomic passage in the traditional haggadah has been shown to be of two distinct patterns. The more common pattern does not really expound on the biblical passages but just quotes biblical prooftexts that substantiate the Deuteronomic passage.[41] Thus, for instance, the verse that states that the Jews went to Egypt "with meager numbers" (Deut. 26:5) is substantiated by quoting another verse, "Your ancestors went down to Egypt seventy persons in all; and now the Lord your God has made you as numerous as the stars of heaven" (Deut. 10:22). The prooftext is introduced by "as it is said" and there is no further explanation. It is noteworthy that this type of midrash, which might be called "primitive midrash," does not appear in the *Eretz Yisra'el* version. It has been suggested that this form of midrash is actually the later one.[42]

The other pattern follows more traditional midrash, adding explanations to the main text without prooftexts. An example of this is a text that we have men-

39. For examples of mutual influence see Rovner, "An Early Passover Haggadah According to the Palestinian Rite."

40. *Siddur R. Saadja Gaon* [in Hebrew], edited by I. Davidson, S. Assaf, and B. I. Joel (Jerusalem: Mekize Nirdamim, 1941), 243.

41. See David Henshke, "The *Midrash* of the Passover *Haggadah*" [in Hebrew], *Sidra* 4 (1988): 33–52. Henshke argues that this was the original part of the midrash.

42. Rovner, "A New Version of the Eres Israel Haggadah Liturgy and the Evolution of the Eres Israel 'Miqra' Bikkurim' Midrash."

tioned above. The haggadah adds to the verse "And he went down into Egypt" (Deut. 26:5) the explanation: "compelled by the [Divine] word." This is a remarkable example as there is nothing in the verse itself that mandates this interpretation and the interpretation cries out for a prooftext to verify its statement.[43] Another example of this type of midrash is the opening passage of our midrash, identifying the biblical Aramean as Laban, attempting to destroy the incipient Jewish nation, which is also explanatory, without any prooftext at all. However, this example does not follow the regular pattern of first quoting the verse and then giving the explanation but instead reverses it by first quoting the explanation and then bringing the biblical verse as a quasi prooftext for the explanation.

Many of the expositions are conflations of the two methods. Thus we read "'and sojourned there' (Deut. 26:5)—this teaches that Jacob our father did not go down to settle but to sojourn there, as it is said: 'For to sojourn in the land are we come; for thy servants have no pasture for their flocks; for the famine is sore in the land of Canaan: now therefore, we pray thee, let thy servants dwell in the land of Goshen' (Gen. 47:4)." Here we have an explanation about the intent of Jacob, followed by a verse that seems to have been meant to justify the explanation, but really adds nothing.

We have one example of a parallel between the Babylonian version and the *Eretz Yisra'el* version that demonstrates clearly the issue of conflated midrash. The Babylonian text reads: "'And the Lord brought us forth out of Egypt' (Deut. 26:8)—not by an angel; not by a seraph; nor by a messenger but the Holy One, Blessed be He, in His own glory and He alone as it says: 'For that night I will go through the land of Egypt and strike down every first-born in the land of Egypt, both man and beast; and I will mete out punishments to all the gods of Egypt, I the LORD' (Exod. 12:12)." The *Eretz Yisra'el* version lacks the prooftext, ending with "He alone." We cannot be sure what this comparison implies. On the one hand, we might think that the original version of this text was an ordinary midrashic text, as it appears in the *Eretz Yisra'el* version, and the Babylonian version added a prooftext to make its pattern conform to the pattern of the majority of the other midrashim. On the other hand, it is possible that the *Eretz Yisra'el* version eliminated this prooftext. This passage has been discussed as a component of the Jewish-Christian polemic in its stressing that Moses was not the redeemer, "thereby refuting the view that Moses is an archetype of Jesus."[44] It is noteworthy that the polemic, if it really

43. See Kasher, *Hagadah Shelemah,* 34.

44. Yuval, "Easter and Passover as Early Christian Dialogue," 110. Cf. P. Winter, "*Ou Dia Xeir Presbews oude Dia Xeir Serape oude Dia Angelou: Isa lxiii:9* [in Greek] (the Septuagint reading for Isaiah 63:9), and the Passover Haggadah *Vetus Testamentum* 4 (1954): 439–441; Judah Goldin, "Not by Means of an Angel and Not by Means of a Messenger," in *Religions in Antiquity: Essays in Memory of Erwin Ramsdale Goodenough,* Studies in the History of Religions XIV (Leiden: Brill, 1968), 412–424; idem, *Studies in Midrash and Related Literature* (Philadelphia: Jewish Publication Society, 1988), 163–173.

exists, is much stronger in the Babylonian version, where anti-Christian polemic would seem much less important than it is in the *Eretz Yisra'el* version, the home of such polemic as existed.

We may now turn to the opening phrase of the Mishnah, which calls on the reader to begin with lowly origins and end with glory. This rhetorical pattern, beginning with lowly origin to stress the heights to which one has risen, is obvious and was well known in antiquity.[45] However, it is not clear whether the mishnaic call to use this pattern is meant to describe the exposition of the biblical *bikkurim* passage mentioned in the Mishnah immediately afterward or rather calls to recite another text, only after which one is to expound the biblical passage. The presumed original interpretation of this *bikkurim* passage, that the ancestors were wandering nomads who have finally, through the grace of God, reached their homeland, fits well with this pattern. The interpretation preserved in the traditional haggadah, that the ancestors were persecuted by Laban and finally rescued by God from the hands of Pharaoh, does not fit the rhetoric pattern as well as the other.

The Other *Maggid* Texts That Are in Common Use

I will now turn to the other, ancillary, texts of the *maggid* section. The section opens with an Aramaic presentation of the matzah used at the seder as the "bread of distress (or: affliction) eaten by our ancestors in Egypt." The opening of the *maggid* with an explanation of the significance of the matzah has been considered as of great antiquity. Attempts have been made to show a parallel to this statement in Philo,[46] and others have discerned in it an anti-Christian polemic.[47] However, the fact that this introduction does not appear in *Eretz Yisra'el* versions of the haggadah suggests that it is late material and of Babylonian origin. It does not appear in the siddur of Rav Saadiah Gaon, but the conclusion of the passage, expressing the hope that the participants will yet be free men and will return to the Land of Israel, does appear in his siddur.[48] The expression of this hope also argues for a non–*Eretz Yisra'el* provenance.

The Passover of the Sages

The next texts to be considered are the texts that come between the story of the Exodus as suggested by Samuel and the story of the Exodus as suggested by Rav. Here we find two interpolations. The first interpolation consists of two units. The first unit consists of two stories about sages who discussed the

45. For the influence of this direction on Christian thought see Everett Ferguson, "The Disgrace and the Glory: A Jewish Motif in Early Christianity," *Studia Patristica* 21 (1989): 86–94.

46. Cohen *Philo Judaeus,* 306.

47. Yuval, "Easter and Passover as Early Christian Dialogue," 105–106.

48. *Siddur R. Saadiah Gaon,* 136.

Exodus. These two stories are introduced by the statement that "even if we are all wise, we are all understanding, we are all elders, we all know the Torah, we are obligated to tell the story of the Exodus from Egypt. Everyone who lengthens the discussion is praiseworthy." These passages are not found in *Eretz Yisra'el haggadot* or in the haggadah of Rav Saadiah Gaon. They are found in the *haggadot* of Rav Natronai, Rav Amram, and Maimonides and in all later *haggadot* that have been examined.

Although the two stories come from different sources, they combine in a thematic whole. The first story tells us of sages who were discussing the story of the Exodus throughout the night until their students came and told them that it was time to recite the morning *Shema:*

> One time R. Eliezer, R. Joshua, R. Eliezer b. Azaryah, R. Akiva, and R. Tarfon were participating in a festive meal in B'nei B'rak and were discussing the Exodus throughout the night, until their students came and said to them: "Our masters, it is time to recite the morning *Shema*." (See p. 85)

This passage is not found in any rabbinical source other than the haggadah. There is a similar story in the Tosefta (*Pesachim* 10:11, pp. 198–199) that also tells of a banquet of sages that seems to have taken place on Passover eve. This story reads:

> Once R. Gamliel and sages were gathered together in the home of Ben Zonin in Lydda and they were engaged in the laws of Passover all night until the cock crowed. The tables were removed and they went to the bet midrash.

The Toseftan story has several points in common with the story in the haggadah. Both stories took place in the land of Judaea, not far from each other, in the first decades after the destruction of the Second Temple, and they both purport to tell us how the sages celebrated the Passover eve. They both tell of a banquet of sages, without telling us whether others, such as women and children, were present. Both tell us that the sages' discussion continued until the morning, although one version implies that they would have continued on if the students had not interrupted them. The significant difference is that the story in the Tosefta tells us that the sages devoted themselves to the study of law whereas the story in the haggadah tells us that they talked about the Exodus. These two versions seem to reflect two different approaches to what type of discussion was appropriate for the evening. The approach that was accepted in the standard haggadah was to deal with history and legend rather than with *halakhah*. However, the halakhic approach appears even in the standard haggadah: the response to the wise child is to teach him the laws of Passover.

This unit continues with a second story, taken from the Mishnah (*Berachot* 1:5). This story tells us of a discussion by rabbis whether there was an obligation to remember the Exodus in the evening. The context of the story is ambiguous. In the context of the Mishnah it is clear that this discussion has nothing to do with Passover but is rather a discussion about the obligation to remember the

Exodus on every night of the year. It is brought in the Mishnah to document how the sages reached the decision, stated in the prior Mishnah, that one is obligated to remember the Exodus in the evening. In the present-day evening prayer there are two mentions of the Exodus. The first is found in the third chapter of the *Shema* and the second is found in the penultimate blessing of the *Shema*. In the *Eretz Yisra'el* version of the *Shema,* the third chapter was not recited in the evening and, therefore, the ruling of the Mishnah must be referring to the mention of the *Shema* in the penultimate blessing. However, many commentators, neglecting to take the *Eretz Yisra'el* custom into consideration, thought that the reference in the Mishnah was to the mention of the Exodus in the third chapter of the *Shema*. Be that as it may, the context of the story in the haggadah makes it seem as if this story were a continuation of the prior story about the Passover celebration of the sages. Indeed, some versions add the words "to them," reading: "Rabbi Eleazar ben Azariah said to them," making it very clear that this story is a continuation of the prior story. Although the composition is historically inaccurate, the combination of the two stories offers us a narrative that is typical of later sympotic literature. The sages were discussing the Exodus when their students arrived to tell them that it was time to recite the morning *Shema*. Rather than getting up to recite the *Shema,* the incident provoked a discussion about proper times for the fulfillment of the commandment to remember the Exodus. It is instructive to note that the discussion in the second story is not of the Exodus but of the laws related to the Exodus. Similar stories, in which events at the meal provoke discussion connected with those events, are found in sympotic literature. The purpose of this combined story, within the framework of the haggadah, is to tell us that one should discuss the Exodus at length and, therefore, although the bare history of the Exodus has already been completed, the haggadah now turns to other versions of the story.[49]

The Four Children

The second interpolation is also a composite passage, presenting us with four different types of children and explaining how one should relate to each type.[50] The function of this interpolation here may be understood as a justification for continuing with different versions of the Exodus as each individual must understand the message of the Exodus in his own way. The previous passage focused on sages and their lengthy discussions even though they are presumed to know it all. Now it is necessary to explain the story to everyone according to his understanding and tendencies. This is exemplified by the various types of individuals found in each family.

49. In the commentary, I will discuss the age of R. Eleazar ben Azariah and the continuation of the *derashah*.

50. See F. O. Francis, "The Baraita of the Four Sons," *Journal of the American Academy of Religion* 42 (1974): 280–297; *Proceedings of the Society of Biblical Literature* 1 (1972): 245–283.

The passage about the four children is found in all Babylonian versions of the haggadah and, with minor variations, in the *Mekhilta de-Rabbi Ishmael* (Pisha 18, ed. Lauterbach, pp. 166–167), the midrash *halakhah* to Exodus. We shall refer to it as a *baraita,* a term commonly used for material that is assumed to be of *tannaitic* origin even though it is not found in the Mishnah. This *baraita* is found also in the Jerusalem Talmud (JT *Pesachim* 10:4, 37d), with greater variations. Nevertheless, it is not found in the *Eretz Yisra'el haggadot*.

Most of the *haggadot* introduce this interpolation with an expression of thanks to God who has given the Torah to His people: "Blessed is the *Makom,* Blessed is He; Blessed is He who gave the Torah to His people, Blessed is He."

The *baraita* of the four children is a complex passage based on biblical interpretation and rabbinical patterns of rhetoric. The Torah contains five passages that talk about transmitting the message of the Exodus and the events connected with it to future generations. Three of these passages utilize the Exodus in contexts that are not connected to Passover. In one of them, a parent is commanded to respond to a child's question about the redemption of firstborn boys with the statement that God took the Children of Israel out of Egypt with force, killing the Egyptian's firstborn when Pharaoh refused to let the people go (Exod. 13:14–16). The second verse tells a parent to respond to the child's question about the meaning of the commandments with the statement that God freed the Jews from Egyptian slavery and gave them the Land of Israel, which justifies His demand to observe all the commandments (Deut. 6:21). The third verse is an aside about the purpose of hardening the heart of Pharaoh "that you may recount in the hearing of your sons and of your sons' sons how I made a mockery of the Egyptians . . . in order that you may know that I am the Lord" (Exod. 10:1–2). None of these three verses specifies that these statements are to be used at the paschal celebration. Nevertheless, the first two are included in the *baraita* of the four children as responses to children whereas the third is totally ignored in the haggadah.

The two other verses are more directly connected to Passover. The first (Exod. 12:26–27) talks about the sacrifice of the paschal lamb in the Land of Israel. When the children ask, "What do you mean by this rite?" you should reply, "It is the Passover sacrifice to the LORD, because He passed over the houses of the Israelites in Egypt when He smote the Egyptians, but saved our houses." The final verse tells us that, while observing the seven-day matzah festival, "you shall explain to your son on that day, 'It is because of what the LORD did for me when I went free from Egypt'" (Exod. 13:8).

The four verses that serve as the base of this *baraita* do not explicitly distinguish between the types of children who are the springboard for the discussion. However, some linguistic and stylistic differences between the passages may be the source of the rabbinical exegesis. The clearest example of this is the passage "And you shall explain to your son on that day, 'It is because of what the LORD did for me when I went free from Egypt'" (Exod. 13:8). Since this passage contains nothing about this statement being a response to the child's asking, it was clear to the sages that this child was not capable of asking questions.

It is also fairly easy to understand how the sages assumed that one of the three remaining passages referred to a wicked child. Two of the three begin with a child's asking (*yishal*) while one begins with a child's saying (*yomru;* Exod. 12:26). This fact may have been joined with the content of the statement, "What do you mean by this rite?" to facilitate the understanding that the inquirer is a difficult child. Comparing this question to the similar question, "What does this mean?" (Exod. 13:14) could bring us to understand, as the sages did, that the first question shows a lack of personal interest and involvement in what is going on.

Finally, we are left with two questions in which the Torah actually uses the verb "ask." They are "What does this mean?" (Exod. 13:14) and "What mean the decrees, laws, and rules that the Lord our God has enjoined upon you?" (Deut. 6:21). If we have to assign one question to a wise person and one to a less sophisticated questioner, the choice is clear.

The question that remains to be asked is why there have to be four children. Why not three (not distinguishing between the two who ask) or five (including the verse that is ignored)? This question is related to another problem connected with the division of the four children. The division into four is not on the same level. Two of the four children are clearly graded according to their intellectual level: wise, and one who is not capable of framing a question. The place of the "simple" child is ambiguous. Does "simple" (*tam*) represent simple piety or does it represent a simple mind? The Jerusalem Talmud has, in this place, a "foolish" (*tippesh*) child, which is clearly an intellectual attribute. The wicked child clearly represents a personality characteristic and should be in apposition to a good or pious child. This has led scholars to posit that our text is a conflated one composed of two earlier texts. One of the earlier texts referred to the wicked child alone, or perhaps compared the wicked one to a pious child. Another text referred to three children of various intellectual levels: a wise child who asks intelligent questions, an intermediate child who asks innocuous questions, and a simple child who does not know how to inquire at all. In the conflation of these texts, the wise child and the pious child were coalesced into one figure.

Several scholars have offered another theory. The typology of four children is based on a pattern common among the sages of listing four combinations of two qualities. In this case, the qualities under consideration are wisdom and piety. The wise child has it all; the wicked child is intelligent but impious; the third child is pious but has no wisdom and so cannot ask intelligent questions; the fourth child is a blank slate from both standpoints. This approach helps explain the order of the children, which does not follow the biblical order. The list starts with one who has all the good qualities, followed by the two who have one good quality apiece, ending with the one who has no qualities at all. This approach also explains why one verse was totally ignored. The starting point of the *baraita* is not the Bible but rather a list of four types of children for whom appropriate verses were found in the Bible.

We may now turn to the response given to each child, noting that the text of the haggadah strays from the biblical text. The answer to each statement in the haggadah is usually different from the answer given in the Torah. Much of the commentary on this passage attempts to explain why this is so. I will describe the problem and suggest a solution based on a historical-critical approach.

The most obvious discrepancies between the responses in the haggadah and those in the Torah relate to the wise child and to the wicked child. The response to the wise child in the Torah is:

> We were slaves to Pharaoh in Egypt and the LORD freed us from Egypt with a mighty hand. The LORD wrought before our eyes marvelous and destructive signs and portents in Egypt, against Pharaoh and all his household; and us He freed from there, that He might take us and give us the land that He had promised on oath to our fathers (Deut. 6:21–23).

But the haggadah ignores this and tells us that the proper response to the wise child is to teach him the laws of Passover. The haggadah mentions the prohibition of eating after the meal as an example of the laws of Passover, and it has often been suggested that the intention was to demand the teaching of all the laws of Passover, ending with the last detail—that one is not to eat after the paschal meal. Some texts actually add the word "until," reading: "teach him the laws of Passover, until 'one may not eat after the paschal meal.'"

The response to the wicked child in the Torah is "It is the passover sacrifice to the LORD, because He passed over the houses of the Israelites in Egypt when He smote the Egyptians, but saved our houses" (Exod. 12:27). This is replaced in the haggadah by the verse "It is because of what the LORD did for me when I went free from Egypt" (Exod. 13:8), which is the statement to be made to the child who does not ask anything. This verse appears again in this *baraita* in its proper place, apparently as the statement to be made to the child who does not ask. However, a significant number of *haggadot* lack a definite response to this child, satisfying themselves with the statement "You should begin [the explanation] as it says: 'And you should tell your child on that day.'"[51]

It is noteworthy that the verses that are omitted, the responses to the wise child and to the wicked child, appear prominently elsewhere in the haggadah. The response to the wise child is the first version of the story that appears in the haggadah, and the response to the wicked child is used as the prooftext for R. Gamliel's explanation of the significance of the paschal sacrifice. It is thus

51. For the information on the *haggadot* that follow this version, see Kasher, *Hagadah Shelemah,* 25–26, and Safrai and Safrai, *Haggadah of the Sages,* 212.

conceivable that the compiler of this *baraita* did not wish to use verses that appear elsewhere in the haggadah as a general text in the context of a specific response to one of the children. In the case of the response to the wise child, the response selected by the sages was eminently appropriate to the question—perhaps even more appropriate than the response supplied by the Torah. The sages interpreted the question not as "What mean the decrees, laws, and rules that the LORD our God has enjoined upon you?" but as "What are the decrees, laws, and rules that the LORD our God has enjoined upon you?" The obvious response is to teach him the laws of Passover.

This explanation, that the biblical response to the wise child was ignored because it appears elsewhere in the haggadah, fits in well with the observation that this *baraita* appears only in *haggadot* that begin the *maggid* section with this verse. The corollary to this is that this *baraita* was created within the framework of the haggadah and that its appearance in the midrash to the book of Exodus is secondary.

We have noted that the *baraita* of the four children is found in the *Mekhilta de-Rabbi Ishmael* (Pisha 18, ed. Lauterbach, pp. 166–167) with only minor variations. However, two of the variations are of great interest. One is just stylistic. Where the haggadah expounds the response to the wicked child as "to me and not to him, if he had been there he would not have been redeemed," the *Mekhilta* reads this in a more confrontational way: "to me and not to you; if you had been there you would not have been redeemed."

The other difference seems to be much more significant. The *Mekhilta* quotes the wise child's question as: "What mean the decrees, laws, and rules that the LORD our God has enjoined upon us?" However, the masoretic text of the Bible reads here "enjoined upon you." The reading of the *Mekhilta* helps resolve an exegetical problem. The fault of the wicked child, as expounded in the text of the haggadah, is that he talks to his parents in an excluding manner: "What do you mean by this rite?" emphasizing that he has nothing to do with it. However, according to the standard texts, the wise child also speaks in an excluding manner: "What mean the decrees, laws, and rules that the LORD our God has enjoined upon you?" It is true that this statement is not as confrontational as that of the wicked child for the wise child includes himself among the others by recognizing that it is "our God" who has commanded these things. Nevertheless, commentators have thought that the reading of the *Mekhilta* is the one on which this exposition is based, strengthening this position by noting that other texts also have this reading. Many copies of the Maimonidean text have this reading, and it is also the reading of the parallel text in the Jerusalem Talmud. Most notably, this is also the reading of the Septuagint, which is followed by the Vulgate. This point is also meant to enhance the antiquity of the midrash by making it rely on a Septuagint type of Hebrew text that had long disappeared. However, it has been argued that the reading of the Septuagint is an internal error, based on the similarity of "upon us" and "upon you" in Greek. If this is true, the changed version of the biblical text would be additional proof that this *baraita* is not really biblical exegesis but is rather a type of rabbinical rhetoric.

As we have noted, this *baraita* also appears in the Jerusalem Talmud. There are some minor differences between the sources. One of the more interesting ones is that the statement of the wicked child is expanded more defiantly: "What is this inconvenience (or 'trouble') with which you inconvenience us every year?" More significant is a change in the answers to the wise child and the simple child. The response to the simple child, here called "foolish" (*tippesh*), is to teach him the laws of Passover, whereas the wise child receives the answer assigned to the simple child in the other sources: "It was with a mighty hand that the LORD brought us out from Egypt, the house of bondage." The reason for this change is not obvious. It is possible that this change reflects the difference regarding what is thought to be the proper mode of discussion on the Passover eve, as we noted above. The standard haggadah texts think that wise people should discuss the laws of Passover, whereas the Jerusalem Talmud thinks that even wise people should talk about the miracles of the Exodus. This left the answer about teaching the laws to the foolish child, presumably one who does not have the basic knowledge of how to fulfill the commandments of Passover.

For the most part, the *baraita* of the four children consists of quotes from biblical verses. Only in the section about the wicked child do we find midrashic expansion, and here we find it both in the question and the answer. An explanation is added to the question, enabling us to understand why his question entitles him to the title of wicked child, and an explanation is added to the answer, explaining how vitriolic it is. At the conclusion of the *baraita* we have a midrashic expansion of the verse about the child who does not know how to ask. This midrash, which explains that the proper time to tell about the Exodus is when matzah and *maror* are on the table, does not appear as a continuation of the *baraita* of the four children in either the Jerusalem Talmud or in the *Mekhilta* mentioned above, However, it does appear in another section of the *Mekhilta* (Pisha 17, p. 149) as an independent midrash on this verse.

As noted above, the *Eretz Yisra'el* version of the haggadah does not have this *baraita,* nor does it have the texts that preceded it. In the place of the *baraita*—that is, as an introduction to the story of the Exodus based on Joshua—the *Eretz Yisra'el* text has a quote from the Mishnah: "One teaches the child according to the child's ability." Functionally, this serves the same purpose as the *baraita,* explaining why various versions of the Exodus story are necessary. In a way, the *baraita* may be considered as just an expansion of this text.

The Plagues at the Sea

The midrash of Deuteronomy 26 ends by expounding the last verse as a reference to the Ten Plagues. In the associative manner common to talmudic literature, the haggadah appends here another midrash that compares the Ten Plagues to the breaching the sea for the crossing of the Jews. The thrust of the passage is that the affliction of the Egyptians at the breaching of the sea was much greater than their suffering during the Ten Plagues. This passage is found in the *Mekhilta* and it is presented by Rav Saadiah Gaon as a passage that people were accustomed to reciting at this point in the seder. This is one of the three passages that Rav Saadiah notes that one is permitted to add, although he remarks that it is not obligatory.

The List of Thanksgiving (*Dayenu*)

The midrash that compares the breaching of the sea to the Ten Plagues is followed by an itemized list of the good things that God did for His people, beginning with the Exodus and concluding with the building of the Temple. The list appears not in the form of a story but rather in the form of an expression of thanksgiving to God for all the benefits He bestowed on His people. The list appears twice, first as a litany in which every phrase ends with the response *Dayenu* (It would have been sufficient), and the second time as prose. A litany is "A liturgical prayer consisting of a series of petitions recited by a leader alternating with fixed responses by the congregation."[52] A litany is thus a communal song; and, at times, the sense of the text takes second place to the musical requirements. Thus the litany ends with the statement that it would have been sufficient for the Jews if God had brought them to the Land of Israel but had not built the Holy Temple. Some versions added an additional member to the list, inserting the Meeting Tent between the entrance into the Land of Israel and the building of the Temple. In either case, there is no formal expression of thanks for the final good—that is, the building of the Temple. Indeed, in this form of the litany the final statement would always include some benefice for which no gratitude would be expressed. Perhaps it was this that made it necessary to repeat the whole list in prose form.

Although the list begins with the Exodus, and would thus seem to be a continuation of that story, it includes a number of flashbacks that describe events immediately preceding the Exodus. A similar list appears in Psalm 136, also in the form of a litany, and it is part of the closing section of the haggadah.

It had been assumed for many years that the *dayenu* passage is one of the earliest elements of the haggadah. The reason for this assumption is that the list of benefits given by God concludes with the entrance into the Land of Israel and the building of the Temple. It was taken for granted that this meant that the list must have been composed while the Temple still existed for, otherwise, it was inconceivable that no mention would be made here of expectations for the return to Israel and the reconstruction of the Temple. Eric Werner, convinced of the antiquity of this passage, thought that a portion of Christian liturgy, known as the Improperia or Reproaches, was based on *Dayenu*. The Improperia, sung on Good Friday, were a reproach to the Jewish people for

52. Houghton Mifflin eReference Suite. CD-ROM ed. Based on *The American Heritage Dictionary of the English Language*, 4th ed. (Boston: Houghton Mifflin, 2000, 2004).

repaying the good things done by God for the Jews with evil actions. These reproaches were presented as the words of Jesus, dying on the cross. Thus, for instance, they were reproached: "I have opened the sea for you; and you have opened my body with a lance." The refrain of the litany was "My people, what have I done to you . . . ?" (Mic. 6:3). The good things listed were mostly connected with the Exodus from Egypt. Werner was the first to call attention to the similarity of this list of benefits to the list of benefits given by God to the Jews in *Dayenu* and, due to his dating, considered the Improperia as actually a Christian parody of this passage.[53] Recently, Yisrael Yuval rejected Werner's claim, noting that *Dayenu* is first documented in the tenth-century siddur of Rav Saadiah Gaon—as a voluntary text—making it very unlikely that a Christian text dated much earlier is a response to the presumably late *Dayenu*. Yuval accepted the connection between the texts but, due to his dating, argued that the relationship should be reversed: *Dayenu* is a response to the Reproaches.[54] However, since the text of *Dayenu* has not been found in any *Eretz Yisra'el haggadot,* its appearance in the Babylonian *haggadot* of the tenth century seems to imply that it is of Babylonian provenance. It is unlikely that Babylonian Jewry, who lived first under Sassanian rule and then under Muslim rule, should be involved in responses to Christian liturgy.

The Other *Maggid* Texts That Are Specific to Certain Communities

This section mentions expansions of the *maggid* section that are in use, or have been in use, in various communities but have not been universally accepted. It is the nature of the haggadah that people add selections from other texts and their own explanations that may, at times, become part of the family tradition. We discuss here only passages that have achieved broader acceptance, either by being included in manuscripts that have survived or by being printed in published *haggadot*. The order of the discussion follows the order in which the passages appear in the haggadah.

Mah Chbar

Many communities translated the haggadah into the vernacular. The Yemenite community added a section in Arabic that immediately followed the questions asked at the seder. It opened *Mah chbar hada elleila min gamia allieali* (How is this night different from all other nights?) and continued with a short description (less than a hundred words) of the suffering in Egypt, the Ten Plagues and the redemption. It closed with the introduction to the continuation of the haggadah: "This is the answer."

53. Eric Werner, "Melito of Sardis, the First Poet of Deicide," *Hebrew Union College Annual* 37 (1966): 191–210.

54. Yuval, "Easter and Passover as Early Jewish Christian Dialogue," 104–105.

Utkol

In some Tunisian communities, a long passage dealing with Abraham's recognition of God was inserted immediately after the declaration that our forefathers were idol worshipers. There are two versions of this text, both in Arabic. Both texts begin with *Utkol* (And you shall say) and they are cited by this word. The longer version began with the creation of the world, described how humanity descended into idolatry, and concluded with the recognition of God by Abraham. This version was common in Gafsa, on the northeast coast of Tunisia near Gabes, and was known as *Utkol Gafsa.* The shorter version began with Enosh, in whose time idol worship began, and skipped to Abraham. This version was common in Jerba, an island off the coast of Tunisia that harbored an important Jewish community, and was known as *Utkol Jerba.* Both texts have been translated into English by Guggenheimer[55] and the Jerban text has been translated into Hebrew in a modern haggadah published in Israel.[56]

I Am the Lord

Following the passage in the *Arami oved avi* midrash that proclaims that God Himself saved the Jews in Egypt, we find a passage that portrays the attempt of the angels to punish Egypt. God rejects their attempt, stating that He wishes to avenge His children personally. This passage was known in France, as Rashi rejects it since it does not appear in the *Mekhilta* and it is not part of the haggadah.[57] Rashi's authority was very great and it is very likely that his rejection is the reason that this text does not appear in European *haggadot*. But it does appear in the Old English haggadah, and it later appears in a Baghdad haggadah. Goldschmidt (p. 86) published the text with variant readings from the various sources.

He Gave Us Their Money

A text that discusses the booty taken from Egypt is interpolated into the *dayenu* text, in the passage where it says, "If he had just given us their money." It is thus an interpolation into an addition. The passage is a conflation of two midrashim. The first midrash explains that the Jews cleaned out Egypt, and the second explains why the booty taken at the sea was more highly thought of than that taken from Egypt. The first midrash is found in the Babylonian Talmud (BT *Berachot* 9b), whereas the complete midrash is found in the *Mekhilta of Rabbi Shimon b. Yohai* (p. 32). The passage is found in the siddur of R. Saadiah

55. Guggenheimer, *The Scholar's Haggadah,* 154–179.

56. *Ha-Haggadah ha-Meduyeket Ish Mazliach* (B'nei Brak: Machon Harav Mazliah, 5758 [1998]), 135–139. See also Nahem Ilan, "*Midrash al Avraham Avinu Ba-Haggadah Shel Pesach shel Yehudei Jerba*", *Sefunot,* 6:21 (5753 [1993]): 167–196.

57. *Machzor Vitri,* edited by Aryeh Goldschmidt (Jerusalem: Ozar Ha-Poskim, 5764 [2004]), 428–429.

Gaon as an integral part of *Dayenu,*[58] and it appears in *haggadot* of Yemen, Baghdad, India, and other communities.

Emunim Arckhu Shevah

One of the most recent expansions of the haggadah is a poem by Aharon Cohen, who is otherwise unknown. Goldschmidt surmises that he lived in the fifteenth or sixteenth century. His poem *Emunim arkhu shevah* (Goldschmidt, p. 105) is based on the verse, *va'amartem zevah pesach* (Exod. 12:27), and it was recited immediately after the reading of this verse. It is found in a haggadah used by the Jews of Baghdad and in *haggadot* printed in Leghorn and Jerusalem, all with translations into Arabic.

The Psalms Before the Meal

Two psalms are sung or recited at the end of the *maggid* section: Psalms 113 and 114. In modern liturgy, these psalms are the first two psalms in the liturgical unit known as *Hallel,* which consists of Psalms 113–118. The recitation of these two psalms during the paschal evening belongs to one of the earliest strata of the haggadah, as they are both mentioned in the description of the seder in the Mishnah. The Mishnah tells us that a psalm beginning "Hallelujah" was sung or recited during the evening ceremony. From the continuation of the Mishnah, it is clear that the Mishnah is referring to Psalm 113, which begins "Hallelujah. O servants of the LORD, give praise; praise the name of the LORD." This psalm is a generic praise of God and has no clear connection with the Exodus. It calls on all servants of God to praise God and continues with general praises of God. Rabbinical interpretation connected it with the Exodus by explaining that the term "servants of God" is meant to imply that the singers are no longer servants or slaves of Pharaoh (JT *Pesachim* 5:5, 32c).

The second psalm has a more direct connection with the Exodus as it begins: "When Israel went forth from Egypt." However, its main content deals not with the Exodus but with the events that came after the Exodus. This psalm was the subject of a disagreement between the houses of Hillel and Shammai. The house of Hillel thought that this psalm should be included in the *Hallel* of the evening, but the house of Shammai objected to this. The reason for this objection is not given in the Mishnah. However, the Tosefta (*Pesach* 10:9, p. 198) reports that the Shammaites responded to the Hillelites: "Have they already left Egypt, that they mention the Exodus?" In other words, this psalm refers to the Exodus, which had not yet taken place at the original paschal celebration and so it should not be said. This response shows that there was a fundamental difference between the houses in the understanding of the paschal meal. The Shammaites assumed that the meal was not a celebration of the Exodus but rather a reenactment of the first paschal meal. The Hillelites answered that the

58. *Siddur R. Saadiah Gaon,* 143.

Shammaites were being inconsistent. According to their reasoning, they should not recite the blessing of redemption either.

The Mishnah does not give us sufficient information to determine whether this psalm was said before eating the paschal meal or afterward. However, the continuation of the toseftan dialogue between the houses implies that both houses were arguing about the place of Psalm 114. The Shammaites did not totally reject the reading of Psalm 114 but thought that it should be postponed until after the meal. The Hillelites held that the postponement was pointless since the Exodus did not take place immediately after the meal but only in the morning. Although there is little doubt that the Mishnah presents an authentic disagreement between the houses, it is possible, and even likely, that the toseftan dialogue reflects later thought about the organization of the seder.[59]

One of the important implications of the disagreement between the houses of Hillel and Shammai about the extent of the *Hallel* that was to be sung at the paschal celebration is that it aids us in dating this ritual. Since the houses flourished during the last century of the Second Temple, we may assume that these psalms were part of the paschal liturgy, while the Temple still existed. This fits in well with the other evidence from the time of the Second Temple, which spoke mostly of song during the evening.

It should be noted, in this context, that the Mishnah tells us that *Hallel* was also recited in the Temple when the paschal lamb was being slaughtered. Although the Mishnah uses the generic term "*Hallel*," which might refer to any collection of psalms, the Mishnah mentions, in a side remark, that Psalm 116 was part of the *Hallel* sung at this occasion. It is thus reasonable to assume that, according to the Mishnah, the *Hallel* sung during the sacrifice consisted of, at least, Psalms 113–116.

The Blessing over Wine: The Blessing of Redemption

The blessing over the second cup is known as the blessing of redemption since its main theme is praise of God for redeeming Israel. The closing formula is "Blessed art Thou, God, Redeemer of Israel." This blessing is mentioned in the Mishnah as the subject of a disagreement between R. Tarfon and R. Akiva. According to R. Tarfon, the text of this blessing was "[Blessed art Thou, O God, our LORD,] who has redeemed us and our ancestors from Egypt and has brought us to this night." Some of the ancient Mishnah manuscripts have a continuation "to eat matzah and *maror*." In any case, this is a short blessing with no additional closing formula. The purpose of this blessing is not clear, and it may have been thought necessary just to give a spiritual meaning to the

59. For a general discussion of this problem see Moshe Weiss, "The Authenticity of the Explicit Discussions in Bet Shammai—Bet Hillel Disputes" [in Hebrew], *Sidra* 4 (1988): 53–66.

second cup of wine. This cup may be considered as concluding the story of the Exodus or as ending the *Hallel* that had just preceded it. The content of this blessing is actually double. On the one hand, it is specifically a blessing of thanks and praise for the redemption of the People of Israel. On the other hand, it seems to be a type of *Shehecheyanu* blessing; expressing personal gratitude for having lived to this time of the year. Both motifs repeat ideas mentioned in the *Kiddush* but with further refinement. The Exodus is no longer an ancient event that is commemorated; it is turned into a present event. The *Shehecheyanu* is not tied to a present, unmodified time but is related to the performance of specific commandments.

R. Akiva's version of this blessing is presented as "So may our LORD and the LORD of our ancestors bring us to coming pilgrimage festivals in peace, rejoicing in the eternal Temple, to eat of the paschal sacrifices and of other sacrifices whose blood will be dashed against the sides of the altar acceptably and we shall thank you for our redemption. Blessed art Thou, O God, Redeemer of Israel." R. Akiva's version is apparently an addition to R. Tarfon's version and an expansion of it. It would seem that R. Tarfon's version reflects a version that existed before the destruction of the Temple, and thus it did not contain a prayer for the future restoration. If his version included the words "to eat matzah and *maror*," it must have been edited to remove the reference to the flesh of the paschal lamb. R. Akiva, who lived in the time of Bar Kokhba and was active in the rebellion, felt it necessary to include a prayer for the redemption in the ancient version. The addition of this prayer lengthened the blessing to an extent that it was necessary to add a closing formula.

The expression "of the paschal sacrifices and of other sacrifices" (*min hapesahim u-min ha-zevahim*) has been the subject of much discussion. The expression seems to refer to the hope that the paschal sacrifice will be restored together with the restoration of the sacrificial ritual. However, many commentators thought that the "other sacrifices" that were referred to were the *Hagigah* sacrifices that accompanied the paschal sacrifice. Since, according to theory, the *Hagigah* should be eaten before the paschal lamb, many preferred the reverse order "the other sacrifices and the paschal sacrifices." This, in turn, led to a distinction between the reading of this text when Passover fell on a weekday and when it fell on a *Shabbat*. Since the *Hagigah* was not offered in the latter case, some thought that, in this case, the paschal sacrifice should take precedence in the order of the words.

The text of the concluding formula was the subject of a grammatical comment by Rava, a third-generation Babylonian sage. He thought that the Hebrew participle *go'el,* meant "who redeems" rather than "Redeemer of Israel." Since he thought that this blessing was primarily thanks for the past redemption, he insisted on using a past verbal form, *ga'al.* His demand was accepted in the Babylonian tradition, and we even have earlier texts that read *go'el* and that have been emended to read *ga'al.*

The Rituals of the Meal

Before the Meal (*Rahtzah, Motzi,* Matzah, *Maror, Korekh*)

When the paschal lamb was no longer offered, the meal itself lost its sacramental character. Although it was, of course, a festive meal, its festive nature was not really different from the festive nature of meals served at other holidays and on special occasions. The meal began with hand washing, just like any other meal. The only real difference between this meal and other festive meals was the consumption of matzah rather than leavened bread. However, the beginning of the meal was marked by special rites. To the blessing recited over bread (*Motzi*) at the beginning of every meal was added a blessing praising God for the commandment to eat matzah. The bitter herbs commanded by the Torah were no longer a side dish to be eaten together with the meat of the paschal lamb, but they were ceremoniously eaten at the beginning of the meal, also accompanied by a blessing praising God for the commandment to eat bitter herbs. Indeed, the sages understood that the Torah did not command one to eat bitter herbs without the flesh of the sacrifice. The postdestruction custom of eating bitter herbs was considered a rabbinical ordination.

Another custom enacted as a symbolic memorial for the paschal sacrifice is connected to the name of Hillel, who flourished approximately a century before the destruction of the Temple. Both Talmuds report that Hillel was accustomed to making a sandwich of matzah and *maror* (*korekh*) and eating them together (JT *Challah* 1:1, 57b; BT *Pesachim* 115a). We should point out that Athenaeus, who lived at the end of the second century C.E. (i.e., about two hundred years after Hillel but some decades before those who documented Hillel's custom), tell us that the Greeks had a kind of bread called "lettuce bread", which is translated as sandwich bread.[60] The assumption is that the bread was meant for eating with lettuce in it, and one may assume that it might have had the shape of lettuce, somewhat similar to the idea of a modern hot dog roll or hamburger bun. Although one might suspect that Hillel's custom was just a convenient way of eating the food, the Babylonian Talmud maintains that he ate the food this way in order to fulfill the commandment: "They shall eat it with unleavened bread and bitter herbs" (Num. 9:11).[61] Although the Jerusalem Talmud mentions specifically that Hillel's sandwich included the meat of the sacrifice, the implication of the Babylonian Talmud is that his sandwich consisted solely

---

60. Athenaeus, *Deipnosohistae* 3:114; edited by Charles B. Gulick (London-Cambridge, Mass.: Loeb Classical Library, 1927–1941), ii:38–39.

61. It has been pointed out that the relevancy of this verse is somewhat problematic since it refers to the paschal sacrifice offered, in certain circumstances, on the fourteenth of Iyyar, a month after the regular Passover. A more relevant verse would be: "They shall eat it roasted over the fire, with unleavened bread and with bitter herbs" (Exod. 12:8). This last verse seems to imply that all three foods should be eaten together.

of matzah and *maror*. The Jerusalem Talmud reports that R. Yochanan, a sage who lived in the third century C.E., used to make a sandwich of matzah and *maror*, omitting the flesh of the sacrifice only because at that time there was no longer a sacrifice (JT *Challah* 1:1, 57b).

According to the Babylonian Talmud (*Pesachim* 115a), eating matzah and *maror* as a sandwich was feasible only while the Temple existed. After its destruction, one could not eat such a sandwich because the two foods were no longer of equal status. *Maror* was an adjunct of the paschal sacrifice, which was performed in the Temple. Without the Temple, eating *maror* was considered a rabbinical commandment. Therefore, the status of *maror* was diminished, so it had to be eaten separately from the matzah. Once they were eaten separately, the obligation to eat both matzah and *maror* was fulfilled, so eating a sandwich of both foods together became unnecessary. Thus the eating of such a sandwich was solely a commemoration of a Temple custom.

Although *Eretz Yisra'el haggadot* do not include instructions for eating a sandwich, the blessings that appear in some of these *haggadot* imply that they did eat the foods together. The *Dropsie Haggadah*,[62] for instance, includes the following blessing: "Blessed art Thou, O LORD, our God, King of the Universe, who has commanded us to eat matzah and *maror* on this night, to remember the power of the King of Kings, Blessed be He, who has performed miracles for our ancestors at this time for the sake of Abraham, Isaac, and Jacob. Blessed art Thou, who remembers the covenant." Blessings of this type appear, with several variations, in a number of ancient *haggadot*. The most important variation is the inclusion of "roasted meat" in the blessing, together with the matzah and *maror*. This shows that roast meat was eaten at the seder in commemoration of the paschal sacrifice, as is evidenced also by the retention of the question about roast meat until gaonic times.

It is not clear whether the *maror* eaten as part of the sandwich must also be dipped in *haroset*. The cultural milieu of eating a sandwich seems very different from that of the hors d'oeuvres. However, according to the talmudic rationale for the *haroset*, *maror* would always require *haroset*. Opinions differed about this and the final decision was that this sandwich was to be eaten *belo tibbul uvelo brakha* (without dipping and without a blessing). This instruction was included in many *haggadot* and became an expression for something that was completely unembellished.

The Meal (*Shulchan Orekh*)

The meal itself is mostly an ordinary festive meal. Ashkenazim are accustomed to begin the meal with eggs in salt water. We have already noted that the Roman equivalent of the phrase "from soup to nuts" is "from eggs to apples." It has been suggested that the Ashkenazic custom derives from this Roman table

62. See p. xiv, n. 7.

custom. Others thought that the egg that was to be eaten was the one that was found on the seder plate, and it was eaten in commemoration of the *Hagigah* sacrifice symbolized by this egg. The earliest documentation of this custom is by Rabbi Moses Isserles, in *Shulchan Arukh* (*Orach Chayyim* 476:2); Isserles reports that it is the custom in some places.

The custom of eating roast meat persevered in some communities, especially among the Sephardim. However, even they refrained from roasting a whole lamb for this might be misunderstood as a paschal lamb. The Ashkenazic custom was not to eat any roasted flesh, even roast chicken (see *Shulchan Arukh, Orach Chayyim* 476).

After the Meal (*Tzafun, Baruch*)

There are two rituals performed at the end of the meal: (1) the eating of the *afikoman* and (2) the reciting of the grace and drinking the cup of wine associated with it.

The consumption of the piece of matzah called *afikoman* as the last thing eaten at the meal has been discussed above. Although the original theory for this requirement was to retain the taste of the matzah in one's mouth until the end of the evening, it gained an additional significance as a surrogate for the paschal lamb. This custom is known as *tzafun*, which means "hidden" (see above, p. 15).

The recitation of grace is often preceded by washing hands, which has been discussed above (p. 21). The grace is said over a cup of wine, just like the *Kiddush* of the first cup and the blessing of redemption of the second cup. The practice of reciting the grace over a cup of wine was, at one time, the general practice at every meal. However, this custom is no longer generally practiced but remains at the seder for it is counted as one of the four obligatory cups.

The After-Dinner Songs (*Hallel, Nirtzah*)

1. *Shfokh Chamatkha*

The after-dinner program of the seder begins, in later tradition, with four verses (a typological number in the haggadah) that call on God to wreak vengeance on the gentiles. These are:

> Pour out Your fury on the nations that do not know You, upon the kingdoms that do not invoke Your name, for they have devoured Jacob and desolated his home (Ps. 79:6–7). Pour out Your wrath on them; may Your blazing anger overtake them (Ps. 69:25); O, pursue them in wrath and destroy them from under the heavens of the LORD (Lam. 3:66).

The earliest mention of this custom is probably the version of the haggadah found in *Machzor Vitry* (p. 296). In this version, we find an additional six verses before the final verse from Lamentations: five from Psalms and one from Hosea. This version seems to be a later addition to the *Machzor Vitry* as there is no mention of this custom in the description of the seder attributed to Rashi in this same work (p. 282). It is difficult to determine when this addition was incorporated into the *Machzor Vitry*. The earliest appearance of these verses that can be dated with some certainty is in the work of Eleazar ben Judah of Worms.[63] He mentions them as an aside, considering them an accepted custom. There is, as yet, no evidence for the recital of these verses outside of Germany or France earlier than this, although they have been interpolated into one of the manuscripts of the siddur of R. Amram Gaon.

The recital of these verses in the thirteenth century is well documented. They appear in an old English haggadah, written sometime before the exile in 1270, and they are referred to in the writings of the Provençal Menahem Meiri (1249–1315) and in the writings of the thirteenth-century Spaniards: Bahya ben Asher (Commentary to Exodus, 6:8 and 12:23) and David Abudarham.[64] These facts would support a theory that the call for vengeance was instituted in Germany or France in response to the massacres of the Crusaders. This would have been especially appropriate at the seder, as the massacres began at Easter time.

Although the custom has spread throughout the Jewish world, even in late Yemenite *haggadot,*[65] we find a large number of variations in this custom. *Machzor Roma* has only the first verse of the four[66] and the Spanish and later Yemenite customs have just the first two verses. On the other hand, the old English haggadah, mentioned above, has a total of seventeen such verses.

Of interest is the note of Rabbi Eleazar ben Judah of Worms, in his commentary to the haggadah. He remarks that it was customary to precede these verses with the verse "Display Your faithfulness in wondrous deeds, You who deliver with Your right hand those who seek refuge from assailants" (Ps. 17:7). The purpose of starting with this verse was to prevent beginning this section of the haggadah with affliction. No testimony to this custom has been found in any haggadah to date. Indeed, even his own *derashah* does not mention any verses before *shfokh hamatkha.*[67] However, modern sensibilities have caused even more radical reactions to these verses. Israel Levi, a nineteenth-century

63. See Rabbi Elazar Vormsensis, *Oratio ad Pascam,* 106.
64. Menahem Meiri, *Bet ha-Behirah al Masechet Pesachim,* edited by Yosef Hacohen Klein (Jerusalem: Machon Ha-Talmud Ha-Yisraeli Ha-Shalem, 5726 [1966]), 205
65. Moshe Gavra, *Studies in the Yemenite Prayerbook,* vol. 1: *The Passover Haggadah* (Kiryat Ono: The Institute for the Research of Yemenite Sages and Their Works, 1988), 154. For the date of its introduction into Italian *haggadot,* see Mordechai Glatzer, "The Ashkenazic and Italian Haggadah and the Haggadot of Joel Ben Simeon," in *The Washington Haggadah* (Washington, D.C.: Library of Congress, 1991), 139–169.
66. Early Italian *machzorim* have none of these verses. See Shlomo Zucker, *The Moskowitz Mahzor of Joel Ben Simeon* (Jerusalem: The Jewish National and University Library, 2005), 29.
67. See Rabbi Eleazar Vormsensis, *Oratio ad Pascam,* 106.

Jewish scholar living in Germany, thought that these verses were inappropriate in modern times and he replaced them with verses that call for all nations to return to God. A similar sensibility seems to be behind what one could almost call a hoax. Chayyim Bloch (1881–1973) reported that he found an unusual version of this prayer in a manuscript haggadah that had been compiled in 1521. He states that this manuscript, which included other poems that are not found in standard *haggadot* and differing versions of the text, had disappeared during the Holocaust without a trace. Fortunately, he claims, he retained some notes with this prayer. The text he cites is, in English translation, as follows.

> Pour out Your love on the nations who have known You and on the kingdoms who call upon Your name. For they show lovingkindness to the seed of Jacob, and they defend Your people Israel from those who would devour them alive. May they live to see the prosperity of Your chosen ones and to participate in the joy of Your nation.
>
> Pour out Your fury on the nations that do not know You, and upon the kingdoms that do not invoke Your name, may they be embarrassed and ashamed of all their evil. Vent upon them their malicious acts; rebuke them and lead them in the vastness of the desert and they will no longer be prickling briers and lacerating thorns from their surroundings, for they shall perish forever.[68]

Unlike the original prayer, which is just a collection of biblical verses, this is a free composition, although replete with biblical allusions. Chayyim Bloch has a reputation for presenting new texts as ancient documents, and it is very likely that this prayer is his own composition, expressing his own feelings in the wake of the Holocaust. (He left Vienna and immigrated to the United States in 1938—after he had been arrested by the Gestapo and freed, with the help of an influential non-Jew). Nevertheless, some people recite the first part of his prayer instead of the traditional verses.[69]

On the other hand, after the Holocaust, some people have used the traditional verses as a background for a memory of the Holocaust at the seder. The noted Jewish-American writer Rufus Learsi (pen name of Israel Goldberg) promulgated a text, which he had composed, that concluded with the singing of *Ani Ma'amin*.

A number of homiletic explanations have been given for the origin and meaning of this custom. The custom presents us with two questions: (1) Why

---

68. Moshe Chayyim Bloch, *Heichal le-divrei Chazal u-pitgameyhem* (New York: Pardes Publishing House and Shoulson Press, 1948), 590–591. Bloch reports that he published a lengthy analysis of this prayer and facsimiles of some pages from this haggadah in his book *Der Judenhaas,* but I have not been able to locate a copy of this work.

69. The first part of the prayer was republished by Naphtali Ben Menahem, in *Mahanayim* 80 (5723 [1963]): 95 with a misprint. This first part, with the misprint, was also included in the haggadah published by Mishael Zion and Noam Zion, *Halailah Hazeh Haggadah* (Jerusalem: Halailah Hazeh, Inc., 2004), 120.

are these verses recited, and (2) Why are they recited just before the reading of the second part of the *Hallel*? Most of the explanations assume that the beginning of the second part of the *Hallel* was thought to require the sentiments expressed in these verses. Modern scholars have suggested that since the second part of the *Hallel* talks of the future redemption, it was thought appropriate to preface this with the call to God to avenge His people as part of the future redemption. The attitude of Israel Levi exemplifies the alternate rabbinical approach to the future redemption—that it will come together with the salvation of the nations.[70]

The Structure of the After-Dinner Songs

The fourth cup of the seder is known as the cup of *Hallel*. *Hallel* is a term for praise of God; and the after-dinner songs are, mostly, praises of God. It seems natural that the spiritual experience of the seder and the festive meal would create an atmosphere that people would try to prolong by singing after the meal. The character of song in the traditional seder is sometimes distorted by hasty reading but this cannot alter the fact that this section consists of songs. Indeed, it is common for people to sing additional songs that are not prescribed in the haggadah. Some people continue with songs about the beginning of the spring season while many end the seder with "Hatikvah," a song that expresses hope of a coming redemption. These songs, like the other songs included in the final portion of the seder, are of different natures and have become part of the seder at different historic times.

The earliest unit of song is the *Hallel* itself. Although *Hallel* is a generic term for praise of God, the term is used specifically to designate chapters 113–118 of the book of Psalms, These psalms are sung several times a year, as part of the morning liturgy of the festivals. There is reason to assume that these psalms were not originally an organic unit. *Tannaitic* evidence implies that Psalm 118 was sung on Tabernacles and Psalms 113–114 were specific for Passover. However, these psalms coalesced into a single unit that was recited whenever *Hallel* was called for. Since Psalms 113–114 had been sung before the meal, it would have been natural to complete the *Hallel* by singing Psalms 115–118 after the meal.

These psalms were followed by a blessing. The mishnah that describes the seder prescribes that "the blessing of the song" (*birkat ha-shir*) should be said after the *Hallel*. Two *amoraim* disagreed about the identity of the blessing referred to here (BT *Pesachim* 118a). They both agreed that the blessing referred to here was not one that was unique to the seder but one that was used on other occasions as the final blessing after reading a section of Psalms. A Babylonian *amora,* R. Judah, was of the opinion that the blessing referred to was the one that began with *Yehallelucha,* whereas R. Yochanan, an *Eretz Yisra'el amora,* was of the opinion that the blessing referred to was the one that began with

70. See Yuval, *"Two Nations in Your Womb,"* 140–150.

Nishmat. Both of these blessings are well known outside the haggadah as blessings recited after the reading of Psalms. *Yehallelucha* is the standard blessing recited today after reading of the *Hallel* psalms on festivals; and, in the *Eretz Yisra'el* tradition, it is the blessing that was recited after the daily psalm reading (*pesukei dezimra*). "*Nishmat*" is the opening word of the poetic introduction to the *Yishtabach* blessing that is used today as the final blessing for the reading of psalms on *Shabbat* and festivals. A blessing beginning with "*Nishmat*" appears in the *Eretz Yisra'el* tradition as the closing blessing in the special ritual known as the prayer of the *shir* that was conducted on *Shabbat* mornings. In the *siddurim* of the *Ge'onim*, the *Yishtabach* blessing, without the extended poetic introduction, was the closing blessing of the psalm reading on weekdays. Scholarly theory would tend to reconcile the disagreement between the *amoraim* by suggesting that there were various traditions: some closed with one blessing while others closed with the alternate blessing. Nevertheless, early *haggadot,* both Babylonian and *Eretz Yisra'el,* include only the *Yehallelucha* blessing for the conclusion of the *Hallel*. The opinion of R. Judah was the one followed in all traditions, although R. Yochanan's explanation was not without influence, as we shall see below.

This blessing was immediately followed by drinking the fourth cup; and at one time, this concluded the seder. However, some people were not satisfied with this. They extended the seder by singing another chapter of Psalms and drinking a fifth cup of wine. It is not clear what the true motivation was for adding the fifth cup and its accompanying psalm. Rabbinical sources present this arrangement as a solution for those who wished to drink more wine after finishing the fourth cup. This is based on the premise that it was forbidden to drink wine after the conclusion of the seder, a premise whose basis is somewhat shaky. It is possible that it was an attempt to extend the spiritual experience of the seder.

The psalm chosen for the fifth cup was Psalm 136, a litany of praise to God known as the Great *Hallel*. This litany has a universal framework: it opens with a description of the creation of the world and closes with praise of God who sustains all living things. But the heart of this litany consists of specific deeds that God did for His people. The list starts with the destruction of the Egyptian firstborn and culminates in the grant of the Land of Israel to the Jewish people. This is, of course, what made this psalm so appropriate here as an addition to the seder. It was not considered sufficient just to say the psalm. It was felt necessary to close this singing of a psalm with a blessing, just as the singing of the two psalms over the fourth cup concluded with a blessing. Indeed, the original blessing used in this place was the same *Yehallelukha* that had been recited just before drinking the fourth cup.

There have been recent attempts to revive the custom of drinking a fifth cup, basing it on a midrash. The four cups were related to four expressions of redemption found in the Bible: "I will free you . . . and deliver you . . . I will redeem you. . . . And I will take you to be My people" (Exod. 6:6–7). However, there is a fifth expression of redemption: "I will bring you into the land" (Exod. 6:8), and modern attempts to revive the custom of drinking the fifth cup have based themselves on the idea that this cup is reminiscent of the fifth expression of the redemption: it celebrates the return to the Land of Israel.

In spite of rabbinical statements that the fifth cup is just a concession to those who wish to drink another cup of wine, the custom was widespread and is documented in Spain, France, and Germany. Until the custom eventually died out, it underwent some changes that left their impression on the text of the haggadah.

The first of these changes was the blessing that was recited just before drinking the fifth cup. We have noted that this was just a repetition of the blessing recited before drinking the fourth cup. Repetition of an identical blessing in such a short space of time was anomalous. A substitute was sought for this blessing and the substitute was the *birkat ha-shir* as defined by R. Yochanan—*Nishmat.* In a way that may be considered typical of the development of Jewish customs, the cup of wine disappeared from the table but the psalm remained. The drinking of the fourth cup was postponed until after reciting Psalm 136 and its accompanying blessing.

The text of the fourth cup now presented an unusual situation as far as the blessings were concerned. This text now consisted of two chapters of Psalms, a concluding blessing (*Yehallelukha*), another chapter of Psalms, and another concluding blessing (*Nishmat*). Although there couldn't be too many psalms, there were clearly too many concluding blessings. This was especially anomalous as the doxologies that closed both blessings were identical ("Blessed art Thou, God, King who is acclaimed by praises"). Several solutions to this problem appear in the sources. The most obvious solution was to skip the concluding blessing after the first two psalms: this is found in a number of sources. However, this solution conflicted with the natural tendency to do things as they had always been done and never to eliminate texts. A more moderate solution was just to eliminate the closing doxology of the intermediate blessing while retaining its body. Although this still presented an anomaly, at least it prevented saying unnecessary blessings and this solution is found in many modern *haggadot*.

The solutions suggested above were found unsatisfactory by many as it meant that the traditional blessing for closing the *Hallel* (*Yehallelukha*) was eliminated, either partially or in entirety, from the text. An alternate solution was to postpone the *Yehallelukha* until the end, just before drinking the fourth cup. This solution, by itself, was not sufficient as it would mean that the two closing blessings, *Nishmat* and *Yehallelukha,* were read one immediately after the other. Although the obvious solution would be to eliminate *Nishmat,* which was now redundant, this was not satisfactory as it would mean eliminating a text that had become traditional. The arrangement that was arrived at was to switch the blessings, reciting *Nishmat* after the first two psalms (without its concluding doxology), followed by the Great *Hallel* that concluded with *Yehallelukha.*

Traditional *haggadot* have not arrived at a standard solution to this problem and both of the solutions mentioned above may be found in them. If the participants are using different *haggadot,* some confusion may arise when they reach this point in the haggadah.

The Additional Songs in the Ashkenazic Tradition

We have already remarked that there was a tendency to extend the experience of the seder by adding additional material, notably songs, at the conclusion of the evening. Rabbi Zidkiah b. Abraham (thirteenth century, Italy) writes that it is customary to recite *rahitim* and *piyyutim* (types of synagogal poetry) after the fourth cup.[71]

Rabbi Zidkiah did not mention any specific poems and various communities added different poems. The Ashkenazic community added seven songs that became part of their standard haggadah, and some of them were eventually adopted into the customs of other Jewish communities. One of them, beginning "*chasal seder pesach,*" which was considered a declaration that the seder had ended, was always said after the drinking of the fourth cup. The other six may be categorized in three pairs. The first pair consists of two poems taken from the synagogue liturgy that have, as their refrain, a biblical verse relating to Pesach. The custom was to recite one on the first night of Pesach and the other on the second night.

The following two pairs have nothing to do with Passover. They may be classified as general songs meant to praise God, and they served to enhance the feelings of festivity. The first of these final two pairs consists of two litanies that are basically a list of attributes of God. The final pair consists of two folkloric types of songs: a number song and *Had Gadya*.

These songs were adopted as part of the haggadah in various times. In modern tradition, they songs are all sung after the drinking of the fourth cup. However, in an earlier Ashkenazic custom, from western Germany, when the only additions were the first three songs (besides *Hasal Seder Pesach*), the custom of singing them before drinking the fourth cup developed. This was reported as the custom of Rabbi Meir of Routenburg (*Tashbetz Qatan* 99). The rationale given for this was that he wished to drink the final cup as close to bedtime as possible, as it was considered forbidden to drink after this cup. However, postponing the cup until after the poems also had the effect of making these poems part of the official rite, which was only concluded after drinking the fourth cup. In this western German tradition the fourth cup was drunk after the liturgical poem, and it was followed immediately by *Hasal Seder Pesach,* which was either preceded by the call "next year in Jerusalem" or followed by it.

---

71. *Shibbolei ha-Leket* 218, edited by Shelomoh Buber (Wilna: Rom Publishers, 1886), 200.

The popularity of this custom was great enough that even when they added another song to the seder, *Addir Hu,* many *haggadot* include it also before the fourth cup. However, the custom of postponing the fourth cup until after these poems had been recited was rejected by the Polish rabbi Solomon Luria (c. 1510–1574), whose words were quoted and accepted by Rabbi Joel Sirkes (1561–1640). The extent to which the custom was common may be implied by the stricture of Rabbi Luria that one should not follow the printed editions of *siddurim* and *machzorim* in this.[72] The reason that Rabbi Luria rejected the custom was because he felt that the fourth cup was mandated for the blessing that came immediately after the *Hallel*. Postponing drinking it until after the additional poems had been sung would distort the meaning of the fourth cup.

The custom eventually disappeared from the eastern European tradition, although it still appears in some *haggadot* of the western Ashkenazic tradition. Others of the western tradition have restored the drinking of the cup to its original position but have retained a vestige of the western Ashkenazic custom by retaining the *Hasal Seder Pesach* after the additional songs, rather than immediately after drinking the fourth cup. It is most noteworthy that Goldschmidt's introduction to the haggadah follows the western order,[73] even though the text itself follows the eastern order.

I will now turn to a study of the individual songs.

The first of these songs, in the modern traditional haggadah, is *Hasal Seder Pesach* (The order of the Passover is concluded), which is taken from a lengthy poem of Joseph ben Samuel Bonfils, a French poet of the eleventh century. The complete poem was composed as an addition to the *Amidah* of *Shacharit* on the Great *Shabbat* before Passover. Bonfils composed a poetic summary of the laws of Passover that was to be said just before the *Kedushah*. This summary concluded with the wish: "The order of the Passover is concluded; just as we have been privileged to arrange it [the laws], so may we be privileged to fulfill it." In its context, this wish meant that they hoped to properly observe the Passover ceremony in the coming week. The adoption of this passage into the haggadah gave it a new meaning: "Just as we have been privileged to arrange it [the practice of the seder in the Diaspora], so may we be privileged to fulfill it [the paschal sacrifice in the Temple]." This reinterpretation makes it a suitable conclusion to the seder and fits in well with the theme of "next year in Jerusalem." This passage from the lengthy poem was apparently introduced into the haggadah by Rabbi Shalom of Neustadt, an Austrian scholar who died in the second decade of the fifteenth century.[74] Rabbi Isaac of Tyrnau, a student of

72. *Responsa Maharshal,* 78; *Bayit Hadash,* 480.

73. Goldschmidt, *The Passover Haggadah,* 96–97.

74. See *Decisions and Customs of Rabbi Shalom of Neustadt,* edited by Shlomoh J. Spitzer [in Hebrew] (Jerusalem: Machon Yerushalayim, 1977), 103.

Rabbi Shalom, is apparently the first to mention that one says "next year in Jerusalem" at this point, immediately before *Hasal Seder Pesach.*[75] Modern practice puts "next year in Jerusalem" immediately after *Hasal Seder Pesach.*

The second poem included in the haggadah, *Oz Rov Nissim,* is taken from a poem of Yannai, an *Eretz Yisra'el* poet of the sixth century. The complete poem, which begins *Onei pitrei rahamatayim,* was originally written as a poetic expansion of the *Amidah* for the *Shabbat* on which the Torah reading began with Exodus 12:29: "In the middle of the night."[76] This, of course, explains the use of this verse as the refrain of this poem. However, this verse is not the beginning of a weekly reading according to the Babylonian cycle of completing the reading of the Torah once a year, but it was the beginning of a weekly portion in the *Eretz Yisra'el* three-year cycle, for which Yannai wrote his poetry. The complete poem appears in Ashkenazic *machzorim* as part of the *Amidah* of the Great *Shabbat.*[77] The custom was to say this poem only at the first seder, which was apparently the reason that Davidson thought that this poem might have been said by Ashkenazim on the first day of Passover.[78] The section of the poem that was adopted into the haggadah expounds the opening verse of the reading, recounting other events that occurred in the middle of the night, beginning with the battle of Abraham against the four kings and ending with the sleeplessness of Ahasuerus, even if there is no evidence that all of these events took place on Passover.

The third poem taken from the liturgy is *Ometz G'vurotekha.* This poem is part of a larger poetic expansion of the *Amidah,* which begins *Asirim asher bakosher,* which was written by Rabbi Eleazar Kallir, a disciple of the abovementioned Yannai. This poem was written for the day on which the Torah reading began with Leviticus 22:26–27 ("When an ox or a sheep or a goat is born"). In the *Eretz Yisra'el* custom, for which Rabbi Eleazar Kallir wrote, this portion of the Torah was read on the first day of Passover. However, the custom outside of *Eretz Yisra'el,* where they observed the second festive day known as the second day of the exiles, was to read this portion on the second day of Passover. So the Ashkenazic custom was to relegate this poem to the second

---

75. *Sefer Haminhagim of Rabbi Eisik Tirna,* edited by Shlomoh J. Spitzer (Jerusalem: Machon Yerushalayim, 1979), 54.

76. For the complete poem see Zvi Meir Rabinovitz, *The Liturgical Poems of Rabbi Yannai According to the Triennial Cycle of the Pentateuch and the Holidays* [in Hebrew] (Jerusalem: Bialik Institute, 1985), 296–304. This section of the poem appears on pp. 302–303.

77. *Siddur Avodat Yisrael,* edited by Yizchak ben Aryeh Yosef Dov [Isaac Seligman Baer] [in Hebrew] (Tel Aviv, 1957; modified facsimile of the edition of J. Lehrberger & Co.: Roedelheim, 1868), 705–709.

78. Israel Davidson, *Thesaurus of Medieval Hebrew Poetry* (New York: Jewish Theological Seminary, 1924), 1:89, no. 1921.

day.[79] This explains the custom found in some *haggadot* that this poem was to be said only at the second seder.

The fourth poem, *Addir Bimlukhah,* is known by the ending of its refrain as *Ki lo na'eh*. This poem is the first of those that have no direct connection with Passover. It is an alphabetical litany with each strophe consisting of three terms. The first two terms are appellations of God and the third is an appellation of the congregation, either angels or humans, telling us that they praise God by saying *lekha ulekha*. The refrain has an additional sentence telling us that it is fit to praise God. In the final strophe, the letter *tav* is used three times to round out the total of appellations to 24. The affinity of this poem to *Heikhalot* literature is well known. *Heikhalot* literature is one of the earliest genres of Jewish mystical literature, and we find in it many examples of this type of poem: a series of alphabetical appellations of God and descriptions of how the angels praise God.[80] Nevertheless, this particular poem is not found in any source other than the haggadah. Its earliest appearance is at the end of the haggadah found in the *Etz Hayim,* the work of the English tosafist, Rabbi Yaakov of London, active in the middle of the thirteenth century. The version found here lacks two letters of the alphabet (*kaf* and *lamed*), although the basic structure is not affected. The requisite multiple of three is retained by adding four terms at the end, which form the acrostic of the name Yaakov.[81] It would thus seem that this version has been composed, or at least revised, by Rabbi Yaakov himself. This haggadah has no other poem following the Great *Hallel* and the fourth cup.

The refrain of this poem is particularly problematic. It reads, "To You, and to You; to You for You; to You also for You; to You, God, belongs kingship; for to Him it is fit, to Him it is appropriate" (*Lekha ulekha, lekha ki lekha, lekha af lekha, lekha Adonai ha-mamlakhah, ki lo na'eh, ki lo ya'eh*). Over a hundred years ago it was suggested that the four phrases that begin with "*lecha*" are truncated references to biblical verses that contain this word. An appropriate biblical passage for the first phrase is either 1 Chronicles 29:11–19: "Yours, LORD, are greatness . . . and it is all Yours," or Psalms 65:2: "Praise befits You in Zion, O God; vows are paid to You." For the second phrase Jeremiah 10:7 has been suggested: "Who would not revere You, O King of the nations? For that is appropriate for You" (*ki lecha ya'atah*). Although this passage does not contain an opening *lecha,* it seems appropriate for the end of the refrain is a paraphrase of it: "for Him it is appropriate." For the third phrase we have two possible verses: "The day is Yours, the night is also Yours" (Ps. 74:16) or "The heaven is Yours, the earth is also Yours" (Ps. 89:12). The first verse is cited in

79. Yonah Frankel, *Machzor lepesach* (Jerusalem: Koren, 1993), 35–36.

80. See Meir Bar Ilan, *The Mysteries of Jewish Prayer and Hekhalot* [in Hebrew] (Ramat-Gan: Bar Ilan, 1987), 55–61, and especially 57.

81. Rabbi Jacob ben Jehuda Hazan of London, *The Etz Hayyim,* edited by Israel Brodie (Jerusalem: Mosad Harav Kook, 1962), 1:332.

the poem of Yannai quoted above. Finally, the fourth phrase is clearly a reference to 1 Chronicles 29:11–19: "To You, God, belong kingship," which is part of one of the passages suggested as referenced by the first phrase.

The song *Addir Hu* was added to the haggadah at a later period than the prior ones. Its earliest appearance may be in the fourteenth-century manuscript haggadah found in Darmstadt. It appears in a number of fifteenth-century *haggadot*. Unlike the prior songs, it has never been included as part of the "official" ritual. In the Darmstadt haggadah, for instance, *Hasal Seder Pesach* is said just before this song. It might be considered as a semi-official addition, because *haggadot* that include the counting of the Omer on the second night of Passover schedule the counting after this poem—before *Ehad Mi Yode'a* and *Had Gadya*.

It has already been noted that the *Addir Hu* song has nothing to do with Passover. Zunz noted that this song, together with *Ehad Mi Yode'a*, was a table song for holidays in Avignon. This fact has often been cited with the implication that it was originally a table song for the holidays and from there it was adopted into the haggadah. However, Zunz's source for this was a collection of prayers and songs for the table that was printed in 1765. This collection includes late material, such as poems by Israel Najara (c. 1555–c. 1625). *Addir Hu* actually appears after a song for Shabbat Hanukkah under the rubric "another *piyyut* (poem)." It thus seems most likely that the people of Avignon took this song from the haggadah for a festival table song.

The structure of this poem is very similar to *Ki Lo Na'eh*. It is an alphabetical list of appellations of God, but without any reference to the congregation. The affinity of this poem with *Ki Lo Na'eh* is emphasized by the fact that the alphabetical list of appellations of God is almost identical in both poems, even though there are some variations between the manuscripts. Of course, the appellations of the congregation in *Ki Lo Na'eh* have been replaced by appellations of God. But even in this we find an affinity between the two poems. We find, for instance, that "His righteous ones say to Him" has been replaced by "He is righteous." Even more striking is the replacement of *limudav yomru lo*, with *lamud hu*. *Limudav* is based on Isaiah 54:13: *limudei Adonai*, which is translated "disciples of God." Converting this into an appellation of God would give us *lamud*, which would best be translated as "he is learned," which is not very appropriate. In fact, the Hatam Sofer has said that this appellation is actually heresy. It would seem that the composition of this poem was strongly influenced by the prior poem, at the expense of appropriateness. Nevertheless, it has its own independent existence. We have already noted that this poem is included among table songs for festivals in the Avignon custom.

After each appellation, or after a series of them, there is a refrain. The refrain expresses the wish that He may build His Temple speedily. In the modern tradition, this is followed by a direct request to God to do so. However, in the Darmstadt haggadah, the direct request is not part of the repeated refrain but it appears at the end of the complete poem. In a fourteenth-century manuscript of the haggadah found in Nuremberg, the direct request is totally lacking.[82]

Any discussion of this poem must note that it appeared also in a translation to Yiddish. Instead of being a slavish translation of the Hebrew, the Yiddish version was a reworking of the Hebrew text. The most notable difference is that the list of appellations was not translated, which would have impaired the alphabetical order, but was replaced by Yiddish appellations. Thus the first two are *almechtiger Got, barimdiger Got* (almighty God, merciful God), preserving the order of the Hebrew alphabet. Another notable difference is that the poem is directed to God. The refrain is not in third person: "May He build His Temple" but only in first person: "build Thy Temple." Thus the appellations of God in the Yiddish version should not be thought of as descriptive but should rather be considered as vocatives. This poem is found in a sixteenth-century illuminated manuscript (Paris, 1333) and appears in early printed *haggadot* (Prague, 1527; Mantova, 1560). One might suspect that the Yiddish version is a more likely the original one and the Hebrew version a clumsy attempt to translate it into Hebrew. However, the fact that the Hebrew version appears in earlier sources than the Yiddish version argues against this.

The pair of songs *Ehad Mi Yode'a* and *Had Gadya* is among the most recent additions to the haggadah. Neither of them appears in any of the manuscripts of the *haggadot* written before the sixteenth century, and it is has been assumed that they were both added, if not composed, in the sixteenth century.

The first of the two, *Ehad Mi Yode'a,* is a counting song. It gives a list of numbers, from one to thirteen, finding something of Jewish significance for each number. Most of the song is in Hebrew, but there are some Aramaic forms for some of the items. A special feature of this song is its cumulative nature. At each number, it recounts backward all the numbers that have been counted until now. This feature is not found in all counting songs.

The song has nothing to do with Passover, and it also appears as a table song for festivals in Avignon. To be more precise, it appears there between the *Kiddush* for the first day of Sukkot and the *Kiddush* for Shemini Atzeret. Goldschmidt noted that it was also sung at weddings in Cochin and Senegal, as evidenced in a volume printed in Amsterdam in 1757 for the use of those communities. Records of the Inquisition, from Majorca in 1678, show that this song was considered sort of a Jewish catechism. Some fragments of this song from the Cairo Genizah show that *Shema Yisra'el* was said as a refrain after each number. Although the first publisher of one of these fragments tried to explain why this refrain was used at the seder, it is more likely that this refrain is further evidence that the song was used outside the seder framework. The refrain gives it a catechetical character. These facts emphasize the lack of any connection

82. L. Rosenthal, "*Über zwei handschriftliche Haggadahs,*" *Magazin für die Wissenschaft des Judenthums* 17 (1890): 312–315.

between this song and Passover but, since they all relate to late evidence, they contribute nothing to the dating of the song.

This song has intrigued folklorists and has been the subject of much study and speculation. One of the reasons for the great interest in this song is its many parallels in different cultures. This has led to a number of attempts to discover which culture was the source for this. All that can be said for certain is that this song first appears in the Prague edition of the haggadah of 1590, printed in the house of Mordechai Cohen, the son of the great printer Gershom Cohen. This haggadah has a translation into Yiddish of the three final poems of the haggadah: *Addir Hu, Ehad Mi Yode'a,* and *Had Gadya.* Versions of the text have been found in the Cairo Genizah, which would seem to date the text much earlier, although we cannot say anything definite, for the Cairo Genizah includes much late material, even printed books. It is reported that one of the texts is written on parchment, which would tend to point to an earlier date, but not much earlier for parchment was still used in the fifteenth century, especially in Italy and apparently in Ashkenaz also.[83]

Some of the introductions to the haggadah date this song to the thirteenth century. The evidence for this is remarkable. Rabbi Tia Weill, who served as a rabbi in Karlsruhe in the late eighteenth century, published, in 1795, a commentary on the haggadah called *Marbeh Ledaber.* In it he reported that he had heard that the songs *Ehad Mi Yode'a* and *Had Gadya* were found on a parchment hidden in the study hall of Rabbi Eleazar Rokeah (c. 1185–c. 1230). This would date these poems earlier than the middle of the fourteenth century, when that study hall was rebuilt. So far, this is based on a hearsay statement that first appears in the end of the eighteenth century. However, Rabbi Weill mentions, in another context, that he used a siddur written in 1406 as an aid in writing his commentary. It was assumed that what he had heard about the dating of these songs was actually seen by him in the 1406 siddur. This would date the first report about the finding of the song to some fifty years after the song had presumably been found. The chain of evidence is flimsy and not very compelling, but this dating nonetheless is found in some modern scholarly works.

Some of the numbered items in *Ehad Mi Yode'a* appear in a midrash that has been suggested as a source, or at least a precedent, for our text. According to this midrash, Rabbi Shimon bar Yochai said that thirty-six hours of retribution had been declared when David conducted a census of the people of Israel. This was considered a sin as the people of Israel should not be counted. However, the people of Israel had great credits, which limited the retribution. These credits were the seven days of *Shabbat,* the eight days of circumcision, the five books of the Torah, and the three Patriarchs. To this list were added either the twelve tribes or the Ten Commandments and the two tablets on which they

83. Malachi Beit-Arie, *Hebrew Codicology* (Jerusalem: The Israel Academy of Sciences and Humanities, 1981), 20.

were written. This gave a total of thirty-five credits so the retribution lasted but one hour instead of thirty-six (*Midrash Shemuel* 31:3, ed. Buber, pp. 137–138).

A more cogent parallel to *Ehad Mi Yode'a* in western culture is found in the Formulae of Eucherius, bishop of Lyons in the middle of the fifth century. He gives a list of numbers, explaining their importance and significance. His list is complete for the first fourteen numbers (although he skips number thirteen) and then continues sporadically until one hundred. Some of his interpretations of the number are identical with those of *Ehad Mi Yode'a*. One is God; five refers to the books of Moses; seven refers to the Sabbath; ten refers to the Decalogue. Most of the others are all christological, although there are some that are neutral: six refers to the six days of Creation. Interestingly, this explanation for six is also the one found in the inquisitory source mentioned above and in an Islamic list of numbers.

One of the important aspects of our song is that it is composed as questions and answers. Number riddles are not a modern invention. Parallels to number songs, composed in the form of questions and answers, have been found in many cultures. A number riddle appears in an ancient midrash. Schoolchildren in Jerusalem posed a riddle to an Athenian: "What is 'nine go out; eight go in; two pour; one drinks; twenty-four serve?'" The Athenian did not know the answer and the explanation was given to him by R. Yochanan: nine months of pregnancy, eight days until the circumcision, two breasts give milk, one child drinks for twenty-four months.[84]

A large number of parallels have been collected from many cultures: Islamic and Christian, Persian and Kirghese, European and American. Some are of religious content and some are of frivolous nature. Some of those of Christian religious nature have items in common with the Hebrew song. The outcome of it all is that the idea of a number riddle of this sort appears in many communities and it is usually difficult, if not impossible, to determine the directions of influence.

Finally, some mention should be made of the differences between the version of this song found in the haggadah and the versions found in the Cairo Genizah fragments that have been published by Sharvit and Fuchs. Sharvit pointed out that some of the variants also appear in the version used for weddings in Cochin, and he therefore referred to these versions as the "Oriental version." In these versions, God is described as "God in heaven" and His presence on earth is ignored. Instead of the Hebrew expression *yarchei leidah,* for the nine-month period of pregnancy, they use the Aramaic expression *yarchei bitna*. Sharvit points out that this is a common saying in Aramaic but not in Hebrew. The number eleven, as used here, refers to the eleven brothers of Joseph, but in the standard version, this number refers to eleven stars (although, there is one *genizah* fragment that contains has the standard version).

84. *Eichah Rabbah,* edited by S. Buber (Vilna 5659 [1899]), 48–49. There are variant readings in the text. I have given the gist of the idea.

The meaning is probably the same, as most commentators explain that the eleven stars are the ones seen by Joseph in his dream. Finally, we may note that the eastern version has only twelve stanzas compared to the thirteen of the standard version.[85]

The final song in the Ashkenazic tradition is *Had Gadya*. This song belongs to the genre of cumulative songs, each stanza adding something before repeating the whole series. One of the most famous of these is the Mother Goose rhyme "This Is the House That Jack Built." The basic idea of the version of the song in the haggadah is that every deed will find its retribution and for every strong thing there is something stronger. A parallel to this last motif is found in the midrash. When Nimrod asked Abraham to worship fire, Abraham replied that water is stronger than fire for it extinguishes fire. Nimrod was agreeable and suggested that they should worship water. Abraham responded that clouds should be worshiped as they contain water and that wind should be worshiped because it moves the clouds and that humans should be worshiped as they contain the wind (a play on Hebrew *ruach*). At which point Nimrod lost his patience and tried to show Abraham the power of fire by throwing him into the fire (*Bereshit Rabbah* 38:28, p. 363).

This song, as the prior one, has many parallels in different cultures. One of the most pertinent is a version found in New England. It tells of a peasant woman who, while cleaning her house, found two pennies with which she decided to buy a pig. The pig balked at crossing a stile on the way home so she ordered a dog to bite the pig. The dog refused so she ordered a stick to beat the dog, followed by fire, water, an ox, a butcher, a rope to hang the butcher, a rat to gnaw the rope, and a cat to kill the rat. The cat asks for milk, which the woman gives to it, and then the cat proceeds to kill the rat, who reconsiders and gnaws the rope . . . until the pig decides to go over the stile and the woman reaches home. In other versions, the pig is replaced by a kid. All the documentation for these tales is late and it is conceivable that they were all based on the Jewish tale, although a scholar has suggested that the original form of this song originated in France in the twelfth century.[86] It is remarkable that the Jewish tale has a final end that provides vengeance but does not resolve the injury done to the kid, while the other versions return to the original problem and present a resolution.

Until the middle of the twentieth century, it was thought that the first appearance of this song in the haggadah was in the same 1590 edition in which *Ehad Mi Yode'a* first appeared. However, Chone Szmeruk discovered a manu-

85. The most recent discussion of this song is that of Menachem (Harry) Fox, "About the History of the Songs *Ehad Mi Yodea* and *Had Gadya* in Israel and Among the Nations" [in Hebrew], *Asufot: Annual for Jewish Studies* 2 (5748 [1988]): 201–226. Fox includes references to all the relevant literature.

86. William Wells Newell, "The Passover Song of the Kid and an Equivalent from New England," *Journal of American Folklore* 18 (1905): 33–48.

script haggadah that is dated between the beginning of the fifteenth century and the beginning of the sixteenth century that contains this song (but not *Ehad Mi Yode'a*). The song appears here in Aramaic and in Yiddish. Szmeruk maintains, based on linguistic analysis of the two versions, that the Aramaic version has been translated from the Yiddish. An interesting difference between this version and the standard version is that the goat is eaten by a mouse, rather than a cat, and the mouse is eaten by the cat. The strength of the association of this song with the seder is shown by the fact that the words "*hasal seder pesach*" appear after this song—a phenomena that I have not found in any other haggadah.[87]

Another manuscript that contains this song, dated about the same time as the other but representing the Provençal custom, was discovered by Harry Fox.[88] Here we find a version, in good Aramaic only, and the chain is slightly different. We have a kid, a dog, a stick, fire, water, an ox, a rope, a rat, and a cat. Here the song breaks off and it is not clear whether there was a continuation. Fox argues that this song was the source for the standard tradition. However, the theosophic end of the standard tradition would be a major change.

Had Gadya has become a major symbol of the Passover seder. Some thought it frivolous. Rabbi Chayim Yosef David Azulai, known as the Chida, one of the great Sephardic sages of the eighteenth century, railed against someone who had belittled *Had Gadya,* claiming that he who did so was belittling tens of thousands of Jews in Poland and Ashkenaz, among them Torah giants (*Chayim Sha'al* 1:28). Defending the poem, many people have found hidden significance in the song and at least thirteen monographs have been written for this purpose.[89] Nathan Alterman wrote a poem about this poem, ending with the father and the kid waiting for a better time, which will surely arrive. The kid has entered the haggadah in many non-Ashkenazic communities who have not absorbed any of the other Ashkenazic songs. It has been translated into Ladino and into Greek.

Additional Songs in Other Traditions

Other communities also added songs after the conclusion of the official seder. In France, before the exile, they used to say a poem that compared the Passover at the Exodus with the Passover that was being celebrated, expressing the difficult times in which they were living. The refrain of the poem called on God to awaken and see their tribulation. The poem, which begins "*Pesach mitzrayim asirai yazeu hofshim,*" was republished by Goldschmidt (p. 99). A poem found in

87. C. Szmeruk, "The Earliest Aramaic and Yiddish Version of the 'Song of the Kid' (Chad Gadya)," in *The Field of Yiddish: Studies in Language, Folklore and Literature,* edited by Uriel Weinreich (New York: Linguistic Circle of New York, 1954), 214–218.

88. See p. 67, n. 85.

89. For a list see M. Haberman, "Had Gadya" [in Hebrew], *Mahanayim* 55 (Erev Pesach 5721 [1961]): 142.

the custom of Avignon and Carpentras is *Mibet aven shevet medanai.* The poem is based on the verse from the Song of Songs: "Arise, my darling; My fair one, go!" (Songs 2:13). The first part of each line opens with a description of the exile and ends with "Arise [from there], my darling." The second part has a description of the Land of Israel and concludes: "My fair one, go!" This poem has also been republished by Goldschmidt (pp. 101–102).

Romaniot communities ended the seder with a poem taken from the next morning's prayer book, *Oseh Fele Be-Mitzrayim.* The poem was a *piyyut* that expanded the blessing of redemption that is said just before the *Amidah*. It described the wonders that God had done to save the Jews from Egypt, and it implored Him to do similar wonders to save them from the yoke of Edom (Goldschmidt, p. 104).

Many people, especially in Sephardic communities, read the Song of Songs after the seder. This book of the Bible is printed in many Sephardic *haggadot;* and, in some of them, it appears before *Had Gadya.* This custom was accepted by many Ashkenazim. However, in the Ashkenazic *haggadot* Song of Songs follows *Had Gadya.* Others read the short midrashic work known as *Sefer ha-Yashar.*

Several modern *haggadot* end the seder with "Hatikvah." The earliest source in which I found this is a haggadah printed in the United States in 1927 with the compliments of a commercial bank. For proper balance, "The Star-Spangled Banner" also appears here.[90] "Hatikvah" appears also in a haggadah printed in Italy in 1948 and in a haggadah printed in the United States in 1953. The inclusion of "Hatikvah" is meant to symbolize the idea that the redemption is not just a past event but one toward which Jews look eagerly. Thus they restore the original paschal meal in Egypt. The ceremony is not just a remembrance of the past; it is also a step toward the future.

90. In two other *haggadot* printed in that year the two anthems are printed in the front of the haggadah (Yudlov 3109, 3110). These *haggadot* were also meant to be in the nature of commercial advertisements.

The Passover Haggadah

A Note About the Translation

The translation is a new translation, trying to use modern English, but it does retain some archaic language, based on traditional English translations. Biblical texts are quoted from the NJPS translation, except where the text of the haggadah reflects a different understanding of the biblical passages. In those cases, the translation has been adapted accordingly.

The translation of the name of God has been a problem since antiquity. The unique name of the God of the Jews, who is the God of all humanity, is the Tetragrammaton (YHVH). All the other terms for God, such as *Adonai, El/Elohim, Tzevaot,* and so on, are names that are used also for human entities. Their use as terms for God is meant to imply that God is the Supreme Being. However, already in ancient times, it was considered improper to pronounce the Tetragrammaton and the term LORD (*Adonai*) was substituted for it. The Septuagint consistently translates the Tetragrammaton by *kurios* (LORD), using *theos* (God) to translate *Elohim*. This is reflected in English translations that use "LORD" as the substitute for the Tetragrammation and "God" for "*Elohim*." Some early Greek manuscripts used a different method, actually copying the Hebrew letters of the Tetragrammaton within the Greek text. I have decided to follow this convention in a more modern form, as practiced in a recent translation of the siddur, transliterating the Hebrew substitute for the Tetragrammaton, *Adonai*. This enables us to use the term "LORD" as the translation of "*Elohim,*" which better reflects its true meaning.

The translation of "*melekh ha-olam*" is also problematic as it is not absolutely clear whether "*olam*" is spatial, and the term should be translated "King of the universe," or "*olam*" is temporal and the term should be translated "Eternal King." We have accepted the traditional English translation: King of the universe.

Traditional blessings end with a praise of God in a participial form. Thus, for instance, the blessing before eating vegetables ends with "*borei p'ri ha-adamah*." This may be translated either as "who creates fruit of the ground" or as "creator of the fruit of the ground." Although traditional translations generally used the first form, I think that the second form reflects more accurately the idea that the sages were trying to convey.

Preparing for the Seder

Traditional *haggadot* begin the instructions for the evening with instructions for the preparation of the seder plate. The plate has its own history. In the times of the Mishnah and Talmud, people reclined either before small tables or before bases for tables. The food for each course was brought either on a tray that was placed on the table or on a tabletop that was placed on the base. The removal of the tray or tabletop after the first dipping was meant to provoke the children to wonder why the food was being removed before they had eaten. When people began to use big tables that were set before the people sat down, they retained the custom of removing the food by placing the special foods that were to be used at the seder on a tray or in a basket that could then be brought in and removed as part of the ritual. Rav Saadiah Gaon prescribes bringing a table (that is, tray) with only the vegetables and the dip necessary for the first dipping. Afterward, he writes that they should bring the matzah and the other foods on a separate table or they should put these things on the table in front of them.

The first one to suggest any particular arrangement for the foods on the table was apparently Maharil (Germany, ?1360–1427). Maharil addressed two issues. His first requirement was that all the special foods should be on the tray that was to be removed. For example, one should not put some of the matzah on the table, rather than on the tray, for then those matzot would not be removed when it was time to remove the food. The second issue was how the foods should be arranged on the tray. Here he merely insisted that the vegetable for the first dipping should be closer to the master of ceremonies than was the matzah. The reason for this was not practical but halakhic. One should not pass over a mitzvah that is in front of one for the sake of another mitzvah. Thus if the matzah were closer to the master of ceremonies than the vegetable, one would be required to take the matzah before the vegetable, disrupting the planned order of the seder. This idea was further developed by R. Moses Isserles (Poland, d. 1572), who added that the matzah should be closer than the *maror* and the *haroset* while farthest should be the egg (which was often eaten at the meal) and the shank bone (which was, in his time, primarily for display) (*Shulchan Arukh, Orach Chayyim* 473:4). This led to the development of artistic seder plates, which were decorated in a way that enabled one to see exactly where each item should be put.

The arrangement would be as follows:

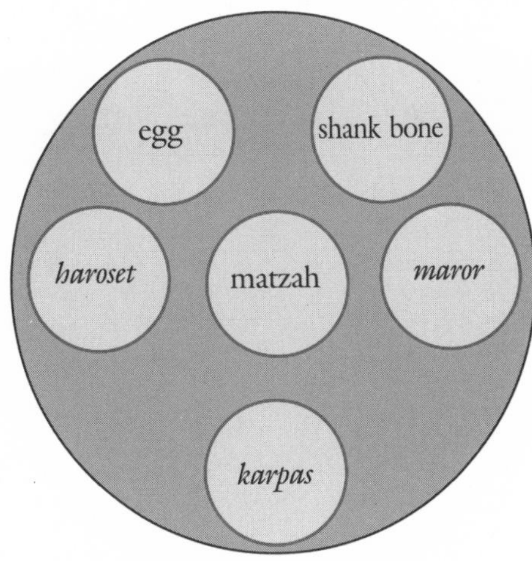

There is no preference expressed, in the early sources, between the right-hand side of the plate and the left side. Presumably, the items used first should be on the right side. Maharil did not mention the liquid (salt water/vinegar) that was used for dipping the *karpas* and, therefore, it was not included in the plate. Others who felt that it should be included reached the following arrangement:

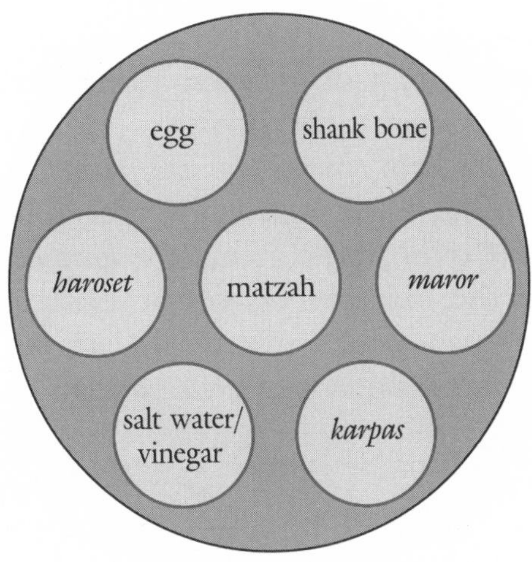

In practice, the matzah was often put in the center of the plate with the other items surrounding it in the prescribed order. Due to the size of the matzah, it was not always feasible or practical to include it on the plate and some place it on separate plates.

Rabbi Isaac Luria (Ari), the renowned sixteenth-century kabbalist, suggested another arrangement of the plate. His arrangement was based on the idea that the plate and its items represent the Ten Emanations of God. The number ten was reached by adding together the three matzot, the other six food items, and the plate itself as an organizing principle. One of the basic principles of the Ten Emanations was that there was an emanation from the right, followed by one from the left, followed by a third that mediated between them or synthesized them. This gives us the following arrangement:

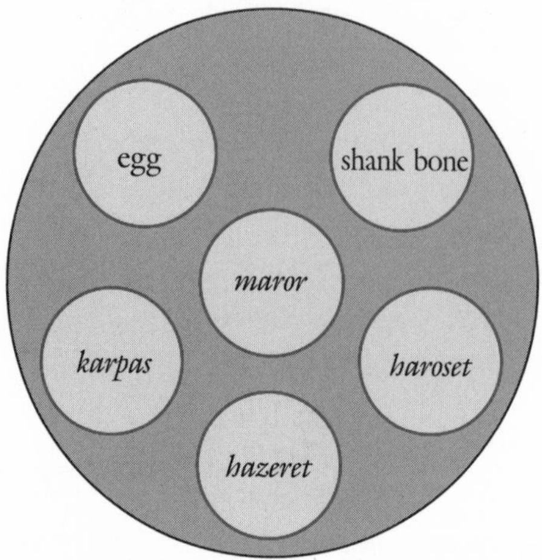

Note that, according to the Ari, there is no salt water on the plate but there is *hazeret*. This follows the European custom of using two different kinds of vegetables as bitter herbs. Due to the difficulty of getting lettuce at the paschal season in northern Europe, people used horseradish to supplement the lettuce. One vegetable was used when the bitter herbs were eaten by themselves, immediately after eating the matzah, and the other was used when they ate the bitter herbs as part of the *korech* sandwich. As noted above, the three matzot were placed under these foods.

Another arrangement was suggested by the Vilna Gaon. The *karpas* itself was not included on the plate for, according to the Gaon, the plate was brought to the table only after dipping the *karpas*. The remaining four items were arranged at the four corners of the plate, around the matzah. The *maror* and *haroset* were above the matzah and the shank bone and egg were below the matzah, actually underneath the matzah.

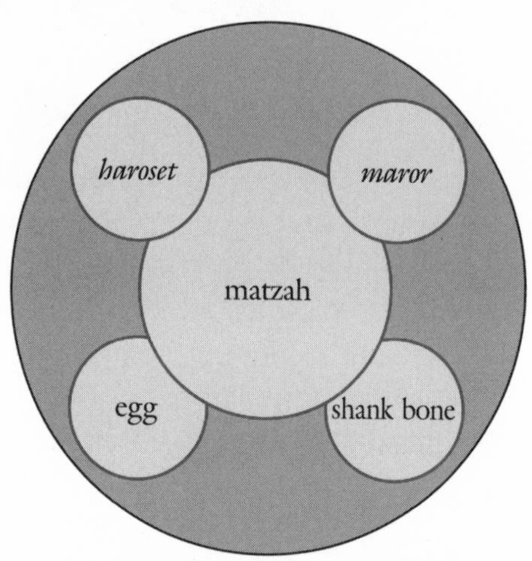

It is customary to arrange three matzot on the seder plate. In gaonic times only two matzot were used and this is the custom prescribed by Maimonides. It was customary, at all *Shabbat* and festival meals, to set the table with two loaves of bread. This was explained as a commemoration of the double portion of manna that the Jews received on Friday during their forty years in the desert. It was assumed that a double portion was received also on the eve of festivals. The Talmud mentioned that on Passover it was not necessary to have whole loaves at the table since the matzah commemorated the bread of affliction, and a broken loaf was appropriate. For this reason, it was customary to break one of the two loaves before the meal, either immediately before reciting the blessing over the matzah, according to Maimonides, or just before beginning the reading of the main part of the haggadah, according to most customs. However, this presented a problem when Passover fell on Friday night, as it was felt that a broken loaf was not appropriate for *Shabbat*. To solve this problem, an additional matzah was added when Passover fell on *Shabbat,* giving a total of three matzot. Eventually, putting three matzot on the table became customary at every seder. Some Yemenites still follow the custom of Maimonides and set the table with two matzot, and the Vilna Gaon also restored the ancient ruling that only two matzot should be included on the seder plate. Nevertheless, it is almost a universal custom to use three loaves, utilizing the broken half for the *afikoman*.

Recite the *Kiddush* / קַדֵּשׁ

One recites the Kiddush *over the first of the four cups of wine. The basic* Kiddush *consists of two blessings: a short one over wine and a long one about the sanctity of the day. It is of interest to note that the long blessing begins by addressing God in the second person, continues addressing Him in the third person, and returns to the second person. When Passover falls on Friday night, mention of the* Shabbat *is integrated into the blessing about the sanctity of the day. When Passover falls on Saturday night, two blessings are added. The first is a blessing whose motif is the distinction between sacred and secular on the one hand, and between various degress of sanctity on the other hand. The second is a blessing over a candle, which may be lit when* Shabbat *is over. In all cases, the Kiddush closes with the* Shehecheyanu *blessing, thanking God for having survived to participate in this joyous event. (For further details on the structure of the* Kiddush, *see pp. 17–21.)*

There is an introductory sentence, starting with "Pay attention," which is meant to call the participants to listen to the Kiddush. *When everybody recites the* Kiddush *together, as is often done at the seder, this sentence is unnecessary.*

When Passover falls on Friday night, it is customary to preface the Friday night Kiddush *with the recital of Genesis 2:1–3, which tells of the first* Shabbat *of Creation. It is a kabbalistic custom to say, before beginning these sentences, the closing words of the previous sentence (*yom ha-shishi; *Gen. 1:31). The reason for this is that the first letters of these two words, taken together with the first letters of the first two words of Genesis 2:1, form an acrosticon of the Tetragrammaton. To avoid saying two words out of context, some begin several words before this: "and it was evening and it was morning." The nature of this passage as an addition is emphasized by the fact that the call to attention is still recited before the blessing over the wine, after reading this paragraph.*

When Passover falls on a Friday night, begin here. On any other day, skip to the next paragraph.

Genesis 2:1–3

The sixth day. The heaven and the earth were finished, and all their array. On the seventh day the LORD finished the work that He had been doing, and He ceased on the seventh day from all the work that He had done. And the LORD blessed the seventh day and declared it holy, because on it the LORD ceased from all the work of creation that He had done.

יוֹם הַשִּׁשִּׁי וַיְכֻלּוּ הַשָּׁמַיִם וְהָאָרֶץ
וְכָל צְבָאָם: וַיְכַל אֱלֹהִים בַּיּוֹם הַשְּׁבִיעִי
מְלַאכְתּוֹ אֲשֶׁר עָשָׂה וַיִּשְׁבֹּת בַּיּוֹם הַשְּׁבִיעִי
מִכָּל מְלַאכְתּוֹ אֲשֶׁר עָשָׂה: וַיְבָרֶךְ אֱלֹהִים
אֶת יוֹם הַשְּׁבִיעִי וַיְקַדֵּשׁ אֹתוֹ כִּי בוֹ שָׁבַת
מִכָּל מְלַאכְתּוֹ אֲשֶׁר בָּרָא אֱלֹהִים לַעֲשׂוֹת:

Attention, Ladies and Gentlemen

Blessed art Thou, *Adonai* our LORD, creator of the fruit of the vine.

בָּרוּךְ אַתָּה יי אֱלֹהֵינוּ מֶלֶךְ הָעוֹלָם בּוֹרֵא פְּרִי הַגָּפֶן.

On *Shabbat*, one adds the words in parentheses:

Blessed art Thou, *Adonai,* our LORD, King of the universe, who has chosen us among the nations and has exalted us from all languages and has sanctified us by His commandment. And You have given us, *Adonai* our LORD, in love, (Sabbaths for rest and) appointed times for joy, festivals and times for rejoicing, (this day of Sabbath and) this day of the matzah festival, the time of our freedom, (in love,) a holy convocation, a memorial of the Exodus from Egypt. For You have chosen us and it us whom You have sanctified from the nations and You have granted us (Sabbath and) Your holy appointed times in (love and in grace), in joy and in gladness. Blessed art Thou, *Adonai,* Sanctifier of Israel and the [special] times.

בָּרוּךְ אַתָּה יי אֱלֹהֵינוּ מֶלֶךְ הָעוֹלָם, אֲשֶׁר בָּחַר בָּנוּ מִכָּל עָם וְרוֹמְמָנוּ מִכָּל לָשׁוֹן וְקִדְּשָׁנוּ בְּמִצְוֹתָיו. וַתִּתֶּן לָנוּ יי אֱלֹהֵינוּ בְּאַהֲבָה (שַׁבָּתוֹת לִמְנוּחָה וּ) מוֹעֲדִים לְשִׂמְחָה, חַגִּים וּזְמַנִּים לְשָׂשׂוֹן, אֶת (יוֹם הַשַּׁבָּת הַזֶּה וְאֶת) יוֹם חַג הַמַּצּוֹת הַזֶּה, זְמַן חֵרוּתֵנוּ (בְּאַהֲבָה), מִקְרָא קֹדֶשׁ, זֵכֶר לִיצִיאַת מִצְרָיִם. כִּי בָנוּ בָחַרְתָּ וְאוֹתָנוּ קִדַּשְׁתָּ מִכָּל הָעַמִּים, (וְשַׁבָּת) וּמוֹעֲדֵי קָדְשְׁךָ (בְּאַהֲבָה וּבְרָצוֹן), בְּשִׂמְחָה וּבְשָׂשׂוֹן הִנְחַלְתָּנוּ. בָּרוּךְ אַתָּה יי, מְקַדֵּשׁ (הַשַּׁבָּת וְ) יִשְׂרָאֵל וְהַזְּמַנִּים.

When Passover falls on any night except Saturday night, skip to the last blessing. When Passover falls on Saturday night, the following two blessings (one for the lighting of the candle and the second to separate the outgoing Shabbat *from the incoming festival) are added to the above:*

Blessed art Thou, *Adonai* our LORD, King of the universe, creator of the lights of the fire.

בָּרוּךְ אַתָּה יי אֱלֹהֵינוּ מֶלֶךְ הָעוֹלָם, בּוֹרֵא מְאוֹרֵי הָאֵשׁ.

Blessed art Thou, *Adonai* our LORD, King of the universe, who separates (or distinguishes) between holy and profane, between light and darkness, between Israel and the nations, between the seventh day of the week and the six days of activity. You have distinguished between the sanctity of *Shabbat* and the sanctity of the festival and you have sanctified the seventh day of the week over the six days of activity. You have separated your people, Israel, from the nations and have sanctified them with Your sanctity. Blessed art Thou, LORD, who distinguishes between sanctity and sanctity.

בָּרוּךְ אַתָּה יי אֱלֹהֵינוּ מֶלֶךְ הָעוֹלָם הַמַּבְדִּיל בֵּין קֹדֶשׁ לְחֹל, בֵּין אוֹר לְחֹשֶׁךְ, בֵּין יִשְׂרָאֵל לָעַמִּים, בֵּין יוֹם הַשְּׁבִיעִי לְשֵׁשֶׁת יְמֵי הַמַּעֲשֶׂה. בֵּין קְדֻשַּׁת שַׁבָּת לִקְדֻשַּׁת יוֹם טוֹב הִבְדַּלְתָּ, וְאֶת יוֹם הַשְּׁבִיעִי מִשֵּׁשֶׁת יְמֵי הַמַּעֲשֶׂה קִדַּשְׁתָּ. הִבְדַּלְתָּ וְקִדַּשְׁתָּ אֶת עַמְּךָ יִשְׂרָאֵל בִּקְדֻשָּׁתֶךָ. בָּרוּךְ אַתָּה יי הַמַּבְדִּיל בֵּין קֹדֶשׁ לְקֹדֶשׁ.

The last blessing:

Blessed art Thou, *Adonai* our LORD, King of the universe, who has kept us alive, sustained us, and brought us to this time.

בָּרוּךְ אַתָּה יי אֱלֹהֵינוּ מֶלֶךְ הָעוֹלָם, שֶׁהֶחֱיָנוּ וְקִיְּמָנוּ וְהִגִּיעָנוּ לַזְּמַן הַזֶּה.

One should drink most of the cup while leaning.

וּרְחַץ

One washes one's hands without reciting a blessing.

כַּרְפַּס

One should dip a vegetable that requires the adamah *blessing in a liquid, customarily vinegar or salt water, and recite the blessing over the vegetable:*

Blessed art Thou, *Adonai* our LORD, King of the universe, creator of the fruit of the land.

בָּרוּךְ אַתָּה יי אֱלֹהֵינוּ מֶלֶךְ הָעוֹלָם, בּוֹרֵא פְּרִי הָאֲדָמָה.

יַחַץ

The master of ceremonies breaks the middle matzah into two parts and puts away the larger part for later consumption as the afikoman.

מַגִּיד

This is the beginning of the story of slavery and redemption:

[1,2]**B**ehold, the bread of distress that
our ancestors ate while in Egypt.
Let anyone who is hungry
come and eat.
Let anyone who wishes to observe
the paschal ritual come and
participate.
Today we are here;
next year in the Land of Israel.
Today we are slaves;
next year we shall be free.

[1,2]**הָא לַחְמָא עַנְיָא**
דִּי אֲכַלוּ אַבְהָתָנָא בְּאַרְעָא דְמִצְרָיִם.
כָּל דִּכְפִין יֵיתֵי וְיֵיכֻל,
כָּל דִּצְרִיךְ יֵיתֵי וְיִפְסַח.
הָשַׁתָּא הָכָא,
לְשָׁנָה הַבָּאָה בְּאַרְעָא דְיִשְׂרָאֵל.
הָשַׁתָּא עַבְדֵי,
לְשָׁנָה הַבָּאָה בְּנֵי חוֹרִין.

1 **Behold, the bread of distress** Except for *Had Gadya,* this passage (which appears only in *haggadot* of Babylonian origin) is the only one in the haggadah that appears in Aramaic. The final section of this passage is a mixture of Aramaic and Hebrew, although some texts present the final statement only in Aramaic. It has been traditionally assumed that this text was composed in Aramaic because it was a common Jewish language when this passage was written and the author wanted to make sure that everybody understood it. This passage consists of three discrete statements. The first presents the three matzot, one of which has just been broken. Note, however, that this statement appears in the haggadah of Maimonides, even though he did not break the matzah at the beginning of the seder. The use of broken bread at a festival table is normally discouraged. Thus this statement may be understood as a justification for using broken bread by explaining that the broken matzah represents the "bread of distress," which our ancestors ate in Egypt. This description contradicts the declaration of Rabbi Gamliel, as expressed in the presentation of the matzah just before the meal, that matzah is eaten as a symbol of the bread that the Jews ate after they left Egypt, not as a symbol of the bread they ate while they were slaves in Egypt. Some versions of the haggadah emend this first sentence to read "this is the bread of distress which our ancestors ate when they left Egypt," in order to reconcile this statement with that of R. Gamliel. However, even after this emendation, the bread remains "bread of distress." We might say that the bread is transformed from a symbol of distress to a symbol of freedom through the telling of the Passover story. Matzah may be considered both a symbol of distress and a symbol of freedom in the context of the haggadah. The reason that this is so is because matzah is bread baked when there is no time to allow the dough to rise. Slaves in Egypt had to get back to work and they had no time to wait for the dough to rise. The Jews who left Egypt in haste also had no time to wait. They were told to leave Egypt immediately, not allowing them time to permit the dough to rise so that they could bake proper bread for the journey. The lack of time is the common element to slavery and the Exodus, and it serves to symbolize the change in the status of the Jews—their time is now devoted to God and not to Pharaoh. They have been transformed from slaves of Pharaoh to servants of God.

The second statement is a twofold invitation: first, a general invitation to a meal, and second, to the paschal meal specifically. The Talmud tells us that R. Huna was accustomed

One removes the seder plate, fills the cup for the second time, and then one of the children, or another person, asks the following questions.

[3] **מַה נִּשְׁתַּנָּה**
הַלַּיְלָה הַזֶּה מִכָּל הַלֵּילוֹת?

שֶׁבְּכָל הַלֵּילוֹת אָנוּ אוֹכְלִין חָמֵץ וּמַצָּה,
הַלַּיְלָה הַזֶּה – כֻּלּוֹ מַצָּה.

שֶׁבְּכָל הַלֵּילוֹת אָנוּ אוֹכְלִין שְׁאָר יְרָקוֹת,
הַלַּיְלָה הַזֶּה – מָרוֹר.

שֶׁבְּכָל הַלֵּילוֹת אֵין אָנוּ מַטְבִּילִין אֲפִילוּ
פַּעַם אֶחָת,
הַלַּיְלָה הַזֶּה – שְׁתֵּי פְעָמִים.

שֶׁבְּכָל הַלֵּילוֹת אָנוּ אוֹכְלִין בֵּין יוֹשְׁבִין
וּבֵין מְסֻבִּין, הַלַּיְלָה הַזֶּה – כֻּלָּנוּ מְסֻבִּין.

[3] **W**hy is this night different from all other nights?

On all other nights we may eat both leavened bread and matzah; on this night we eat only matzah.

On all other nights, we eat all kinds of vegetables; on this night we eat bitter herbs.

On all other nights we do not dip even once; on this night we dip twice [once we dip *karpas* in either salt water or vinegar and the second time we dip bitter herbs in *haroset*].

On all other nights we may eat either sitting or leaning; on this night we all eat only while leaning.

to extending such invitations at the beginning of every meal (*Ta'anit* 20b). One of the *Ge'onim* mentions that it was an ancient custom to extend such invitations specifically during the paschal meal. Yet, the second part of this invitation, which mentions the paschal meal, cannot be referring to the meal at which a paschal sacrifice was offered. The Mishnah requires that the guest list for this meal be finalized before the lamb is slaughtered. Thus, because invitations to the "paschal ritual" must be given before the animal is killed, this phrase must be understood as an invitation to the nonsacrificial seder rite. In any case, this passage is out of place and should have been said before the *Kiddush,* as the invitees are also required to participate in the *Kiddush* and the other rituals that precede this statement.

The third section compares the situation at the time this passage was composed with hopes for the future. The situation at the time was exile and subjection, with expectations of freedom in the Land of Israel sometime in the future. Therefore, the traditional haggadah's closing wish, "Next year in Jerusalem," becomes a frame for the haggadah.

Finally, it should be noted that the *haggadah* of Maimonides and some Sephardic *haggadot,* open this passage with another statement in Aramaic: "we left Egypt in haste" (*bivhilu yatzanu mi-mitzrayim*). The function of this statement here is unclear. Rabbi Shimon b. Zemah Duran has suggested that this statement is part of the introduction of the matzah, based on the verse: "For seven days thereafter you shall eat unleavened bread, bread of distress—for you departed from the land of Egypt hurriedly" (Deut. 16:3). However, it appears also in *haggadot* that refer to the matzah not as bread eaten in haste but as bread eaten by slaves, with the emphasis on the Jews' captivity.

2 **Behold** The Aramaic "*ha*" is generally translated as "this." However, "*ha*" as a demonstrative pronoun is feminine and bread is masculine. It is thus better to translate "*ha*" as "behold" or, possibly, "here is."

The seder plate is returned to the table and the matzot are uncovered.

[4,5]We were slaves to Pharaoh in Egypt and *Adonai,* our Lord, freed us from Egypt with a mighty hand (Deut. 6:21) and an outstretched arm (Deut. 5:15).

[4,5]**עֲבָדִים הָיִינוּ** לְפַרְעֹה בְּמִצְרָיִם,
וַיּוֹצִיאֵנוּ יי אֱלֹהֵינוּ מִשָּׁם
בְּיָד חֲזָקָה וּבִזְרוֹעַ נְטוּיָה.

And if the Holy One, blessed be He, had not taken our ancestors out of Egypt, we, our children, and our children's children would be subjugated to Pharaoh.

וְאִלּוּ לֹא הוֹצִיא הַקָּדוֹשׁ בָּרוּךְ הוּא
אֶת אֲבוֹתֵינוּ מִמִּצְרַיִם,
הֲרֵי אָנוּ וּבָנֵינוּ וּבְנֵי בָנֵינוּ
מְשֻׁעְבָּדִים הָיִינוּ לְפַרְעֹה בְּמִצְרָיִם.

Therefore, even if we are all wise, we are all understanding, we are all elders, we all know the Torah, we are obligated to tell the story of the Exodus from Egypt.

וַאֲפִילוּ כֻּלָּנוּ חֲכָמִים, כֻּלָּנוּ נְבוֹנִים,
כֻּלָּנוּ זְקֵנִים, כֻּלָּנוּ יוֹדְעִים אֶת הַתּוֹרָה,
מִצְוָה עָלֵינוּ לְסַפֵּר בִּיצִיאַת מִצְרָיִם.

Everyone who lengthens the discussion is praiseworthy.

וְכָל הַמַּרְבֶּה לְסַפֵּר בִּיצִיאַת מִצְרַיִם
הֲרֵי זֶה מְשֻׁבָּח.

3 **Why is this night different** There are several ways of interpreting this paragraph, known as the Four Questions. We have followed the traditional translation of the first sentence. This leaves us two different ways of understanding the following four phrases. One is that these four phrases give a list of differences, substantiating the questioner's statement that this night is different and requiring an explanation of why it is different. A general answer, such as "We are celebrating the Exodus" would be sufficient. However, there is a second, preferable way of understanding the four phrases. These four phrases are the actual questions. The questioner wishes to know why these specific things are different from on any other night. Many commentators have suggested that the first sentence should be translated as: "In what ways is this night different from all other nights?" We may then assume that what follows are not questions but answers explaining the four differences between this night and all other nights.

4 **We were slaves to Pharaoh in Egypt** This biblical passage is considered by many to be the answer to the preceding question. In many Sephardic *haggadot* this passage is prefaced by the statement, "This is the answer." This passage is an appropriate answer if the question is taken to mean "Why is this night different . . . ?" However, it does not explain the connection between the specific acts mentioned and the redemption of Israel from Egypt.

5 **We were slaves to Pharaoh in Egypt** The verse cited is a conflation of two verses. The first verse ends with "a mighty hand" and the second has the phrase "a mighty hand and an outstretched arm."

[6]One time R. Eliezer, R. Joshua, R. Eleazar ben Azariah, R. Akiva, and R. Tarfon were participating in a festive meal in B'nei B'rak and were discussing the Exodus throughout the night, until their students came and said to them: "Our masters, it is time to recite the morning *Shema*."

[6]**מַעֲשֶׂה** בְּרַבִּי אֱלִיעֶזֶר וְרַבִּי יְהוֹשֻׁעַ וְרַבִּי אֶלְעָזָר בֶּן עֲזַרְיָה וְרַבִּי עֲקִיבָא וְרַבִּי טַרְפוֹן שֶׁהָיוּ מְסֻבִּין בִּבְנֵי בְרַק, וְהָיוּ מְסַפְּרִים בִּיצִיאַת מִצְרַיִם כָּל אוֹתוֹ הַלַּיְלָה עַד שֶׁבָּאוּ תַלְמִידֵיהֶם וְאָמְרוּ לָהֶם: רַבּוֹתֵינוּ, הִגִּיעַ זְמַן קְרִיאַת שְׁמַע שֶׁל שַׁחֲרִית.

[7]R. Eleazar ben Azariah said: [8]I am about seventy years old and [9]I had never convinced anyone that the Exodus should be mentioned every evening until Ben Zoma expounded this, as it says: "so that you may remember the day of your departure from the land of Egypt all the days of your life" (Deut. 16:3); "the days of your life"—daytimes; "all the days of your life"—nighttimes. But the sages say: "the days of your life"—this world; "all the days of your life"—to include the world to come.

[7]אָמַר רַבִּי אֶלְעָזָר בֶּן עֲזַרְיָה: [8]הֲרֵי אֲנִי כְּבֶן שִׁבְעִים שָׁנָה, [9]וְלֹא זָכִיתִי שֶׁתֵּאָמֵר יְצִיאַת מִצְרַיִם בַּלֵּילוֹת עַד שֶׁדְּרָשָׁהּ בֶּן זוֹמָא: שֶׁנֶּאֱמַר "לְמַעַן תִּזְכֹּר אֶת יוֹם צֵאתְךָ מֵאֶרֶץ מִצְרַיִם כֹּל יְמֵי חַיֶּיךָ"; יְמֵי חַיֶּיךָ – הַיָּמִים, כֹּל יְמֵי חַיֶּיךָ – הַלֵּילוֹת. וַחֲכָמִים אוֹמְרִים: יְמֵי חַיֶּיךָ – הָעוֹלָם הַזֶּה, כֹּל יְמֵי חַיֶּיךָ – לְהָבִיא לִימוֹת הַמָּשִׁיחַ.

6 **One time, R. Eliezer** This story does not appear in any other source. Its situation in the haggadah suggests that it took place on Passover eve, when there was a special obligation to discuss the Exodus. The scholars mentioned in the story all flourished in the period shortly before the Bar Kokhba rebellion. R. Akiva is especially known as a supporter of Bar Kokhba. Some commentators have suggested that the story should be understood as an enigmatic reference to these scholars' discussions of plans for the rebellion. However, there is no way to substantiate this interpretation. For a comparison of this story with a similar story found in the Tosefta, see the introduction.

7 **R. Eleazar ben Azariah said** This passage is taken from the Mishnah (*Berakhot* 1:5). The discussion has nothing to do with Passover; it refers to the regular evening reading of the *Shema* and its blessings. Many traditional commentators explain that the discussion is about the evening reading of the third part of *Shema,* in which the Exodus is mentioned. However, it seems more likely that the discussion is about mentioning the Exodus in the blessing that immediately follows the *Shema.* In either circumstance, the story has nothing to do with Passover and it is incorporated here merely because it discusses the importance of remembering the Exodus. See pp. 37–39.

8 **R. Eleazar ben Azariah said: I am about seventy years old** Some earlier translations read, "I am like seventy years old." This is based on the legend that, when he was appointed as head of the Sanhedrin at a young age, R. Eleazar aged immediately so that he would appear wise and age appropriate for this prestigious task. However, the Jerusalem Talmud assumes that he was really "about" seventy years old. This expression appears elsewhere as a statement of age.

[10]**B**lessed is the Omnipresent, blessed is He. Blessed is He who gave the Torah to His people, Israel, blessed is He.

[10]**בָּרוּךְ** הַמָּקוֹם, בָּרוּךְ הוּא. בָּרוּךְ שֶׁנָּתַן תּוֹרָה לְעַמּוֹ יִשְׂרָאֵל, בָּרוּךְ הוּא.

[11]**T**he Torah refers to four children:
one—wise;
one—wicked;
one—simple;
and one who does not know how to ask a question.

[11]**כְּנֶגֶד אַרְבָּעָה בָנִים** דִּבְּרָה תוֹרָה.
אֶחָד חָכָם,
וְאֶחָד רָשָׁע,
וְאֶחָד תָּם,
וְאֶחָד שֶׁאֵינוֹ יוֹדֵעַ לִשְׁאוֹל.

What does the wise one say?
[12]"What are the decrees, laws, and rules that *Adonai* our Lord has enjoined upon you?" (Deut. 6:20). And you should say to him, according to the laws of Passover, "one may not indulge in revelry after the paschal meal."

חָכָם מָה הוּא אוֹמֵר?
[12]מָה הָעֵדוֹת וְהַחֻקִּים וְהַמִּשְׁפָּטִים אֲשֶׁר צִוָּה יי אֱלֹהֵינוּ אֶתְכֶם? וְאַף אַתָּה אֱמֹר לוֹ כְּהִלְכוֹת הַפֶּסַח: אֵין מַפְטִירִין אַחַר הַפֶּסַח אֲפִיקוֹמָן.

9 **I had never convinced anyone** This translation assumes that R. Eleazar ben Azariah was a proponent of this idea. The parallel passage in the Tosefta implies that the issue had never arisen until Ben Zoma raised it.

10 **Blessed is the Omnipresent**: *Makom*, which means "place," is usually translated as "Omnipresent." This is based on a midrashic idea that this term is used for God to signify that He is the place of the world, rather than His having a place in the world. However, scholarly thought is that this term was originally used to refer to God as residing in His place, the Holy Temple, It is a metonym for "He who resides in this place," much as in present time the captain of a ship may be known by the name of his ship (see E. E Urbach, *The Sages, Their Concepts and Beliefs;* translated from the Hebrew by Israel Abrahams [Cambridge Mass.: Harvard University Press, 1979], pp. 66–79). The passage about the four children begins with a blessing of God who gave the Torah to His people. It is not an official blessing so it does not follow the regular pattern of blessings. The words "blessed is He" were probably meant as a response to the reader's mention of God's name.

11 **The Torah refers to four children:** For an analysis of this passage see pp. 39–45.

12 **"What are the decrees . . ."** According to the NJPS translation, the biblical verse quoted as the wise child's question centers on the meaning of the laws. This fits the context, as the biblical response talks about the reasons for observing the laws. Taking the question out of context, it is best translated, "What are the laws?" Many scholars have suggested that the response is not meant to imply that forbidding the *afikoman* is the most important law of Pesach. It should rather be understood as quoting the last law in the Mishnah (*Pesach* 10:8), which deals with the seder. Thus the implication is that one should teach the wise child all the laws, until the very last one. In the Jerusalem Talmud, this response is given to the simple, or foolish, son.

What does the wicked one say?
"What does this rite mean to you?" (Exod. 12:26). "To you" and not to him. And since he excluded himself from the community, he is a heretic. [13]And you should blunt his teeth and say to him, "It is because of what *Adonai* did for me when I went free from Egypt" (Exod. 13:8); "for me" and not for him—if he had been there he would not have been redeemed.

רָשָׁע מָה הוּא אוֹמֵר?
מָה הָעֲבֹדָה הַזֹּאת לָכֶם? לָכֶם – וְלֹא לוֹ. וּלְפִי שֶׁהוֹצִיא אֶת עַצְמוֹ מִן הַכְּלָל – כָּפַר בָּעִקָּר. וְאַף אַתָּה [13]הַקְהֵה אֶת שִׁנָּיו וֶאֱמֹר לוֹ: בַּעֲבוּר זֶה עָשָׂה יי לִי בְּצֵאתִי מִמִּצְרָיִם. לִי – וְלֹא לוֹ. אִלּוּ הָיָה שָׁם, לֹא הָיָה נִגְאָל.

[14]**W**hat does the simple one say?
"What does this mean?" And you shall say to him: "It was with a mighty hand that *Adonai* brought us out from Egypt, the house of bondage" (Exod. 13:14).

[14]**תָּם** מָה הוּא אוֹמֵר?
מַה זֹּאת? וְאָמַרְתָּ אֵלָיו: בְּחֹזֶק יָד הוֹצִיאָנוּ יי מִמִּצְרַיִם, מִבֵּית עֲבָדִים.

And to the one who does not know how to ask a question—
you take the initiative, as it says: "And you shall explain to your son on that day, 'It is for this that *Adonai* did [these things] for me when I went free from Egypt'" (Exod. 13:8).

וְשֶׁאֵינוֹ יוֹדֵעַ לִשְׁאוֹל –
אַתְּ פְּתַח לוֹ, שֶׁנֶּאֱמַר: וְהִגַּדְתָּ לְבִנְךָ בַּיּוֹם הַהוּא לֵאמֹר, בַּעֲבוּר זֶה עָשָׂה יי לִי בְּצֵאתִי מִמִּצְרָיִם.

13 **And you should blunt his teeth** This term appears in the Bible to describe the feeling of one who eats unripe grapes: his teeth are blunted (Jer. 31:29; Ezek. 18:1). Earlier translations of the Bible say: his teeth are set on edge. Both refer to the unpleasant feeling of the teeth caused by of eating unripe grapes. The meaning of the metaphor is clear: one should respond sharply to the wicked child in a way that will put him in his place. Perhaps there is an allusion to the biblical verse in Jeremiah, implying that the wicked child's teeth are blunted due to the sins of parents, who did not raise the child properly.

14 **What does the simple one say?** This is the only clear case where the response in the haggadah is the same as in the Bible. In the parallel passage in the Jerusalem Talmud, the response to the simple child is that which the haggadah prescribes for the wise child. It should be noted that the Jerusalem Talmud refers to this child not as the simple one but as the foolish one (*tippesh*).

[15,16]One could think that it [the obligation to tell the story of the Exodus] begins on the first of the month, therefore it says: "on that day." Based on this, I could think that it begins during the day, therefore its says: "for this." I cannot say "for this" except '— when I have the matzah and *maror* ["this"] before me.

[15,16]יָכוֹל מֵרֹאשׁ חֹדֶשׁ – תַּלְמוּד לוֹמַר בַּיּוֹם הַהוּא; אִי בַּיּוֹם הַהוּא, יָכוֹל מִבְּעוֹד יוֹם – תַּלְמוּד לוֹמַר בַּעֲבוּר זֶה – בַּעֲבוּר זֶה לֹא אָמַרְתִּי, אֶלָּא בְּשָׁעָה שֶׁמַּצָּה וּמָרוֹר מֻנָּחִים לְפָנֶיךָ.

[17]In the beginning, our ancestors were idol worshipers and now the Omnipresent has drawn us to His worship. As it says: "Then Joshua said to all the people, 'Thus said *Adonai,* the LORD of Israel: In olden times, your forefathers, Terah, father of Abraham and father of Nahor, lived beyond the Euphrates and worshiped other gods. But I took your father Abraham from beyond the Euphrates and led him through the whole land of Canaan and multiplied his offspring. I gave him Isaac, and to Isaac I gave Jacob and Esau. I gave Esau the hill country of Seir as his possession, while Jacob and his children went down to Egypt' (Josh. 24:2–4)."

[17]**מִתְּחִלָּה** עוֹבְדֵי עֲבוֹדָה זָרָה הָיוּ אֲבוֹתֵינוּ, וְעַכְשָׁיו קֵרְבָנוּ הַמָּקוֹם לַעֲבֹדָתוֹ, שֶׁנֶּאֱמַר: וַיֹּאמֶר יְהוֹשֻׁעַ אֶל כָּל הָעָם, כֹּה אָמַר יי אֱלֹהֵי יִשְׂרָאֵל: בְּעֵבֶר הַנָּהָר יָשְׁבוּ אֲבוֹתֵיכֶם מֵעוֹלָם, תֶּרַח אֲבִי אַבְרָהָם וַאֲבִי נָחוֹר, וַיַּעַבְדוּ אֱלֹהִים אֲחֵרִים. וָאֶקַּח אֶת אֲבִיכֶם אֶת אַבְרָהָם מֵעֵבֶר הַנָּהָר וָאוֹלֵךְ אוֹתוֹ בְּכָל אֶרֶץ כְּנָעַן, וָאַרְבֶּה אֶת זַרְעוֹ וָאֶתֶּן לוֹ אֶת יִצְחָק, וָאֶתֵּן לְיִצְחָק אֶת יַעֲקֹב וְאֶת עֵשָׂו. וָאֶתֵּן לְעֵשָׂו אֶת הַר שֵׂעִיר לָרֶשֶׁת אֹתוֹ, וְיַעֲקֹב וּבָנָיו יָרְדוּ מִצְרָיִם.

15 **One could think that it... begins on the first of the month** This exposition has nothing to do with the child who does not know how to ask a question. It is an exposition of the verse that also appears in the *Mekilta de-Rabbi Ishmael* (ed. Lauterbach, p. 1490), without any mention of the child who does not know how to ask. It serves here as an interesting counterpoint to the story of R. Eleazar ben Azariah. The final point made there is that the Exodus must be remembered all the time, day and night, and even in the world to come. However, here it says that one does not fulfill the obligation to tell the story of the Exodus unless one does so on the evening of the fifteenth, with matzah and *maror* on the table.

16 **One could think that it... begins on the first of the month** The reason that one might think the obligation begins on the first of the month is because the biblical passage in which this phrase appears states, "you shall observe in this month the following practice" (Exod. 13:5–6; the festival of matzah), without giving a more precise date.

17 **In the beginning, our ancestors were idol worshipers** This passage is the story of the Exodus as prescribed by Rav (see p. 32).

Blessed is He who keeps His promise to Israel, Blessed is He. For the Holy one, blessed be He, calculated the end, to do as He had promised Abraham in the covenant between the pieces. As it says: "And He said to Abram, 'Know well that your offspring shall be strangers in a land not theirs, and they shall be enslaved and oppressed four hundred years; but I will execute judgment on the nation they shall serve, and in the end they shall go free with great wealth'" (Gen. 15:13–14).

בָּרוּךְ שׁוֹמֵר הַבְטָחָתוֹ לְיִשְׂרָאֵל, בָּרוּךְ הוּא. שֶׁהַקָּדוֹשׁ בָּרוּךְ הוּא חִשַּׁב אֶת הַקֵּץ, לַעֲשׂוֹת כְּמוֹ שֶׁאָמַר לְאַבְרָהָם אָבִינוּ בִּבְרִית בֵּין הַבְּתָרִים, שֶׁנֶּאֱמַר: וַיֹּאמֶר לְאַבְרָם, יָדֹעַ תֵּדַע כִּי גֵר יִהְיֶה זַרְעֲךָ בְּאֶרֶץ לֹא לָהֶם, וַעֲבָדוּם וְעִנּוּ אֹתָם אַרְבַּע מֵאוֹת שָׁנָה. וְגַם אֶת הַגּוֹי אֲשֶׁר יַעֲבֹדוּ דָּן אָנֹכִי וְאַחֲרֵי כֵן יֵצְאוּ בִּרְכֻשׁ גָּדוֹל.

According to a late tradition (see the introduction), the following statement is made after covering the matzah and holding the cup in one's hand.

And it is this promise that has
sustained us, for not just once
did somebody try to destroy us
for in every generation
they have tried to destroy us,
but the Holy One, blessed be He,
saves us from them.

וְהִיא שֶׁעָמְדָה לַאֲבוֹתֵינוּ וְלָנוּ,
שֶׁלֹּא אֶחָד בִּלְבָד עָמַד עָלֵינוּ לְכַלּוֹתֵנוּ,
אֶלָּא שֶׁבְּכָל דּוֹר וָדוֹר
עוֹמְדִים עָלֵינוּ לְכַלּוֹתֵנוּ,
וְהַקָּדוֹשׁ בָּרוּךְ הוּא מַצִּילֵנוּ מִיָּדָם.

Put down the cup and uncover the matzah.

Go forth and see what Laban the Aramean tried to do to our ancestor, Jacob. For Pharaoh's decree was only against the males while Laban tried to destroy everything. As it is said:

צֵא וּלְמַד מַה בִּקֵּשׁ לָבָן הָאֲרַמִּי לַעֲשׂוֹת לְיַעֲקֹב אָבִינוּ. שֶׁפַּרְעֹה לֹא גָזַר אֶלָּא עַל הַזְּכָרִים וְלָבָן בִּקֵּשׁ לַעֲקוֹר אֶת הַכֹּל, שֶׁנֶּאֱמַר:

18"**An Aramean tried to destroy my father. He went down to Egypt and sojourned there with meager numbers; but there he became a great and very populous nation**" (Deut. 26:5).

18**אֲרַמִּי אֹבֵד אָבִי, וַיֵּרֶד מִצְרַיְמָה וַיָּגָר שָׁם בִּמְתֵי מְעָט, וַיְהִי שָׁם לְגוֹי גָּדוֹל, עָצוּם וָרָב.**

18 **An Aramean tried to destroy my father** This passage is a midrash based on Deuteronomy 26:5–9, the biblical passage that was read by those who brought their firstfruits to the priest in the Temple. It begins the central story of the Exodus as prescribed by the Mishnah (see pp. 33–37). This is one of the few texts in the Bible that one is required to read. At the seder, it is not sufficient merely to read the text; the Mishnah commands that it should also be midrashically expanded. There is a pattern for this midrash in the haggadah. First, the verse is quoted in its entirety. Then, specific words are quoted so that they may be

[19]**He went down to Egypt**—forced to do so by the word [of God]

[19]**וַיֵּרֶד מִצְרַיְמָה** – אָנוּס עַל פִּי הַדִּבּוּר.

and sojourned there—this teaches us that our forefather Jacob did not intend to settle in Egypt but just to live there temporarily. As it is said: "'We have come,' they told Pharaoh, 'to sojourn in this land, for there is no pasture for your servants' flocks, the famine being severe in the land of Canaan. Pray, then, let your servants stay in the region of Goshen'" (Gen. 47:4).

וַיָּגָר שָׁם – מְלַמֵּד שֶׁלֹּא יָרַד יַעֲקֹב אָבִינוּ לְהִשְׁתַּקֵּעַ בְּמִצְרַיִם אֶלָּא לָגוּר שָׁם, שֶׁנֶּאֱמַר: וַיֹּאמְרוּ אֶל פַּרְעֹה, לָגוּר בָּאָרֶץ בָּאנוּ, כִּי אֵין מִרְעֶה לַצֹּאן אֲשֶׁר לַעֲבָדֶיךָ, כִּי כָבֵד הָרָעָב בְּאֶרֶץ כְּנָעַן, וְעַתָּה יֵשְׁבוּ נָא עֲבָדֶיךָ בְּאֶרֶץ גֹּשֶׁן.

with meager numbers—as it is said: "Your ancestors went down to Egypt seventy persons in all; and now *Adonai* your LORD has made you as numerous as the stars of heaven" (Deut. 10:22).

בִּמְתֵי מְעָט – כְּמָה שֶׁנֶּאֱמַר: בְּשִׁבְעִים נֶפֶשׁ יָרְדוּ אֲבוֹתֶיךָ מִצְרָיְמָה, וְעַתָּה שָׂמְךָ יי אֱלֹהֶיךָ כְּכוֹכְבֵי הַשָּׁמַיִם לָרֹב.

[20]**but there he became a . . . nation**—this teaches us that the Israelites were distinguished there.

[20]**וַיְהִי שָׁם לְגוֹי** – מְלַמֵּד שֶׁהָיוּ יִשְׂרָאֵל מְצֻיָּנִים שָׁם.

explained. The explanation is short, often followed by a prooftext, a passage that is used to justify the explanation. In some cases, there is no explanation, but the quote is immediately followed by a prooftext. The prooftext does not always provide additional content, often serving as a verse that simply repeats what is in the original quote Scholars have suggested that this midrash is a conflation of a two separate midrashim: one that contained only short explanations and one that contained just prooftexts (see p. 35). This biblical passage also appears in *Eretz Yisra'el haggadot*. However, the midrash there differs in a number of ways, the most notable being that it is much shorter. The only passage that is the same in the midrash of both *haggadot* is the description of the Ten Plagues (see later).

19 **He went down to Egypt—forced to do so by the word [of God]** It is not clear what this statement is referring to, and no prooftext is given for it. Many commentators think it refers to the "Covenant Between the Pieces," mentioned earlier. The exile in Egypt was the only exile that was clearly not a punishment for sin. Rather, it was part of the divine covenant made with Abraham.

Other commentators explain that this statement refers to God telling Jacob: "Fear not to go down to Egypt. . . . I Myself will go down with you to Egypt" (Gen. 46:3–4), which implies that without the word of God, Jacob would not have gone. The midrash stresses that Jacob did not go to Egypt willingly, perhaps because the author of the midrash wished to discourage people from leaving the Land of Israel of their own volition. See Menachem M. Kasher, *Hagadah Shelemah* [in Hebrew] (Jerusalem: Torah Shelema Institute, 1967), 34.

20 **but there he became a . . . nation—this teaches us that the Israelites were distinguished there** This is based on the midrashic idea that the Jews retained specific symbols of Jewish identity, such as their names and their language (*Mekilta de-Rabbi Ishmael,* ed. Lauterbach, Pisha 5, pp. 33–34).

גָּדוֹל, עָצוּם – כְּמוֹ שֶׁנֶּאֱמַר: וּבְנֵי יִשְׂרָאֵל פָּרוּ וַיִּשְׁרְצוּ וַיִּרְבּוּ וַיַּעַצְמוּ בִּמְאֹד מְאֹד, וַתִּמָּלֵא הָאָרֶץ אֹתָם.

great—as it is said: "But the Israelites were fertile and prolific; they multiplied and increased very greatly, so that the land was filled with them" (Exod. 1:7).

[21]**וָרָב** – כְּמָה שֶׁנֶּאֱמַר: רְבָבָה כְּצֶמַח הַשָּׂדֶה נְתַתִּיךְ, וַתִּרְבִּי וַתִּגְדְּלִי וַתָּבֹאִי בַּעֲדִי עֲדָיִים, שָׁדַיִם נָכֹנוּ וּשְׂעָרֵךְ צִמֵּחַ, וְאַתְּ עֵרֹם וְעֶרְיָה. וָאֶעֱבֹר עָלַיִךְ וָאֶרְאֵךְ מִתְבּוֹסֶסֶת בְּדָמָיִךְ, וָאֹמַר לָךְ בְּדָמַיִךְ חֲיִי, וָאֹמַר לָךְ בְּדָמַיִךְ חֲיִי.

[21]**and very populous**—as it is said: "I let you grow like the plants of the field; and you continued to grow up until you attained to womanhood, until your breasts became firm and your hair sprouted. You were still naked and bare" (Ezek. 16:7). "When I passed by you and saw you wallowing in your blood, I said to you: 'Live in spite of your blood.' Yea, I said to you: 'Live in spite of your blood'" (Ezek. 16:6).

וַיָּרֵעוּ אֹתָנוּ הַמִּצְרִים וַיְעַנּוּנוּ, וַיִּתְּנוּ עָלֵינוּ עֲבֹדָה קָשָׁה.

The Egyptians dealt harshly with us and oppressed us; they imposed heavy labor upon us (Deut. 26:6).

וַיָּרֵעוּ אֹתָנוּ הַמִּצְרִים – כְּמוֹ שֶׁנֶּאֱמַר: הָבָה נִתְחַכְּמָה לוֹ פֶּן יִרְבֶּה, וְהָיָה כִּי תִקְרֶאנָה מִלְחָמָה וְנוֹסַף גַּם הוּא עַל שֹׂנְאֵינוּ וְנִלְחַם בָּנוּ, וְעָלָה מִן הָאָרֶץ.

The Egyptians dealt harshly with us—as it is said: "Let us deal shrewdly with them, so that they may not increase; otherwise in the event of war they may join our enemies in fighting against us and rise from the ground" (Exod. 1:10).

21 **and very populous** The first verse quoted from Ezekiel (16:7), which tells us that the Jews grew "like the plants of the field," is the prooftext, showing that "populous" is evidenced in the vision of Ezekiel, which was understood as an allegory depicting the historical relationship between God and Israel. The sages understood the previous verse (Ezek. 16:6) as "Live through your bloods," which was considered a reference to the two signs of blood by which the Jews were redeemed from Israel: the sign of circumcision blood and the sign of blood from the sacrifice on the lintels. Thus the sages' interpretation of the second verse connects it to the Exodus. Rabbi Isaac Luria insisted that this verse be added to the haggadah at this point, based on kabbalistic considerations. He apparently inserted it immediately after the quote from Exodus, "**and very populous,**" before the prooftext from Ezekiel 16:7, which would preserve the order of the verses in Ezekiel. However, most *haggadot* insert this verse (Ezek. 16:6) after the prooftext (Ezek. 16:7), apparently not wishing to separate the quote from Exodus and its prooftext.

and oppressed us—as it is said: "So they set taskmasters over them to oppress them with forced labor; and they built garrison cities for Pharaoh: Pithom and Raamses" (Exod. 1:11).

וַיְעַנּוּנוּ – כְּמָה שֶׁנֶּאֱמַר: וַיָּשִׂימוּ עָלָיו שָׂרֵי מִסִּים לְמַעַן עַנֹּתוֹ בְּסִבְלֹתָם. וַיִּבֶן עָרֵי מִסְכְּנוֹת לְפַרְעֹה, אֶת פִּתֹם וְאֶת רַעַמְסֵס.

they imposed heavy labor upon us—as it is said: "The Egyptians ruthlessly imposed upon the Israelites the various labors that they made them perform" (Exod. 1:13–14).

וַיִּתְּנוּ עָלֵינוּ עֲבֹדָה קָשָׁה – כְּמוֹ שֶׁנֶּאֱמַר: וַיַּעֲבִדוּ מִצְרַיִם אֶת בְּנֵי יִשְׂרָאֵל בְּפָרֶךְ.

We cried to *Adonai,* the Lord of our fathers, and *Adonai* heard our plea and saw our plight, our misery, and our oppression (Deut. 26:7).

וַנִּצְעַק אֶל יי אֱלֹהֵי אֲבֹתֵינוּ, וַיִּשְׁמַע יי אֶת קֹלֵנוּ, וַיַּרְא אֶת עָנְיֵנוּ וְאֶת עֲמָלֵנוּ וְאֶת לַחֲצֵנוּ.

We cried to *Adonai,* the Lord of our fathers—as it is said: "A long time after that, the king of Egypt died. The Israelites were groaning under the bondage and cried out; and their cry for help from the bondage rose up to the Lord" (Exod. 2:23).

וַנִּצְעַק אֶל יי אֱלֹהֵי אֲבֹתֵינוּ – כְּמָה שֶׁנֶּאֱמַר: וַיְהִי בַיָּמִים הָרַבִּים הָהֵם וַיָּמָת מֶלֶךְ מִצְרַיִם, וַיֵּאָנְחוּ בְנֵי יִשְׂרָאֵל מִן הָעֲבוֹדָה וַיִּזְעָקוּ, וַתַּעַל שַׁוְעָתָם אֶל הָאֱלֹהִים מִן הָעֲבֹדָה.

and *Adonai* heard our plea—as it is said: "The Lord heard their moaning, and the Lord remembered His covenant with Abraham and Isaac and Jacob" (Exod. 2:24).

וַיִּשְׁמַע יי אֶת קֹלֵנוּ – כְּמָה שֶׁנֶּאֱמַר: וַיִּשְׁמַע אֱלֹהִים אֶת נַאֲקָתָם, וַיִּזְכֹּר אֱלֹהִים אֶת בְּרִיתוֹ אֶת אַבְרָהָם, אֶת יִצְחָק וְאֶת יַעֲקֹב.

[22]**and saw our plight**—this is the cessation of family life, as it is said: "the Lord looked upon the Israelites, and the Lord took notice of them" (Exod. 2:25).

[22]**וַיַּרְא אֶת עָנְיֵנוּ** – זוֹ פְּרִישׁוּת דֶּרֶךְ אֶרֶץ, כְּמָה שֶׁנֶּאֱמַר: וַיַּרְא אֱלֹהִים אֶת בְּנֵי יִשְׂרָאֵל וַיֵּדַע אֱלֹהִים.

22 **and saw our plight—this is the cessation of family life** This is a prime example of conflated midrash. The explanation is based on the word "*'onyenu,*" which in other contexts is understood as "refraining from sex." The connection between the verse and the prooftext is the phrase "and he saw," which appears in both verses. Some scholars have suggested that there is also a connection between the explanation and the prooftext based on the phrase "and he took notice" (*vayeda*), which in other contexts is taken to mean conjugal knowledge.

our misery—these are the children, as it is said: "Every boy that is born you shall throw into the Nile, but let every girl live" (Exod. 1:22).

וְאֶת עֲמָלֵנוּ – אֵלּוּ הַבָּנִים. כְּמָה שֶׁנֶּאֱמַר: כָּל הַבֵּן הַיִּלּוֹד הַיְאֹרָה תַּשְׁלִיכֻהוּ וְכָל הַבַּת תְּחַיּוּן.

[23]**and our oppression**—this is the persecution, as it is said: "Moreover, I have seen how the Egyptians oppress them" (Exod. 3:9).

[23]**וְאֶת לַחֲצֵנוּ** – זֶה הַדְּחַק, כְּמָה שֶׁנֶּאֱמַר: וְגַם רָאִיתִי אֶת הַלַּחַץ אֲשֶׁר מִצְרַיִם לֹחֲצִים אֹתָם.

***Adonai* freed us from Egypt by a mighty hand, by an outstretched arm and by awesome power, and by signs and portents** (Deut. 26:8).

וַיּוֹצִאֵנוּ יי מִמִּצְרַיִם בְּיָד חֲזָקָה וּבִזְרֹעַ נְטוּיָה, וּבְמֹרָא גָּדֹל, וּבְאֹתוֹת וּבְמֹפְתִים.

***Adonai* freed us from Egypt**—not by an angel, not by a seraph, not by an agent, but the Holy One, blessed be He, in His glory and by Himself, as it is said: "For that night I will go through the land of Egypt and I will strike down every first-born in the land of Egypt, both man and beast; and I will mete out punishments to all the gods of Egypt, I am *Adonai*" (Exod. 12:12).

וַיּוֹצִאֵנוּ יי מִמִּצְרַיִם – לֹא עַל יְדֵי מַלְאָךְ, וְלֹא עַל יְדֵי שָׂרָף, וְלֹא עַל יְדֵי שָׁלִיחַ, אֶלָּא הַקָּדוֹשׁ בָּרוּךְ הוּא בִּכְבוֹדוֹ וּבְעַצְמוֹ, שֶׁנֶּאֱמַר: וְעָבַרְתִּי בְאֶרֶץ מִצְרַיִם בַּלַּיְלָה הַזֶּה, וְהִכֵּיתִי כָל בְּכוֹר בְּאֶרֶץ מִצְרַיִם מֵאָדָם וְעַד בְּהֵמָה, וּבְכָל אֱלֹהֵי מִצְרַיִם אֶעֱשֶׂה שְׁפָטִים. אֲנִי יי.

[24]**For that night I will go through the land of Egypt:** I—and not an angel. and I will strike down every first-born in the land of Egypt: I—and not a seraph. And I will mete out punishments to all the gods of Egypt: I—and not an agent.

[24]**וְעָבַרְתִּי בְאֶרֶץ מִצְרַיִם בַּלַּיְלָה הַזֶּה** – אֲנִי וְלֹא מַלְאָךְ; וְהִכֵּיתִי כָל בְּכוֹר בְּאֶרֶץ מִצְרַיִם – אֲנִי וְלֹא שָׂרָף; וּבְכָל אֱלֹהֵי מִצְרַיִם אֶעֱשֶׂה שְׁפָטִים – אֲנִי וְלֹא הַשָּׁלִיחַ.

23 **and our oppression—this is the persecution** This is another example of what seems to be a conflation of two types of midrash (see p. 89, n. 18). "This is the persecution" is explanatory midrash, using the Hebrew word "*d-h-k*" (persecution) to explain the biblical word "*l-h-z*" (oppression)—both essentially synonymous. The Aramaic translations of the Bible, both *Targum Onkelos* and the targum known as *Targum Jonathan*, frequently use the Aramaic root "*d-h-k*" to translate the root "*l-h-z*." The passage continues with a "prooftext" type of midrash, quoting the verse from Exodus 3:9 that adds nothing to our understanding of the passage but is just a prooftext showing that the story actually happened.

24 **For that night** The following is a midrash within a midrash. The text turns away from the exposition of Deuteronomy 26:8 to expound on the prooftext, Exodus 12:11–12.

אֲנִי יי — אֲנִי הוּא וְלֹא אַחֵר.

I am *Adonai*: I am He, and no other.

בְּיָד חֲזָקָה — זוֹ הַדֶּבֶר, כְּמָה שֶׁנֶּאֱמַר: הִנֵּה יַד יי הוֹיָה בְּמִקְנְךָ אֲשֶׁר בַּשָּׂדֶה, בַּסּוּסִים, בַּחֲמֹרִים, בַּגְּמַלִּים, בַּבָּקָר וּבַצֹּאן, דֶּבֶר כָּבֵד מְאֹד.

by a mighty hand—this is the pestilence, as it is said: "then the hand of *Adonai* will strike your livestock in the fields—the horses, the asses, the camels, the cattle, and the sheep—with a very severe pestilence" (Exod. 9:3).

וּבִזְרֹעַ נְטוּיָה — זוֹ הַחֶרֶב, כְּמָה שֶׁנֶּאֱמַר: וְחַרְבּוֹ שְׁלוּפָה בְּיָדוֹ, נְטוּיָה עַל יְרוּשָׁלָיִם.

by an outstretched arm—this is the sword, as it is said: "with a drawn sword in his hand directed against Jerusalem" (1 Chron. 21:16).

וּבְמֹרָא גָּדֹל — זֶה גִּלּוּי שְׁכִינָה, כְּמָה שֶׁנֶּאֱמַר: אוֹ הֲנִסָּה אֱלֹהִים לָבֹא לָקַחַת לוֹ גוֹי מִקֶּרֶב גּוֹי בְּמַסֹּת בְּאֹתֹת וּבְמוֹפְתִים, וּבְמִלְחָמָה וּבְיָד חֲזָקָה וּבִזְרוֹעַ נְטוּיָה, וּבְמוֹרָאִים גְּדֹלִים, כְּכֹל אֲשֶׁר עָשָׂה לָכֶם יי אֱלֹהֵיכֶם בְּמִצְרַיִם לְעֵינֶיךָ.

by awesome power—this is the revelation of the Divine presence, as it is said: "Or has any god ventured to go and take for himself one nation from the midst of another by prodigious acts, by signs and portents, by war, by a mighty and an outstretched arm and awesome power, as *Adonai* your LORD did for you in Egypt before your very eyes?" (Deut. 4:34).

וּבְאֹתוֹת — זֶה הַמַּטֶּה, כְּמָה שֶׁנֶּאֱמַר: וְאֶת הַמַּטֶּה הַזֶּה תִּקַּח בְּיָדֶךָ, אֲשֶׁר תַּעֲשֶׂה בּוֹ אֶת הָאֹתֹת.

and by signs—this is the staff, as it is said: "And take with you this rod, with which you shall perform the signs" (Exod. 4:17).

A custom first found in twelfth-century Ashkenazic pietist sources is to spill some of the wine at the mention of the plagues. Three drops are spilled when mentioning "blood, fire, and pillars of smoke," one drop for each of the Ten Plagues, and a final three drops when mentioning the three words of R. Judah's mnemonic device for the plagues. The total number of drops is sixteen, which is given various mystical explanations. Others skip the first three drops for a total of thirteen drops. The early sources do not specify how the wine should be spilled and various traditions developed. Some spilled the wine directly from the cup while others thought that a specific finger should be used to drip the wine from the cup: the index finger, the ring finger, or the little finger. *(See also pp. 44–45.)*

וּבְמֹפְתִים — זֶה הַדָּם, כְּמָה שֶׁנֶּאֱמַר: וְנָתַתִּי מוֹפְתִים בַּשָּׁמַיִם וּבָאָרֶץ
דָּם וָאֵשׁ וְתִימְרוֹת עָשָׁן.

and portents—this is the blood, as it is said: "I will set portents in the sky and on earth: **Blood and fire and pillars of smoke**" (Joel 3:3).

Another explanation [of the verse from Deuteronomy]: by a mighty hand—two; by an outstretched arm—two, and by awesome power—two; and by signs—two; and portents—two.

דָּבָר אַחֵר: בְּיָד חֲזָקָה – שְׁתַּיִם, וּבִזְרֹעַ נְטוּיָה – שְׁתַּיִם, וּבְמֹרָא גָּדֹל – שְׁתַּיִם, וּבְאֹתוֹת – שְׁתַּיִם, וּבְמֹפְתִים – שְׁתַּיִם.

These are the Ten Plagues that the Holy One, blessed be He, brought upon the Egyptians in Egypt.

אֵלּוּ עֶשֶׂר מַכּוֹת שֶׁהֵבִיא הַקָּדוֹשׁ בָּרוּךְ הוּא עַל הַמִּצְרִים בְּמִצְרַיִם, וְאֵלּוּ הֵן:

Blood, frogs, lice, swarms of insects,

דָּם, צְפַרְדֵּעַ, כִּנִּים, עָרוֹב,

pestilence, boils, hail, locusts,

דֶּבֶר, שְׁחִין, בָּרָד, אַרְבֶּה,

darkness, death of the first-born.

חֹשֶׁךְ, מַכַּת בְּכוֹרוֹת

R. Judah referred to them by an acrosticon: *detzakh, adash, be-ahab*.

רַבִּי יְהוּדָה הָיָה נוֹתֵן בָּהֶם סִימָנִים:
דְּצַ״ךְ עַדַ״שׁ בְּאַחַ״ב.

R. Yose ha-Galili said: How do you know that the Egyptians suffered ten plagues in Egypt and they suffered fifty plagues at the sea? What does it say in Egypt? "And the magicians said to Pharaoh, "This is the finger of God!" (Exod. 8:15). But what does it say at the sea? "And when Israel saw the powerful hand which *Adonai* had wielded against the Egyptians, the people feared *Adonai;* they had faith in *Adonai* and in His servant Moses" (Exod. 14:31). How much did they suffer from a finger? Ten plagues! Say, therefore, that in Egypt they suffered ten plagues and at the sea they suffered fifty plagues.

רַבִּי יוֹסֵי הַגְּלִילִי אוֹמֵר: מִנַּיִן אַתָּה אוֹמֵר שֶׁלָּקוּ הַמִּצְרִים בְּמִצְרַיִם עֶשֶׂר מַכּוֹת וְעַל הַיָּם לָקוּ חֲמִשִּׁים מַכּוֹת? בְּמִצְרַיִם מַה הוּא אוֹמֵר? וַיֹּאמְרוּ הַחַרְטֻמִּים אֶל פַּרְעֹה: אֶצְבַּע אֱלֹהִים הִוא, וְעַל הַיָּם מַה הוּא אוֹמֵר? וַיַּרְא יִשְׂרָאֵל אֶת הַיָּד הַגְּדֹלָה אֲשֶׁר עָשָׂה יי בְּמִצְרַיִם, וַיִּירְאוּ הָעָם אֶת יי, וַיַּאֲמִינוּ בַּיי וּבְמשֶׁה עַבְדּוֹ. כַּמָּה לָקוּ בְאֶצְבַּע? עֶשֶׂר מַכּוֹת. אֱמוֹר מֵעַתָּה: בְּמִצְרַיִם לָקוּ עֶשֶׂר מַכּוֹת וְעַל הַיָּם לָקוּ חֲמִשִּׁים מַכּוֹת.

R. Eliezer says: How do we know that each and every plague that the Holy One, blessed be He, brought upon the Egyptians was composed of four plagues? As it is said: "He inflicted His burning anger upon them, wrath, indignation, trouble, a band of deadly messengers" (Ps. 78:49–50); wrath—one, indignation—two, trouble—three, a band of deadly messengers—four. Say, therefore, that in Egypt they suffered forty plagues and at the sea they suffered two hundred plagues.

רַבִּי אֱלִיעֶזֶר אוֹמֵר: מִנַּיִן שֶׁכָּל מַכָּה וּמַכָּה שֶׁהֵבִיא הַקָּדוֹשׁ בָּרוּךְ הוּא עַל הַמִּצְרִים בְּמִצְרַיִם הָיְתָה שֶׁל אַרְבַּע מַכּוֹת? שֶׁנֶּאֱמַר: יְשַׁלַּח בָּם חֲרוֹן אַפּוֹ, עֶבְרָה וָזַעַם וְצָרָה, מִשְׁלַחַת מַלְאֲכֵי רָעִים. עֶבְרָה – אַחַת, וָזַעַם – שְׁתַּיִם, וְצָרָה – שָׁלֹשׁ, מִשְׁלַחַת מַלְאֲכֵי רָעִים – אַרְבַּע. אֱמוֹר מֵעַתָּה: בְּמִצְרַיִם לָקוּ אַרְבָּעִים מַכּוֹת וְעַל הַיָּם לָקוּ מָאתַיִם מַכּוֹת.

R. Akiva says: How do we know that each and every plague that the Holy One, blessed be He, brought upon the Egyptians was composed of five plagues? As it said: "He inflicted His burning anger upon them, wrath, indignation, trouble, a band of deadly messengers" (Ps. 78:49–50); burning anger—one, wrath—two, indignation—three, trouble—four, a band of deadly messengers—five. Say, therefore, that in Egypt they suffered fifty plagues and at the sea they suffered two hundred and fifty plagues.

רַבִּי עֲקִיבָא אוֹמֵר: מִנַּיִן שֶׁכָּל מַכָּה וּמַכָּה שֶׁהֵבִיא הַקָּדוֹשׁ בָּרוּךְ הוּא עַל הַמִּצְרִים בְּמִצְרַיִם הָיְתָה שֶׁל חָמֵשׁ מַכּוֹת? שֶׁנֶּאֱמַר: יְשַׁלַּח בָּם חֲרוֹן אַפּוֹ, עֶבְרָה וָזַעַם וְצָרָה, מִשְׁלַחַת מַלְאֲכֵי רָעִים. חֲרוֹן אַפּוֹ – אַחַת, עֶבְרָה – שְׁתַּיִם, וָזַעַם – שָׁלוֹשׁ, וְצָרָה – אַרְבַּע, מִשְׁלַחַת מַלְאֲכֵי רָעִים – חָמֵשׁ. אֱמוֹר מֵעַתָּה: בְּמִצְרַיִם לָקוּ חֲמִשִּׁים מַכּוֹת וְעַל הַיָּם לָקוּ חֲמִשִּׁים וּמָאתַיִם מַכּוֹת.

The following passage is a litany that is meant to be sung or read by a reader and the choir of listeners. The leader reads a changing list of things that had been done by God and the listeners respond with a fixed text: dayenu *(it would have been sufficient). It is possible that the leader may have improvised additional things that had been done by God for which one should be grateful. An early source, the* Midrash Sekhel Tov, *requires one to list at least fifteen deeds, symbolic of the fifteen chapters of Psalms that begin with "A song for ascents." Some texts do include an additional stanza. The nature of the litany is poetic and rhythmic and, at times, the content itself is subjugated to the form. Thus, for instance, it is not easily understandable why one should respond to the statement "If He had brought us before Mount Sinai and had not given us the Torah" that that would have been sufficient, as if arriving at Mount Sinai were, in itself, a benefit for which one should be grateful. Commentators have suggested, in this case, that the feeling of unity that the people sensed at Mount Sinai, as reported by a midrash, is the justification for considering this, in itself, as being a grant of God.*

[25]For how many good deeds are we obligated to the Omnipresent!	[25]**כַּמָּה מַעֲלוֹת** טוֹבוֹת לַמָּקוֹם עָלֵינוּ!
If He had taken us out of Egypt but had not punished them it would have been sufficient	אִלּוּ הוֹצִיאָנוּ מִמִּצְרַיִם, וְלֹא עָשָׂה בָהֶם שְׁפָטִים דַּיֵּנוּ.
If He had punished them but had not destroyed their gods it would have been sufficient	אִלּוּ עָשָׂה בָהֶם שְׁפָטִים, ולֹא עָשָׂה בֵאלֹהֵיהֶם דַּיֵּנוּ.
If He had destroyed their gods but had not killed their first-born it would have been sufficient	אִלּוּ עָשָׂה בֵאלֹהֵיהֶם, וְלֹא הָרַג אֶת בְּכוֹרֵיהֶם דַּיֵּנוּ.
If He had killed their first-born but had not given us their money it would have been sufficient	אִלּוּ הָרַג אֶת בְּכוֹרֵיהֶם, וְלֹא נָתַן לָנוּ אֶת מָמוֹנָם דַּיֵּנוּ.
If He had given us their money but had not separated the sea for us it would have been sufficient	אִלּוּ נָתַן לָנוּ אֶת מָמוֹנָם, וְלֹא קָרַע לָנוּ אֶת הַיָּם דַּיֵּנוּ.

25 **For how many good deeds** For the structure of this litany, see pp. 45–46. The opening sentence is almost impossible to translate. However, *ma'alot tovot* is generally translated as "good qualities," and not as "good deeds." "*Ma'alot*" can also mean "steps," and in most versions there are fifteen stanzas that correspond both to the number of steps that led to the Temple and to the number of psalms that are titled "Song of ascents." Therefore, the use of *ma'alot* may be a pun. Although this litany focuses on the Exodus, its climax is the building of the Temple in Jerusalem.

If He had separated the sea for us but had not brought us through it on dry land
it would have been sufficient

אִלּוּ קָרַע לָנוּ אֶת הַיָּם,
וְלֹא הֶעֱבִירָנוּ בְתוֹכוֹ בֶּחָרָבָה דַּיֵּנוּ.

If He had brought us through it on dry land but had not drowned our enemies in it
it would have been sufficient

אִלּוּ הֶעֱבִירָנוּ בְתוֹכוֹ בֶּחָרָבָה,
וְלֹא שִׁקַּע צָרֵינוּ בְּתוֹכוֹ דַּיֵּנוּ.

If He had drowned our enemies in it but had not provided our needs in the desert for forty years
it would have been sufficient

אִלּוּ שִׁקַּע צָרֵינוּ בְּתוֹכוֹ,
וְלֹא סִפֵּק צָרְכֵּנוּ בַּמִּדְבָּר
אַרְבָּעִים שָׁנָה דַּיֵּנוּ.

If He had provided our needs in the desert for forty years but had not fed us manna
it would have been sufficient

אִלּוּ סִפֵּק צָרְכֵּנוּ בַּמִּדְבָּר אַרְבָּעִים
שָׁנָה, ולֹא הֶאֱכִילָנוּ אֶת הַמָּן דַּיֵּנוּ.

If He had fed us manna but had not given us the *Shabbat*
it would have been sufficient

אִלּוּ הֶאֱכִילָנוּ אֶת הַמָּן,
וְלֹא נָתַן לָנוּ אֶת הַשַּׁבָּת דַּיֵּנוּ.

If He had given us the *Shabbat* and had not brought us before Mount Sinai
it would have been sufficient

אִלּוּ נָתַן לָנוּ אֶת הַשַּׁבָּת,
וְלֹא קֵרְבָנוּ לִפְנֵי הַר סִינַי דַּיֵּנוּ.

If He had brought us before Mount Sinai and had not given us the Torah
it would have been sufficient

אִלּוּ קֵרְבָנוּ לִפְנֵי הַר סִינַי,
וְלֹא נָתַן לָנוּ אֶת הַתּוֹרָה דַּיֵּנוּ.

If He had given us the Torah and had not brought us to the Land of Israel
it would have been sufficient

אִלּוּ נָתַן לָנוּ אֶת הַתּוֹרָה
וְלֹא הִכְנִיסָנוּ לְאֶרֶץ יִשְׂרָאֵל דַּיֵּנוּ.

If He had brought us to the Land of Israel but had not built the Temple for us
it would have been sufficient

אִלּוּ הִכְנִיסָנוּ לְאֶרֶץ יִשְׂרָאֵל
וְלֹא בָנָה לָנוּ אֶת בֵּית הַבְּחִירָה דַּיֵּנוּ.

How much more so are we obligated to the Omnipresent!

He took us out of Egypt, and punished the Egyptians, and destroyed their gods, and killed their first-born and gave us their money, and separated the sea for us, and brought us through it on dry land, and drowned our enemies in it, and provided our needs in the desert for forty years, and fed us manna, and gave us the *Shabbat,* and brought us before Mount Sinai, and gave us the Torah, and brought us to the Land of Israel, and built the Temple for us to atone for our sins.

עַל אַחַת כַּמָּה וְכַמָּה, טוֹבָה כְפוּלָה וּמְכֻפֶּלֶת לַמָּקוֹם עָלֵינוּ:

שֶׁהוֹצִיאָנוּ מִמִּצְרַיִם, וְעָשָׂה בָהֶם שְׁפָטִים, וְעָשָׂה בֵאלֹהֵיהֶם, וְהָרַג אֶת בְּכוֹרֵיהֶם, וְנָתַן לָנוּ אֶת מָמוֹנָם, וְקָרַע לָנוּ אֶת הַיָּם, וְהֶעֱבִירָנוּ בְתוֹכוֹ בֶּחָרָבָה, וְשִׁקַּע צָרֵינוּ בְּתוֹכוֹ, וְסִפֵּק צָרְכֵּנוּ בַּמִּדְבָּר אַרְבָּעִים שָׁנָה, וְהֶאֱכִילָנוּ אֶת הַמָּן, וְנָתַן לָנוּ אֶת הַשַּׁבָּת, וְקֵרְבָנוּ לִפְנֵי הַר סִינַי, וְנָתַן לָנוּ אֶת הַתּוֹרָה, וְהִכְנִיסָנוּ לְאֶרֶץ יִשְׂרָאֵל, וּבָנָה לָנוּ אֶת בֵּית הַבְּחִירָה לְכַפֵּר עַל כָּל עֲוֹנוֹתֵינוּ.

At this point in the text the meaning of the food that is about to be eaten is explained. It is customary to hold the matzah and the maror *to display them while reciting their explanations. The meat or bone, which is symbolic of the paschal sacrifice, is not held to avoid the possibility that people might think of it as a real paschal lamb.*

[26]R. Gamliel used to say: Whoever did not explain these three things on Passover has not fulfilled his duty. They are: *Pesach,* matzah and *maror*.

[26]רַבָּן גַּמְלִיאֵל הָיָה אוֹמֵר: כָּל שֶׁלֹּא אָמַר שְׁלֹשָׁה דְּבָרִים אֵלּוּ בַּפֶּסַח, לֹא יָצָא יְדֵי חוֹבָתוֹ, וְאֵלּוּ הֵן: **פֶּסַח, מַצָּה, וּמָרוֹר.**

The passover lamb that our ancestors ate when the Temple existed—for what reason? Because the Holy One, blessed be He, passed over the homes of our ancestors in Egypt, as it is said: "You shall say, 'It is the passover sacrifice to *Adonai,* because He passed over the houses of the Israelites in Egypt when He smote the Egyptians, but saved our houses.'" The people then bowed low in homage (Exod. 12:27).

פֶּסַח שֶׁהָיוּ אֲבוֹתֵינוּ אוֹכְלִים בִּזְמַן שֶׁבֵּית הַמִּקְדָּשׁ הָיָה קַיָּם, עַל שׁוּם מָה? עַל שׁוּם שֶׁפָּסַח הַקָּדוֹשׁ בָּרוּךְ הוּא עַל בָּתֵּי אֲבוֹתֵינוּ בְּמִצְרַיִם, שֶׁנֶּאֱמַר: וַאֲמַרְתֶּם זֶבַח פֶּסַח הוּא לַייָ, אֲשֶׁר פָּסַח עַל בָּתֵּי בְנֵי יִשְׂרָאֵל בְּמִצְרַיִם בְּנָגְפּוֹ אֶת מִצְרַיִם, וְאֶת בָּתֵּינוּ הִצִּיל. וַיִּקֹּד הָעָם וַיִּשְׁתַּחֲווּ.

26 **R. Gamliel used to say** This passage is taken from the Mishnah, but it has been modified to reflect the fact that there is no paschal sacrifice. "R. Gamliel used to say" replaces "R. Gamliel says," while "The Passover lamb that our ancestors ate when the Temple existed" replaces the mishnaic text, "This paschal lamb which we eat." Here, the explanations are presented as both questions and answers, whereas in the Mishnah they appear as simple declarative statements.

[27]This matzah that we eat—for what reason? Because the dough of our ancestors had not fermented before the King of kings, the Holy One, blessed be He, appeared before them and redeemed them. As it is said: "And they baked unleavened cakes of the dough that they had taken out of Egypt, for it was not leavened, since they had been driven out of Egypt and could not delay; nor had they prepared any provisions for themselves" (Exod. 12:39–40).

[27]**מַצָּה** זוּ שֶׁאָנוּ אוֹכְלִים, עַל שׁוּם מָה? עַל שׁוּם שֶׁלֹּא הִסְפִּיק בְּצֵקָם שֶׁל אֲבוֹתֵינוּ לְהַחֲמִיץ עַד שֶׁנִּגְלָה עֲלֵיהֶם מֶלֶךְ מַלְכֵי הַמְּלָכִים, הַקָּדוֹשׁ בָּרוּךְ הוּא, וּגְאָלָם, שֶׁנֶּאֱמַר: וַיֹּאפוּ אֶת הַבָּצֵק אֲשֶׁר הוֹצִיאוּ מִמִּצְרַיִם עֻגֹת מַצּוֹת, כִּי לֹא חָמֵץ, כִּי גֹרְשׁוּ מִמִּצְרַיִם וְלֹא יָכְלוּ לְהִתְמַהְמֵהַּ, וְגַם צֵדָה לֹא עָשׂוּ לָהֶם.

This *maror* that we eat—for what reason? Because the Egyptians embittered the lives of our ancestors in Egypt, as it is said: "Ruthlessly they made life bitter for them with harsh labor at mortar and bricks and with all sorts of tasks in the field" (Exod. 1:14).

מָרוֹר זֶה שֶׁאָנוּ אוֹכְלִים, עַל שׁוּם מָה? עַל שׁוּם שֶׁמֵּרְרוּ הַמִּצְרִים אֶת חַיֵּי אֲבוֹתֵינוּ בְּמִצְרַיִם, שֶׁנֶּאֱמַר: וַיְמָרְרוּ אֶת חַיֵּיהֶם בַּעֲבֹדָה קָשָׁה, בְּחֹמֶר וּבִלְבֵנִים וּבְכָל עֲבֹדָה בַּשָּׂדֶה אֵת כָּל עֲבֹדָתָם אֲשֶׁר עָבְדוּ בָהֶם בְּפָרֶךְ.

In every generation one is required to see oneself as if he had gone out of Egypt. As it is said: "It is because of what *Adonai* did for me when I went free from Egypt" (Exod. 13:8). Not only our ancestors were redeemed by the Holy One, blessed be He, but we were also redeemed by Him. As it is said: "and us He freed from there, that He might take us and give us the land that He had promised on oath to our fathers" (Deut. 6:23).

בְּכָל דּוֹר וָדוֹר חַיָּב אָדָם לִרְאוֹת אֶת עַצְמוֹ כְּאִלּוּ הוּא יָצָא מִמִּצְרַיִם, שֶׁנֶּאֱמַר: וְהִגַּדְתָּ לְבִנְךָ בַּיּוֹם הַהוּא לֵאמֹר, בַּעֲבוּר זֶה עָשָׂה יי לִי בְּצֵאתִי מִמִּצְרָיִם. לֹא אֶת אֲבוֹתֵינוּ בִּלְבַד גָּאַל הַקָּדוֹשׁ בָּרוּךְ הוּא, אֶלָּא אַף אוֹתָנוּ גָּאַל עִמָּהֶם, שֶׁנֶּאֱמַר: וְאוֹתָנוּ הוֹצִיא מִשָּׁם, לְמַעַן הָבִיא אֹתָנוּ, לָתֶת לָנוּ אֶת הָאָרֶץ אֲשֶׁר נִשְׁבַּע לַאֲבֹתֵינוּ.

27 **This matzah that we eat** The Mishnah has a different explanation for the significance of the matzah. See pp. 29–30.

This concludes the story of the Exodus and now one begins the praise of God, with two chapters of psalms that are the opening chapters of the unit known as Hallel. *The praise of God is in the form of song, and wine and song go together. Therefore, one should hold the cup of wine until the conclusion of this section.*

The following is an introduction to the Hallel, *which serves as a transition between the story and the praise.*

לְפִיכָךְ אֲנַחְנוּ חַיָּבִים לְהוֹדוֹת, לְהַלֵּל, לְשַׁבֵּחַ, לְפָאֵר, לְרוֹמֵם, לְהַדֵּר, לְבָרֵךְ, לְעַלֵּה וּלְקַלֵּס לְמִי שֶׁעָשָׂה לַאֲבוֹתֵינוּ וְלָנוּ אֶת כָּל הַנִּסִּים הָאֵלּוּ: הוֹצִיאָנוּ מֵעַבְדוּת לְחֵרוּת, מִיָּגוֹן לְשִׂמְחָה, וּמֵאֵבֶל לְיוֹם טוֹב, וּמֵאֲפֵלָה לְאוֹר גָּדוֹל, וּמִשִּׁעְבּוּד לִגְאֻלָּה. וְנֹאמַר לְפָנָיו שִׁירָה חֲדָשָׁה: הַלְלוּיָהּ.

Therefore, we are obligated to thank, to acclaim, to praise, to laud, to exalt, to extol, to bless, to applaud, Him who performed all these miracles for our ancestors and for us: He took us from slavery to freedom, from suffering to joy, form mourning to celebration, from darkness to great light, and from subjection to redemption. And we shall sing for Him a new song: Halleluyah.

Psalm 113

הַלְלוּיָהּ הַלְלוּ עַבְדֵי יי, הַלְלוּ אֶת שֵׁם יי. יְהִי שֵׁם יי מְבֹרָךְ מֵעַתָּה וְעַד עוֹלָם. מִמִּזְרַח שֶׁמֶשׁ עַד מְבוֹאוֹ מְהֻלָּל שֵׁם יי. רָם עַל כָּל גּוֹיִם יי, עַל הַשָּׁמַיִם כְּבוֹדוֹ. מִי כַּיי אֱלֹהֵינוּ הַמַּגְבִּיהִי לָשָׁבֶת, הַמַּשְׁפִּילִי לִרְאוֹת בַּשָּׁמַיִם וּבָאָרֶץ? מְקִימִי מֵעָפָר דָּל, מֵאַשְׁפֹּת יָרִים אֶבְיוֹן, לְהוֹשִׁיבִי עִם נְדִיבִים, עִם נְדִיבֵי עַמּוֹ. מוֹשִׁיבִי עֲקֶרֶת הַבַּיִת, אֵם הַבָּנִים שְׂמֵחָה. הַלְלוּיָהּ.

Hallelujah. O servants of *Adonai,* give praise; praise the name of *Adonai*. Let the name of *Adonai* be blessed now and forever. From east to west the name of *Adonai* is praised. *Adonai* is exalted above all nations; His glory is above the heavens. Who is like *Adonai* our LORD, who, enthroned on high, sees what is below, in heaven and on earth? He raises the poor from the dust, lifts up the needy from the refuse heap to set them with the great, with the great men of His people. He sets the childless woman among her household as a happy mother of children. Hallelujah.

Psalm 114

When Israel went forth from Egypt,
the house of Jacob from a people
of strange speech,
Judah became His holy one,
Israel, His dominion.
The sea saw them and fled,
Jordan ran backward,
mountains skipped like rams,
hills like sheep.
What alarmed you, O sea,
that you fled,
Jordan, that you ran backward,
mountains, that you skipped like rams,
hills, like sheep?
Tremble, O earth,
at the presence of *Adonai,*
at the presence of the God of Jacob,
who turned the rock
into a pool of water,
the flinty rock into a fountain.

בְּצֵאת יִשְׂרָאֵל מִמִּצְרָיִם,
בֵּית יַעֲקֹב מֵעַם לֹעֵז,
הָיְתָה יְהוּדָה לְקָדְשׁוֹ,
יִשְׂרָאֵל מַמְשְׁלוֹתָיו.
הַיָּם רָאָה וַיָּנֹס,
הַיַּרְדֵּן יִסֹּב לְאָחוֹר.
הֶהָרִים רָקְדוּ כְאֵילִים,
גְּבָעוֹת – כִּבְנֵי צֹאן.
מַה לְּךָ הַיָּם כִּי תָנוּס,
הַיַּרְדֵּן – תִּסֹּב לְאָחוֹר,
הֶהָרִים – תִּרְקְדוּ כְאֵילִים,
גְּבָעוֹת – כִּבְנֵי צֹאן?
מִלִּפְנֵי אָדוֹן חוּלִי אָרֶץ,
מִלִּפְנֵי אֱלוֹהַּ יַעֲקֹב.
הַהֹפְכִי הַצּוּר אֲגַם מָיִם,
חַלָּמִישׁ – לְמַעְיְנוֹ מָיִם.

One raises the cup until completing the blessing.

Blessed art Thou, *Adonai* our Lord, King of the universe, who redeemed us and redeemed our ancestors from Egypt, and brought us to this night to eat matzah and *maror*. So may *Adonai,* our Lord and the Lord of our ancestors, bring us to other festivals and other pilgrimage festivals, may they come to us in peace, rejoicing in the building of Your city and delighting in Your worship. And we shall eat there from the sacrifices and the paschal lambs whose blood will be sprinkled on Your altar according to Your wish, and we shall praise You with a new song about our redemption and the salvation of our souls. Blessed art Thou, *Adonai,* redeemer of Israel.

בָּרוּךְ אַתָּה יי אֱלֹהֵינוּ מֶלֶךְ הָעוֹלָם, אֲשֶׁר גְּאָלָנוּ וְגָאַל אֶת אֲבוֹתֵינוּ מִמִּצְרַיִם, וְהִגִּיעָנוּ לַלַּיְלָה הַזֶּה לֶאֱכָל בּוֹ מַצָּה וּמָרוֹר. כֵּן יי אֱלֹהֵינוּ וֵאלֹהֵי אֲבוֹתֵינוּ יַגִּיעֵנוּ לְמוֹעֲדִים וְלִרְגָלִים אֲחֵרִים הַבָּאִים לִקְרָאתֵנוּ לְשָׁלוֹם, שְׂמֵחִים בְּבִנְיַן עִירֶךָ וְשָׂשִׂים בַּעֲבוֹדָתֶךָ, וְנֹאכַל שָׁם מִן הַזְּבָחִים וּמִן הַפְּסָחִים אֲשֶׁר יַגִּיעַ דָּמָם עַל קִיר מִזְבַּחֲךָ לְרָצוֹן, וְנוֹדֶה לְּךָ שִׁיר חָדָשׁ עַל גְּאֻלָּתֵנוּ וְעַל פְּדוּת נַפְשֵׁנוּ. בָּרוּךְ אַתָּה יי גָּאַל יִשְׂרָאֵל.

בָּרוּךְ אַתָּה יי אֱלֹהֵינוּ מֶלֶךְ הָעוֹלָם בּוֹרֵא פְּרִי הַגָּפֶן.

Blessed art Thou, *Adonai* our LORD, King of the universe, creator of the fruit of the vine.

One should drink most of the cup, at least, while reclining on the left.

The following rubrics of the haggadah, rachtzah *and motzi matzah, must be treated as one since it is not proper to talk between washing of the hands and eating the matzah. One washes one's hands for eating bread and recites the appropriate blessing. After this, one takes the three matzot in hand and recites the blessing for eating bread. The three matzot are held so that one has two whole matzot in hand, besides the broken one, as festival meals require two whole loaves (lechem mishneh). After reciting this blessing, the lowest matzah is released. One whole matzah and one broken matzah remain and the blessing for eating matzah is then recited. Use of a broken matzah is considered proper for this blessing as a broken loaf represents bread of distress. Although it is customary to salt the bread eaten after the blessing for eating matzah, it is the Ashkenazic tradition to eat unsalted matzah at the seder. Sephardim usually salt the matzah. One should eat, at least, a quantity of matzah equal to the size of an olive.*

רַחְצָה

The blessing for washing one's hands:

בָּרוּךְ אַתָּה יי אֱלֹהֵינוּ מֶלֶךְ הָעוֹלָם, אֲשֶׁר קִדְּשָׁנוּ בְּמִצְוֹתָיו וְצִוָּנוּ עַל נְטִילַת יָדָיִם.

Blessed art Thou, *Adonai* our LORD, King of the universe, who has sanctified us by His commandments and commanded us about washing hands.

מוֹצִיא

The blessings recited before eating the matzah (see instructions above):

בָּרוּךְ אַתָּה יי אֱלֹהֵינוּ מֶלֶךְ הָעוֹלָם הַמּוֹצִיא לֶחֶם מִן הָאָרֶץ.

Blessed art Thou, *Adonai* our LORD, King of the universe, who brings forth bread from the earth.

מַצָּה

בָּרוּךְ אַתָּה יי אֱלֹהֵינוּ מֶלֶךְ הָעוֹלָם אֲשֶׁר קִדְּשָׁנוּ בְּמִצְוֹתָיו וְצִוָּנוּ עַל אֲכִילַת מַצָּה.

Blessed art Thou, *Adonai* our LORD, King of the universe, who has sanctified us by His commandments and commanded us about eating matzah.

מָרוֹר

One takes the bitter herbs (lettuce or other suitable vegetable) and dips it into the haroset. *The main flavor should be that of the bitter herbs so it is the Ashkenazic tradition to shake off the* haroset *from bitter herbs after dipping. One should eat a quantity of the bitter herbs equal to the size of an olive. Since the bitter herbs are a symbol of suffering and slavery, it is not necessary to recline while eating them.*

בָּרוּךְ אַתָּה יי אֱלֹהֵינוּ מֶלֶךְ הָעוֹלָם אֲשֶׁר קִדְּשָׁנוּ בְּמִצְוֹתָיו וְצִוָּנוּ עַל אֲכִילַת מָרוֹר.

Blessed art Thou, *Adonai* our LORD, King of the universe, who has sanctified us by His commandments and commanded us about eating *maror*.

כּוֹרֵךְ

One prepares a sandwich of bitter herbs (according to Ashkenazic tradition, one should not dip the bitter herbs in haroset*) on matzah and says the following:*

[28]זֵכֶר לְמִקְדָּשׁ כְּהִלֵּל. כֵּן עָשָׂה הִלֵּל בִּזְמַן שֶׁבֵּית הַמִּקְדָּשׁ הָיָה קַיָּם: הָיָה כּוֹרֵךְ מַצָּה וּמָרוֹר וְאוֹכֵל בְּיַחַד, לְקַיֵּם מַה שֶּׁנֶּאֱמַר: עַל מַצּוֹת וּמְרֹרִים יֹאכְלֻהוּ.

[28]In commemoration of the Temple, according to Hillel. Thus did Hillel when the Temple still existed: he would wrap matzah and *maror* together and eat them to fulfill what is said: "They shall eat it with unleavened bread and bitter herbs" (Num. 9:11).

One now eats the sandwich. It is customary to recline while eating this sandwich.

28 **In commemoration of the Temple, according to Hillel** The eating of the sandwich is prefaced by the statement that this is a remembrance of the Temple according to the custom of Hillel. This statement is a paraphrase of the talmudic statements made in this context (BT *Pesachim* 115a). It seems that this statement is a note in the haggadah explaining why it was customary to eat this sandwich even though one had already fulfilled the obligations of eating matzah and *maror*. Nevertheless, this explanation became part of the text of the haggadah. Rabbi Joseph Caro says explicitly that one is to say that this is a commemoration of the Temple according to Hillel (*Shulchan Arukh*, *Orach Chayyim* 475:1), although it has been suggested that the text has been corrupted (see *Bi'ur Halakhah,* loc. cit.). Presumably, a commemoration would not be recognized as such unless there was an announcement that this act was a commemoration. However, a short declaration, "in memory of the Temple," would have been sufficient. The rest of the text that explains Hillel's custom seems to have been instructional rather than as a text to be read as part of the haggadah. However, the custom was to read the whole text out loud, and many also recited the additional instruction, *belo tibbul uvelo bracha*.

שֻׁלְחָן עוֹרֵךְ

One eats and drinks, taking into consideration that one has to eat the final matzah known as afikoman.

צָפוּן

After the meal, each person should eat a piece of matzah, equal in size to at least an olive. This is done for two reasons. One is to ensure fulfillment of the requirement that the taste of matzah be left in one's mouth. The second reason is in commemoration of the paschal lamb, which, according to rabbinical theory, was the last food eaten at the meal.

בָּרֵךְ

One pours the third cup for grace after the meal. It is customary to sing or recite the following psalm before grace on Sabbath and festivals.

Psalm 126:1–6

שִׁיר הַמַּעֲלוֹת: בְּשׁוּב יי אֶת שִׁיבַת צִיּוֹן הָיִינוּ כְּחֹלְמִים. אָז יִמָּלֵא שְׂחוֹק פִּינוּ וּלְשׁוֹנֵנוּ רִנָּה. אָז יֹאמְרוּ בַגּוֹיִם: הִגְדִּיל יי לַעֲשׂוֹת עִם אֵלֶּה. הִגְדִּיל יי לַעֲשׂוֹת עִמָּנוּ, הָיִינוּ שְׂמֵחִים. שׁוּבָה יי אֶת שְׁבִיתֵנוּ כַּאֲפִיקִים בַּנֶּגֶב. הַזֹּרְעִים בְּדִמְעָה, בְּרִנָּה יִקְצֹרוּ. הָלוֹךְ יֵלֵךְ וּבָכֹה נֹשֵׂא מֶשֶׁךְ הַזָּרַע, בֹּא יָבֹא בְרִנָּה נֹשֵׂא אֲלֻמֹּתָיו.

A song of ascents. When *Adonai* restores the fortunes of Zion—we see it as in a dream—our mouths shall be filled with laughter, our tongues, with songs of joy. Then shall they say among the nations, "*Adonai* has done great things for them!" *Adonai* will do great things for us and we shall rejoice. Restore our fortunes, *Adonai,* like watercourses in the Negeb. They who sow in tears shall reap with songs of joy. Though he goes along weeping, carrying the seed-bag, he shall come back with songs of joy, carrying his sheaves.

Blessed art Thou, *Adonai* our LORD, King of the universe, who nourishes the entire world in His goodness, with grace and charity and mercy He gives bread to all flesh, for His steadfast love is eternal. And in His great goodness we have never lacked, nor will we lack food, forever, for the sake of His great name, for He is a LORD who nourishes and supports all and is good to all, and He prepares food for all His creatures that He has created. Blessed art Thou, *Adonai,* who nourishes all.

We thank you, *Adonai* our LORD, for giving our ancestors a desirous, good, and spacious land, and for bringing us out of Egypt, and for redeeming us from a house of slavery, and for the covenant that You have engraved in our flesh, and for Your Torah that You have taught us, and for Your laws that You have informed us, and for life, grace, and charity that You have granted us, and for the eating of food by which You nourish and support us constantly, every day, every time, and every moment. And for all, *Adonai* our LORD, we thank You and we bless You, may Your name be blessed by all life constantly and forever as it says: "When you have eaten your fill, give thanks to *Adonai* your LORD, for the good land which He has given you" (Deut. 8:10). Blessed art Thou, *Adonai,* for the land and for the food.

Have mercy, *Adonai* our LORD, on Your people Israel and on Your city, Jerusalem, and on Zion, the abode of Your glory, and on the kingdom of the house of David, Your anointed one, and on the great and holy house that is called by Your name. Our LORD, our Father, shepherd us, nourish us, support us and help us prosper, and relieve us, *Adonai* our LORD, from all our troubles.

בָּרוּךְ אַתָּה יי אֱלֹהֵינוּ מֶלֶךְ הָעוֹלָם הַזָּן אֶת הָעוֹלָם כֻּלּוֹ בְּטוּבוֹ בְּחֵן בְּחֶסֶד וּבְרַחֲמִים הוּא נוֹתֵן לֶחֶם לְכָל בָּשָׂר כִּי לְעוֹלָם חַסְדּוֹ. וּבְטוּבוֹ הַגָּדוֹל תָּמִיד לֹא חָסַר לָנוּ, וְאַל יֶחְסַר לָנוּ מָזוֹן לְעוֹלָם וָעֶד. בַּעֲבוּר שְׁמוֹ הַגָּדוֹל, כִּי הוּא אֵל זָן וּמְפַרְנֵס לַכֹּל וּמֵטִיב לַכֹּל, וּמֵכִין מָזוֹן לְכָל בְּרִיּוֹתָיו אֲשֶׁר בָּרָא. בָּרוּךְ אַתָּה יי הַזָּן אֶת הַכֹּל.

נוֹדֶה לְּךָ יי אֱלֹהֵינוּ עַל שֶׁהִנְחַלְתָּ לַאֲבוֹתֵינוּ אֶרֶץ חֶמְדָּה טוֹבָה וּרְחָבָה וְעַל שֶׁהוֹצֵאתָנוּ יי אֱלֹהֵינוּ מֵאֶרֶץ מִצְרַיִם, וּפְדִיתָנוּ מִבֵּית עֲבָדִים, וְעַל בְּרִיתְךָ שֶׁחָתַמְתָּ בִּבְשָׂרֵנוּ, וְעַל תּוֹרָתְךָ שֶׁלִּמַּדְתָּנוּ, וְעַל חֻקֶּיךָ שֶׁהוֹדַעְתָּנוּ, וְעַל חַיִּים חֵן וָחֶסֶד שֶׁחוֹנַנְתָּנוּ, וְעַל אֲכִילַת מָזוֹן שָׁאַתָּה זָן וּמְפַרְנֵס אוֹתָנוּ תָּמִיד, בְּכָל יוֹם וּבְכָל עֵת וּבְכָל שָׁעָה: וְעַל הַכֹּל יי אֱלֹהֵינוּ אֲנַחְנוּ מוֹדִים לָךְ וּמְבָרְכִים אוֹתָךְ, יִתְבָּרַךְ שִׁמְךָ בְּפִי כָּל חַי תָּמִיד לְעוֹלָם וָעֶד: כַּכָּתוּב, וְאָכַלְתָּ וְשָׂבָעְתָּ וּבֵרַכְתָּ אֶת יי אֱלֹהֶיךָ עַל הָאָרֶץ הַטּוֹבָה אֲשֶׁר נָתַן לָךְ. בָּרוּךְ אַתָּה יי עַל הָאָרֶץ וְעַל הַמָּזוֹן:

רַחֵם נָא יי אֱלֹהֵינוּ עַל יִשְׂרָאֵל עַמֶּךָ וְעַל יְרוּשָׁלַיִם עִירֶךָ וְעַל צִיּוֹן מִשְׁכַּן כְּבוֹדֶךָ וְעַל מַלְכוּת בֵּית דָּוִד מְשִׁיחֶךָ וְעַל הַבַּיִת הַגָּדוֹל וְהַקָּדוֹשׁ שֶׁנִּקְרָא שִׁמְךָ עָלָיו: אֱלֹהֵינוּ אָבִינוּ, רְעֵנוּ זוּנֵנוּ פַּרְנְסֵנוּ וְכַלְכְּלֵנוּ וְהַרְוִיחֵנוּ, וְהַרְוַח לָנוּ יי אֱלֹהֵינוּ מְהֵרָה מִכָּל צָרוֹתֵינוּ.

And please, *Adonai* our LORD, do not put us in need of gifts from humans nor of their loans, but only Your full hand, holy and vast, that we may never be shamed or embarrassed.

וְנָא אַל תַּצְרִיכֵנוּ יי אֱלֹהֵינוּ, לֹא לִידֵי מַתְּנַת בָּשָׂר וָדָם וְלֹא לִידֵי הַלְוָאתָם, כִּי אִם לְיָדְךָ הַמְּלֵאָה הַפְּתוּחָה הַקְּדוֹשָׁה וְהָרְחָבָה, שֶׁלֹּא נֵבוֹשׁ וְלֹא נִכָּלֵם לְעוֹלָם וָעֶד.

On the Sabbath the following paragraph is added:

Accept and strengthen us, *Adonai* our LORD, in Your commandments and in the commandment of the seventh day, this great and holy *Shabbat,* for it is a great and holy day before You, to cease from work and to rest on it, in love, according to the commandment of Your will. And, in Your will, allow us, *Adonai* our LORD, to have no distress or suffering or sighing on our day of rest. And show us, *Adonai* our LORD, the comforting of Zion, Your city, and the building of Jerusalem, Your Holy City, for You are the master of salvations and the master of comforts.

רְצֵה וְהַחֲלִיצֵנוּ יי אֱלֹהֵינוּ בְּמִצְוֹתֶיךָ וּבְמִצְוַת יוֹם הַשְּׁבִיעִי הַשַּׁבָּת הַגָּדוֹל וְהַקָּדוֹשׁ הַזֶּה, כִּי יוֹם זֶה גָּדוֹל וְקָדוֹשׁ הוּא לְפָנֶיךָ לִשְׁבָּת בּוֹ וְלָנוּחַ בּוֹ בְּאַהֲבָה כְּמִצְוַת רְצוֹנֶךָ. וּבִרְצוֹנְךָ הָנִיחַ לָנוּ יי אֱלֹהֵינוּ שֶׁלֹּא תְהֵא צָרָה וְיָגוֹן וַאֲנָחָה בְּיוֹם מְנוּחָתֵנוּ. וְהַרְאֵנוּ יי אֱלֹהֵינוּ בְּנֶחָמַת צִיּוֹן עִירֶךָ וּבְבִנְיַן יְרוּשָׁלַיִם עִיר קָדְשֶׁךָ כִּי אַתָּה הוּא בַּעַל הַיְשׁוּעוֹת וּבַעַל הַנֶּחָמוֹת.

Our LORD and the LORD of our ancestors, may our memory and our recollection, and the memory of the anointed son of your servant, David, and the memory of Jerusalem Your Holy City, and the memory of all of Your people, the house of Israel, arise and come, and reach and be seen and be accepted and be heard and be recollected and remembered before You for salvation, for good and grace, for mercy and compassion, for life and peace, on this day of the matzah festival. Remember us on it, *Adonai* our LORD, for good and recollect us for blessing and save us for life. As for salvation and compassion, spare us, be graceful to us, be compassionate to and save, for our eyes are turned to You, for You are a graceful and compassionate LORD and King.

אֱלֹהֵינוּ וֵאלֹהֵי אֲבוֹתֵינוּ, יַעֲלֶה וְיָבֹא וְיַגִּיעַ וְיֵרָאֶה וְיֵרָצֶה וְיִשָּׁמַע וְיִפָּקֵד וְיִזָּכֵר זִכְרוֹנֵנוּ וּפִקְדוֹנֵנוּ, וְזִכְרוֹן אֲבוֹתֵינוּ, וְזִכְרוֹן מָשִׁיחַ בֶּן דָּוִד עַבְדֶּךָ, וְזִכְרוֹן יְרוּשָׁלַיִם עִיר קָדְשֶׁךָ, וְזִכְרוֹן כָּל עַמְּךָ בֵּית יִשְׂרָאֵל לְפָנֶיךָ, לִפְלֵיטָה לְטוֹבָה לְחֵן וּלְחֶסֶד וּלְרַחֲמִים, לְחַיִּים וּלְשָׁלוֹם בְּיוֹם חַג הַמַּצּוֹת הַזֶּה זָכְרֵנוּ יי אֱלֹהֵינוּ בּוֹ לְטוֹבָה וּפָקְדֵנוּ בוֹ לִבְרָכָה וְהוֹשִׁיעֵנוּ בוֹ לְחַיִּים. וּבִדְבַר יְשׁוּעָה וְרַחֲמִים חוּס וְחָנֵּנוּ וְרַחֵם עָלֵינוּ וְהוֹשִׁיעֵנוּ, כִּי אֵלֶיךָ עֵינֵינוּ, כִּי אֵל מֶלֶךְ חַנּוּן וְרַחוּם אָתָּה.

And build Jerusalem, the Holy City, speedily in our own days. Blessed art Thou, *Adonai* our LORD, builder of Jerusalem in His mercy. Amen.

וּבְנֵה יְרוּשָׁלַיִם עִיר הַקֹּדֶשׁ בִּמְהֵרָה בְיָמֵינוּ. בָּרוּךְ אַתָּה יי בּוֹנֵה בְרַחֲמָיו יְרוּשָׁלָיִם. אָמֵן.

Blessed art Thou, *Adonai* our LORD, King of the universe, the LORD, our Father, our King, our Powerful One, our Creator, our Redeemer, He who formed us, our Holy One, the Holy One of Jacob, our Shepherd, Shepherd of Israel, the King who is good and is good to all. For on every day He did good, He does good, and He will do good for us. He has granted us, He grants us, and He will grant us grace, mercy, compassion, prosperity, safety and success, blessing and salvation, comfort, support, and maintenance, compassion and life and peace and all good things and He will never deprive us of any good thing.

בָּרוּךְ אַתָּה יי אֱלֹהֵינוּ מֶלֶךְ הָעוֹלָם, הָאֵל אָבִינוּ מַלְכֵּנוּ אַדִּירֵנוּ בּוֹרְאֵנוּ גֹּאֲלֵנוּ יוֹצְרֵנוּ קְדוֹשֵׁנוּ קְדוֹשׁ יַעֲקֹב רוֹעֵנוּ רוֹעֵה יִשְׂרָאֵל הַמֶּלֶךְ הַטּוֹב וְהַמֵּטִיב לַכֹּל שֶׁבְּכָל יוֹם וָיוֹם הוּא הֵטִיב, הוּא מֵטִיב, הוּא יֵיטִיב לָנוּ. הוּא גְמָלָנוּ הוּא גוֹמְלֵנוּ הוּא יִגְמְלֵנוּ לָעַד, לְחֵן וּלְחֶסֶד וּלְרַחֲמִים וּלְרֶוַח הַצָּלָה וְהַצְלָחָה, בְּרָכָה וִישׁוּעָה נֶחָמָה פַּרְנָסָה וְכַלְכָּלָה וְרַחֲמִים וְחַיִּים וְשָׁלוֹם וְכָל טוֹב, וּמִכָּל טוּב לְעוֹלָם עַל יְחַסְּרֵנוּ.

The compassionate one, may He rule over us forever.

הָרַחֲמָן הוּא יִמְלוֹךְ עָלֵינוּ לְעוֹלָם וָעֶד.

The compassionate one, may He be blessed in heaven and earth.

הָרַחֲמָן הוּא יִתְבָּרַךְ בַּשָּׁמַיִם וּבָאָרֶץ.

The compassionate one, may He be praised for all generations, and may He take pride in us for all eternity, and may He glory in us forever.

הָרַחֲמָן הוּא יִשְׁתַּבַּח לְדוֹר דּוֹרִים, וְיִתְפָּאַר בָּנוּ לָעַד וּלְנֵצַח נְצָחִים, וְיִתְהַדַּר בָּנוּ לָעַד וּלְעוֹלְמֵי עוֹלָמִים.

The compassionate one, may He support us in honor.

הָרַחֲמָן הוּא יְפַרְנְסֵנוּ בְּכָבוֹד.

The compassionate one, may He shatter the yoke from our necks, may He lead us, upright, to our land.

הָרַחֲמָן הוּא יִשְׁבּוֹר עֻלֵּנוּ מֵעַל צַוָּארֵנוּ, וְהוּא יוֹלִיכֵנוּ קוֹמְמִיּוּת לְאַרְצֵנוּ.

The compassionate one, may He send us abundant blessing to this house and to the table on which we have eaten.

הָרַחֲמָן הוּא יִשְׁלַח לָנוּ בְּרָכָה מְרֻבָּה בַּבַּיִת הַזֶּה, וְעַל שֻׁלְחָן זֶה שֶׁאָכַלְנוּ עָלָיו.

The compassionate one, may He send us His prophet Elijah, of blessed memory, and announce good news, salvation, and comfort.

הָרַחֲמָן הוּא יִשְׁלַח לָנוּ אֶת אֵלִיָּהוּ הַנָּבִיא זָכוּר לַטּוֹב, וִיבַשֶּׂר לָנוּ בְּשׂוֹרוֹת טוֹבוֹת יְשׁוּעוֹת וְנֶחָמוֹת.

It is customary to insert here a blessing for the host. Children who are at their parents' home say the following version. Others should adapt the blessing to fit the occasion.

The compassionate one, may He bless my father, my teacher, master of this house and my mother, my teacher, mistress of this house, them, their family and all their offspring and all that they have, us and all that we have, as He blessed our forefathers, Abraham, Isaac, and Jacob, with all and with everything, so may He bless us all together with a complete blessing and let us say: Amen.

הָרַחֲמָן הוּא יְבָרֵךְ אֶת אָבִי מוֹרִי בַּעַל הַבַּיִת הַזֶּה, וְאֶת אִמִּי מוֹרָתִי בַּעֲלַת הַבַּיִת הַזֶּה, אוֹתָם וְאֶת בֵּיתָם וְאֶת זַרְעָם וְאֶת כָּל אֲשֶׁר לָהֶם. אוֹתָנוּ וְאֶת כָּל אֲשֶׁר לָנוּ, כְּמוֹ שֶׁנִּתְבָּרְכוּ אֲבוֹתֵינוּ אַבְרָהָם יִצְחָק וְיַעֲקֹב בַּכֹּל מִכֹּל כֹּל, כֵּן יְבָרֵךְ אוֹתָנוּ כֻּלָּנוּ יַחַד בִּבְרָכָה שְׁלֵמָה, וְנֹאמַר, אָמֵן.

May those on high present them and us in a most favorable light that will bring us an era of peace. We shall receive blessing from *Adonai* and justice from our saving LORD, and we shall find favor and grace in the eyes of the LORD and of humanity.

בַּמָּרוֹם יְלַמְּדוּ עֲלֵיהֶם וְעָלֵינוּ זְכוּת שֶׁתְּהֵא לְמִשְׁמֶרֶת שָׁלוֹם. וְנִשָּׂא בְרָכָה מֵאֵת יי, וּצְדָקָה מֵאלֹהֵי יִשְׁעֵנוּ, וְנִמְצָא חֵן וְשֵׂכֶל טוֹב בְּעֵינֵי אֱלֹהִים וְאָדָם.

The compassionate one, may He grant us a day that is totally good.

הָרַחֲמָן הוּא יַנְחִילֵנוּ יוֹם שֶׁכֻּלּוֹ טוֹב.

The compassionate one, may He grant us the Messianic Era and the life of the world to come.

הָרַחֲמָן הוּא יְזַכֵּנוּ לִימוֹת הַמָּשִׁיחַ וּלְחַיֵּי הָעוֹלָם הַבָּא.

He accords great victories to His king, keeps faith with His anointed, with David and his offspring forever (Ps. 18:51). He who imposes peace in His heights (Job 25:2), may he impose peace upon us and all of Israel and say: Amen (2 Sam. 22:51).

מִגְדּוֹל יְשׁוּעוֹת מַלְכּוֹ וְעֹשֶׂה חֶסֶד לִמְשִׁיחוֹ לְדָוִד וּלְזַרְעוֹ עַד עוֹלָם. עֹשֶׂה שָׁלוֹם בִּמְרוֹמָיו, הוּא יַעֲשֶׂה שָׁלוֹם עָלֵינוּ וְעַל כָּל יִשְׂרָאֵל וְאִמְרוּ, אָמֵן.

Fear *Adonai,* you His consecrated ones, for those who fear Him lack nothing (Ps. 34:10). Lions have been reduced to starvation, but those who turn to *Adonai* shall not lack any good (Ps. 34:11). Praise *Adonai,* for He is good, His steadfast love is eternal (Ps. 118:1). You give it openhandedly, feeding every creature to its heart's content (Ps. 145:16).

יְראוּ אֶת יי קְדשָׁיו, כִּי אֵין מַחְסוֹר לִירֵאָיו. כְּפִירִים רָשׁוּ וְרָעֵבוּ, וְדֹרְשֵׁי יי לֹא יַחְסְרוּ כָל טוֹב. הוֹדוּ לַיי כִּי טוֹב כִּי לְעוֹלָם חַסְדּוֹ. פּוֹתֵחַ אֶת יָדֶךָ, וּמַשְׂבִּיעַ לְכָל חַי רָצוֹן.

Blessed is he who trusts in *Adonai*, whose trust is *Adonai* alone (Jer. 17:7). I have been young and am now old, but I have never seen a righteous man abandoned, or his children seeking bread (Ps. 37:25). May *Adonai* grant strength to His people; may *Adonai* bestow on His people well-being (Ps. 29:11).

בָּרוּךְ הַגֶּבֶר אֲשֶׁר יִבְטַח בַּיי, וְהָיָה יי מִבְטַחוֹ. נַעַר הָיִיתִי גַּם זָקַנְתִּי, וְלֹא רָאִיתִי צַדִּיק נֶעֱזָב, וְזַרְעוֹ מְבַקֶּשׁ לָחֶם. יי עֹז לְעַמּוֹ יִתֵּן, יי יְבָרֵךְ אֶת עַמּוֹ בַשָּׁלוֹם.

Recite the blessing over the third cup of wine.
At least most of the cup should be drunk while reclining on the left side.

Blessed art Thou, *Adonai* our LORD, King of the universe, creator of the fruit of the vine.

בָּרוּךְ אַתָּה יי אֱלֹהֵינוּ מֶלֶךְ הָעוֹלָם בּוֹרֵא פְּרִי הַגָּפֶן.

It is customary to open the door before reciting these verses.
Some people commemorate the Holocaust at this point.

29 **P**our out Your fury on the nations that do not know You, upon the kingdoms that do not invoke Your name, for they have devoured Jacob and desolated his home (Ps. 79:6–7). Pour out Your wrath on them; may Your blazing anger overtake them (Ps. 69:25); Oh, pursue them in wrath and destroy them from under the heavens of *Adonai* (Lam. 3:66).

29 **שְׁפֹךְ חֲמָתְךָ** אֶל הַגּוֹיִם אֲשֶׁר לֹא יְדָעוּךָ וְעַל מַמְלָכוֹת אֲשֶׁר בְּשִׁמְךָ לֹא קָרָאוּ. כִּי אָכַל אֶת יַעֲקֹב וְאֶת נָוֵהוּ הֵשַׁמּוּ. שְׁפָךְ עֲלֵיהֶם זַעְמֶךָ וַחֲרוֹן אַפְּךָ יַשִּׂיגֵם. תִּרְדֹּף בְּאַף וְתַשְׁמִידֵם מִתַּחַת שְׁמֵי יי.

29 **It is customary to open the door** The earlier custom seems to have been to leave the doors open throughout the evening. Deteriorating security caused people to limit opening their doors to short spans of time while reading these verses.

Hallel הַלֵּל

Psalm 115:1–18

Not to us, *Adonai,* not to us	לֹא לָנוּ, יי, לֹא לָנוּ,
but to Your name bring glory	כִּי לְשִׁמְךָ תֵּן כָּבוֹד,
for the sake of Your love and Your faithfulness.	עַל חַסְדְּךָ, עַל אֲמִתֶּךָ.
2 Let the nations not say,	לָמָּה יֹאמְרוּ הַגּוֹיִם:
"Where, now, is their God?"	אַיֵּה נָא אֱלֹהֵיהֶם?
3 when our God is in heaven	וֵאלֹהֵינוּ בַשָּׁמָיִם,
and all that He wills He accomplishes.	כֹּל אֲשֶׁר חָפֵץ עָשָׂה.
4 Their idols are silver and gold,	עֲצַבֵּיהֶם כֶּסֶף וְזָהָב
the work of men's hands.	מַעֲשֵׂה יְדֵי אָדָם.
5 They have mouths, but cannot speak,	פֶּה לָהֶם וְלֹא יְדַבֵּרוּ,
eyes, but cannot see;	עֵינַיִם לָהֶם וְלֹא יִרְאוּ.
6 they have ears, but cannot hear,	אָזְנַיִם לָהֶם וְלֹא יִשְׁמָעוּ,
noses, but cannot smell;	אַף לָהֶם וְלֹא יְרִיחוּן.
7 they have hands, but cannot touch,	יְדֵיהֶם וְלֹא יְמִישׁוּן,
feet, but cannot walk;	רַגְלֵיהֶם וְלֹא יְהַלֵּכוּ,
they can make no sound in their throats.	לֹא יֶהְגּוּ בִּגְרוֹנָם.
8 Those who fashion them,	כְּמוֹהֶם יִהְיוּ
all who trust in them,	עֹשֵׂיהֶם,
shall become like them.	כֹּל אֲשֶׁר בֹּטֵחַ בָּהֶם.
9 O Israel, trust in *Adonai!*	יִשְׂרָאֵל בְּטַח בַּיי,
He is their help and shield.	עֶזְרָם וּמָגִנָּם הוּא.
10 O house of Aaron, trust in *Adonai!*	בֵּית אַהֲרֹן בִּטְחוּ בַיי,
He is their help and shield.	עֶזְרָם וּמָגִנָּם הוּא.
11 O you who fear *Adonai,* trust in *Adonai!*	יִרְאֵי יי בִּטְחוּ בַיי,
He is their help and shield.	עֶזְרָם וּמָגִנָּם הוּא.
12 *Adonai* is mindful of us.	יי זְכָרָנוּ
He will bless us;	יְבָרֵךְ,

He will bless the house of Israel;	יְבָרֵךְ אֶת בֵּית יִשְׂרָאֵל,
He will bless the house of Aaron;	יְבָרֵךְ אֶת בֵּית אַהֲרֹן,
13 He will bless those who fear *Adonai,*	יְבָרֵךְ יִרְאֵי יי,
small and great alike.	הַקְּטַנִּים עִם הַגְּדֹלִים.
14 May *Adonai* increase your numbers,	יֹסֵף יי עֲלֵיכֶם,
yours and your children's also.	עֲלֵיכֶם וְעַל בְּנֵיכֶם.
15 May you be blessed by *Adonai,*	בְּרוּכִים אַתֶּם לַיי,
Maker of heaven and earth.	עֹשֵׂה שָׁמַיִם וָאָרֶץ.
16 The heavens belong to *Adonai,*	הַשָּׁמַיִם שָׁמַיִם לַיי
but the earth He gave over to man.	וְהָאָרֶץ נָתַן לִבְנֵי אָדָם.
17 The dead cannot praise *Adonai,*	לֹא הַמֵּתִים יְהַלְלוּ יָהּ
nor any who go down into silence.	וְלֹא כָּל יֹרְדֵי דוּמָה.
18 But we will bless *Adonai*	וַאֲנַחְנוּ נְבָרֵךְ יָהּ
now and forever.	מֵעַתָּה וְעַד עוֹלָם.
Hallelujah.	הַלְלוּיָהּ.

Psalm 116

I love *Adonai*	**אָהַבְתִּי** כִּי יִשְׁמַע יי
for He hears my voice, my pleas;	אֶת קוֹלִי, תַּחֲנוּנָי.
2 for He turns His ear to me	כִּי הִטָּה אָזְנוֹ לִי
whenever I call.	וּבְיָמַי אֶקְרָא.
3 The bonds of death encompassed me;	אֲפָפוּנִי חֶבְלֵי מָוֶת
the torments of Sheol overtook me.	וּמְצָרֵי שְׁאוֹל מְצָאוּנִי,
I came upon trouble and sorrow	צָרָה וְיָגוֹן אֶמְצָא.
4 and I invoked the name of *Adonai,*	וּבְשֵׁם יי אֶקְרָא:
"*Adonai,* save my life!"	אָנָּה יי מַלְּטָה נַפְשִׁי!
5 *Adonai* is gracious and beneficent;	חַנּוּן יי וְצַדִּיק,
our LORD is compassionate.	וֵאלֹהֵינוּ מְרַחֵם.
6 *Adonai* protects the simple;	שֹׁמֵר פְּתָאִים יי,
I was brought low and He saved me.	דַּלֹּתִי וְלִי יְהוֹשִׁיעַ.

7 Be at rest, once again,
O my soul, for *Adonai* has been good to you.
8 You have delivered me from death,
my eyes from tears,
my feet from stumbling.
9 I shall walk before *Adonai*
in the lands of the living.
10 I trust *in Adonai;*
out of great suffering I spoke
11 and said rashly,
"All men are false."
12 How can I repay *Adonai*
for all His bounties to me?
13 I raise the cup of deliverance
and invoke the name of *Adonai*.
14 I will pay my vows to *Adonai*
in the presence of all His people.
15 The death of His faithful ones
is grievous in *Adonai*'s sight.
16 *Adonai,*
I am Your servant,
Your servant, the son of Your maidservant;
You have undone the cords that bound me.
17 I will sacrifice a thank offering to You
and invoke the name of *Adonai*.
18 I will pay my vows to *Adonai*
in the presence of all His people,
19 in the courts of the house of *Adonai,*
in the midst of Jerusalem.
Hallelujah.

שׁוּבִי נַפְשִׁי לִמְנוּחָיְכִי,
כִּי יי גָּמַל עָלָיְכִי.
כִּי חִלַּצְתָּ נַפְשִׁי מִמָּוֶת,
אֶת עֵינִי מִן דִּמְעָה,
אֶת רַגְלִי מִדֶּחִי.
אֶתְהַלֵּךְ לִפְנֵי יי
בְּאַרְצוֹת הַחַיִּים.
הֶאֱמַנְתִּי כִּי אֲדַבֵּר,
אֲנִי עָנִיתִי מְאֹד.
אֲנִי אָמַרְתִּי בְחָפְזִי:
כָּל הָאָדָם כֹּזֵב.
מָה אָשִׁיב לַיי
כֹּל תַּגְמוּלוֹהִי עָלָי.
כּוֹס יְשׁוּעוֹת אֶשָּׂא
וּבְשֵׁם יי אֶקְרָא.
נְדָרַי לַיי אֲשַׁלֵּם
נֶגְדָה נָּא לְכָל עַמּוֹ.
יָקָר בְּעֵינֵי יי
הַמָּוְתָה לַחֲסִידָיו.
אָנָּא יי
כִּי אֲנִי עַבְדֶּךָ,
אֲנִי עַבְדְּךָ בֶּן אֲמָתֶךָ,
פִּתַּחְתָּ לְמוֹסֵרָי.
לְךָ אֶזְבַּח זֶבַח תּוֹדָה
וּבְשֵׁם יי אֶקְרָא.
נְדָרַי לַיי אֲשַׁלֵּם
נֶגְדָה נָּא לְכָל עַמּוֹ.
בְּחַצְרוֹת בֵּית יי,
בְּתוֹכֵכִי יְרוּשָׁלָיִם.
הַלְלוּיָהּ.

Psalm 117

Praise *Adonai,* all you nations;
extol Him, all you peoples,
2 for great is His steadfast love toward us;
the faithfulness of *Adonai* endures forever.
Hallelujah.

הַלְלוּ אֶת יי כָּל גּוֹיִם,
שַׁבְּחוּהוּ כָּל הָאֻמִּים.
כִּי גָבַר עָלֵינוּ חַסְדּוֹ,
וֶאֱמֶת יי לְעוֹלָם.
הַלְלוּיָהּ.

Psalm 118

Praise *Adonai,* for He is good,
His steadfast love is eternal.
2 Let Israel declare,
"His steadfast love is eternal."
3 Let the house of Aaron declare,
"His steadfast love is eternal."
4 Let those who fear *Adonai* declare,
"His steadfast love is eternal."
5 In distress I called on *Adonai;*
Adonai answered me and brought me relief.
6 *Adonai* is on my side,
I have no fear;
what can man do to me?
7 With *Adonai* on my side as my helper,
I will see the downfall of my foes.
8 It is better to take refuge in *Adonai*
than to trust in mortals;
9 it is better to take refuge in *Adonai*
than to trust in the great.
10 All nations have beset me;
by the name of *Adonai* I will surely cut them down.

הוֹדוּ לַיי כִּי טוֹב
כִּי לְעוֹלָם חַסְדּוֹ.
יֹאמַר נָא יִשְׂרָאֵל
כִּי לְעוֹלָם חַסְדּוֹ.
יֹאמְרוּ נָא בֵית אַהֲרֹן
כִּי לְעוֹלָם חַסְדּוֹ.
יֹאמְרוּ נָא יִרְאֵי יי
כִּי לְעוֹלָם חַסְדּוֹ.
מִן הַמֵּצַר קָרָאתִי יָּהּ,
עָנָנִי בַמֶּרְחָב יָהּ.
יי לִי,
לֹא אִירָא —
מַה יַּעֲשֶׂה לִי אָדָם?
יי לִי בְּעֹזְרָי
וַאֲנִי אֶרְאֶה בְשֹׂנְאָי.
טוֹב לַחֲסוֹת בַּיי
מִבְּטֹחַ בָּאָדָם.
טוֹב לַחֲסוֹת בַּיי
מִבְּטֹחַ בִּנְדִיבִים.
כָּל גּוֹיִם סְבָבוּנִי,
בְּשֵׁם יי כִּי אֲמִילַם.

11 They beset me, they surround me;
by the name of *Adonai* I will surely cut them down.
12 They have beset me like bees;
they shall be extinguished like burning thorns;
by the name of *Adonai* I will surely cut them down.
13 You pressed me hard,
I nearly fell;
but *Adonai* helped me.
14 *Adonai* is my strength and might;
He has become my deliverance.
15 The tents of the victorious resound with joyous
shouts of deliverance,
"The right hand of *Adonai* is triumphant!
16 The right hand of *Adonai* is exalted!
The right hand of *Adonai* is triumphant!"
17 I shall not die but live
and proclaim the works of *Adonai*.
18 *Adonai* punished me severely,
but did not hand me over to death.
19 Open the gates of victory for me
that I may enter them and praise *Adonai*.
20 This is the gateway to *Adonai*—
the victorious shall enter through it.
21 I praise You, for You have answered me,
and have become my deliverance.
22 The stone that the builders rejected
has become the chief cornerstone.
23 This is *Adonai*'s doing;
it is marvelous in our sight.

סַבּוּנִי גַם סְבָבוּנִי,
בְּשֵׁם יי כִּי אֲמִילַם.
סַבּוּנִי כִדְבוֹרִים,
דֹּעֲכוּ כְּאֵשׁ קוֹצִים,
בְּשֵׁם יי כִּי אֲמִילַם.
דָּחֹה דְחִיתַנִי
לִנְפֹּל,
וַיי עֲזָרָנִי.
עָזִּי וְזִמְרָת יָהּ
וַיְהִי לִי לִישׁוּעָה.
קוֹל רִנָּה וִישׁוּעָה בְּאָהֳלֵי
צַדִּיקִים:
יְמִין יי עֹשָׂה חָיִל,
יְמִין יי רוֹמֵמָה,
יְמִין יי עֹשָׂה חָיִל.
לֹא אָמוּת כִּי אֶחְיֶה,
וַאֲסַפֵּר מַעֲשֵׂי יָהּ.
יַסֹּר יִסְּרַנִּי יָּהּ,
וְלַמָּוֶת לֹא נְתָנָנִי.
פִּתְחוּ לִי שַׁעֲרֵי צֶדֶק,
אָבֹא בָם, אוֹדֶה יָהּ.
זֶה הַשַּׁעַר לַיי,
צַדִּיקִים יָבֹאוּ בוֹ.
אוֹדְךָ כִּי עֲנִיתָנִי
וַתְּהִי לִי לִישׁוּעָה.
אֶבֶן מָאֲסוּ הַבּוֹנִים
הָיְתָה לְרֹאשׁ פִּנָּה.
מֵאֵת יי הָיְתָה זֹּאת
הִיא נִפְלָאת בְּעֵינֵינוּ.

24 This is the day that *Adonai* has made—
let us exult and rejoice on it.
25 *Adonai,* deliver us!
Adonai, let us prosper!
26 May he who enters be blessed in the name of *Adonai;*
we bless You from the House of *Adonai*.
27 *Adonai* is the LORD
He has given us light;
bind the festal offering to the horns of the altar
with cords.
28 You are my LORD and I will praise You;
You are my LORD and I will extol You.
29 Praise *Adonai* for He is good,
His steadfast love is eternal.

זֶה הַיּוֹם עָשָׂה יי
נָגִילָה וְנִשְׂמְחָה בוֹ.
אָנָּא יי, הוֹשִׁיעָה נָּא.
אָנָּא יי, הַצְלִיחָה נָּא.
בָּרוּךְ הַבָּא בְּשֵׁם יי,
בֵּרַכְנוּכֶם מִבֵּית יי.
אֵל יי
וַיָּאֶר לָנוּ,
אִסְרוּ חַג בַּעֲבֹתִים עַד קַרְנוֹת
הַמִּזְבֵּחַ.
אֵלִי אַתָּה וְאוֹדֶךָּ,
אֱלֹהַי – אֲרוֹמְמֶךָּ.
הוֹדוּ לַיי כִּי טוֹב,
כִּי לְעוֹלָם חַסְדּוֹ.

The following is the beginning of the blessing that is said after Hallel. *Some people skip it here and recite it below (there is an appropriate note below). For the history of this custom, see pp. 56–59.*

All your creations will praise You, *Adonai* our LORD, and Your pious ones, righteous ones who do Your will, and all Your people, the house of Israel, with song will praise and bless, sanctify and enthrone Your name, our King, for it is good to praise You and it is fit to sing to Your name, for You are the LORD forever and ever.

יְהַלְלוּךָ יי אֱלֹהֵינוּ כָּל מַעֲשֶׂיךָ, וַחֲסִידֶיךָ צַדִּיקִים עוֹשֵׂי רְצוֹנֶךָ, וְכָל עַמְּךָ בֵּית יִשְׂרָאֵל בְּרִנָּה יוֹדוּ וִיבָרְכוּ, וִישַׁבְּחוּ וִיפָאֲרוּ, וִירוֹמְמוּ וְיַעֲרִיצוּ, וְיַקְדִּישׁוּ וְיַמְלִיכוּ אֶת שִׁמְךָ, מַלְכֵּנוּ. כִּי לְךָ טוֹב לְהוֹדוֹת וּלְשִׁמְךָ נָאֶה לְזַמֵּר, כִּי מֵעוֹלָם וְעַד עוֹלָם אַתָּה אֵל.

Psalm 136

1 **P**raise *Adonai;* for He is good,
His steadfast love is eternal.
2 Praise the LORD of lords,
His steadfast love is eternal.
3 Praise the Master of masters,
His steadfast love is eternal;
4 Who alone works great marvels,
His steadfast love is eternal;
5 Who made the heavens with wisdom,
His steadfast love is eternal;
6 Who spread the earth over the water,
His steadfast love is eternal;
7 Who made the great lights,
His steadfast love is eternal;
8 the sun to dominate the day,
His steadfast love is eternal;
9 the moon and the stars to
dominate the night,
His steadfast love is eternal;
10 Who struck Egypt through their first-born,
His steadfast love is eternal;
11 and brought Israel out of their midst,
His steadfast love is eternal;
12 with a strong hand and outstretched arm,
His steadfast love is eternal;
13 Who split apart the Sea of Reeds,
His steadfast love is eternal;
14 and made Israel pass through it,
His steadfast love is eternal;
15 Who hurled Pharaoh and his army into
the Sea of Reeds,
His steadfast love is eternal;

הודו לַיי כִּי טוֹב
כִּי לְעוֹלָם חַסְדּוֹ.
הודוּ לֵאלֹהֵי הָאֱלֹהִים
כִּי לְעוֹלָם חַסְדּוֹ.
הודוּ לַאֲדֹנֵי הָאֲדֹנִים
כִּי לְעוֹלָם חַסְדּוֹ.
לְעֹשֵׂה נִפְלָאוֹת גְּדֹלוֹת לְבַדּוֹ
כִּי לְעוֹלָם חַסְדּוֹ.
לְעֹשֵׂה הַשָּׁמַיִם בִּתְבוּנָה
כִּי לְעוֹלָם חַסְדּוֹ.
לְרוֹקַע הָאָרֶץ עַל הַמָּיִם
כִּי לְעוֹלָם חַסְדּוֹ.
לְעֹשֵׂה אוֹרִים גְּדֹלִים
כִּי לְעוֹלָם חַסְדּוֹ.
אֶת הַשֶּׁמֶשׁ לְמֶמְשֶׁלֶת בַּיּוֹם
כִּי לְעוֹלָם חַסְדּוֹ.
אֶת הַיָּרֵחַ וְכוֹכָבִים
לְמֶמְשְׁלוֹת בַּלָּיְלָה
כִּי לְעוֹלָם חַסְדּוֹ.
לְמַכֵּה מִצְרַיִם בִּבְכוֹרֵיהֶם
כִּי לְעוֹלָם חַסְדּוֹ.
וַיּוֹצֵא יִשְׂרָאֵל מִתּוֹכָם
כִּי לְעוֹלָם חַסְדּוֹ.
בְּיָד חֲזָקָה וּבִזְרוֹעַ נְטוּיָה
כִּי לְעוֹלָם חַסְדּוֹ.
לְגֹזֵר יַם סוּף לִגְזָרִים
כִּי לְעוֹלָם חַסְדּוֹ.
וְהֶעֱבִיר יִשְׂרָאֵל בְּתוֹכוֹ
כִּי לְעוֹלָם חַסְדּוֹ.
וְנִעֵר פַּרְעֹה וְחֵילוֹ
בְיַם סוּף
כִּי לְעוֹלָם חַסְדּוֹ.

16 Who led His people through the wilderness,	לְמוֹלִיךְ עַמּוֹ בַּמִּדְבָּר
His steadfast love is eternal;	כִּי לְעוֹלָם חַסְדּוֹ.
17 Who struck down great kings,	לְמַכֵּה מְלָכִים גְּדֹלִים
His steadfast love is eternal;	כִּי לְעוֹלָם חַסְדּוֹ.
18 and slew mighty kings,	וַיַּהֲרֹג מְלָכִים אַדִּירִים
His steadfast love is eternal;	כִּי לְעוֹלָם חַסְדּוֹ.
19 Sihon, king of the Amorites,	לְסִיחוֹן מֶלֶךְ הָאֱמֹרִי
His steadfast love is eternal;	כִּי לְעוֹלָם חַסְדּוֹ.
20 Og, king of Bashan,	וּלְעוֹג מֶלֶךְ הַבָּשָׁן
His steadfast love is eternal;	כִּי לְעוֹלָם חַסְדּוֹ.
21 and gave their land as a heritage,	וְנָתַן אַרְצָם לְנַחֲלָה
His steadfast love is eternal;	כִּי לְעוֹלָם חַסְדּוֹ.
22 a heritage to His servant Israel,	נַחֲלָה לְיִשְׂרָאֵל עַבְדּוֹ
His steadfast love is eternal;	כִּי לְעוֹלָם חַסְדּוֹ.
23 Who took note of us in our degradation,	שֶׁבְּשִׁפְלֵנוּ זָכַר לָנוּ
His steadfast love is eternal;	כִּי לְעוֹלָם חַסְדּוֹ.
24 and rescued us from our enemies,	וַיִּפְרְקֵנוּ מִצָּרֵינוּ
His steadfast love is eternal;	כִּי לְעוֹלָם חַסְדּוֹ.
25 Who gives food to all flesh,	נֹתֵן לֶחֶם לְכָל בָּשָׂר
His steadfast love is eternal.	כִּי לְעוֹלָם חַסְדּוֹ.
26 Praise the LORD of heaven,	הוֹדוּ לְאֵל הַשָּׁמָיִם
His steadfast love is eternal.	כִּי לְעוֹלָם חַסְדּוֹ.

The soul of every living thing will bless Your name, *Adonai* our LORD, and the spirit of all flesh will glorify your fame, our King, constantly, eternally, You are the LORD and other than You we have no king, redeemer, and savior, supporter and compassionate in all times of trouble and distress. LORD of the first and the last, LORD of all creatures, LORD of all history, praised with a multitude of praises, who conducts His world with mercy and His creatures with compassion. And *Adonai* will neither

נִשְׁמַת כָּל חַי תְּבָרֵךְ אֶת שִׁמְךָ, יי אֱלֹהֵינוּ, וְרוּחַ כָּל בָּשָׂר תְּפָאֵר וּתְרוֹמֵם זִכְרְךָ, מַלְכֵּנוּ, תָּמִיד, מִן הָעוֹלָם וְעַד הָעוֹלָם אַתָּה אֵל, וּמִבַּלְעָדֶיךָ אֵין לָנוּ מֶלֶךְ גּוֹאֵל וּמוֹשִׁיעַ, פּוֹדֶה וּמַצִּיל וּמְפַרְנֵס וּמְרַחֵם בְּכָל עֵת צָרָה וְצוּקָה. אֵין לָנוּ מֶלֶךְ אֶלָּא אָתָּה. אֱלֹהֵי הָרִאשׁוֹנִים וְהָאַחֲרוֹנִים, אֱלוֹהַּ כָּל בְּרִיּוֹת, אֲדוֹן כָּל תּוֹלָדוֹת, הַמְּהֻלָּל בְּרֹב הַתִּשְׁבָּחוֹת, הַמְנַהֵג עוֹלָמוֹ בְּחֶסֶד וּבְרִיּוֹתָיו

sleep nor slumber—He who awakes sleepers and arouses slumberers, who gives speech to the dumb and frees the fettered and braces the fallen and supports the bowed. To You only we give thanks. If our mouths were full of song as the sea, and our tongues—music as the multitude of the waves, and our lips—praise as the expanse of the firmament, our eyes shining like the sun and the moon, our hands outstretched like those of the eagles of the heaven, our legs nimble as antelope, we would not be capable of thanking You, *Adonai,* our LORD and the LORD of our fathers, or to bless Your name for one thousandth, one hundred thousandth, of all the good that that You did for our ancestors and for us. You redeemed us from Egypt, *Adonai* our LORD, and You saved us from the house of slavery, You nourished us in times of famine, and You supported us in times of prosperity, You saved us from the sword and You rescued us from plague and You delivered us from all real evil diseases. Until now, Your compassion has succored us and Your mercy has not abandoned us and do not abandon us, *Adonai* our LORD—ever. Therefore, all the limbs that You have created in our body, the spirit and the soul that You have breathed into us, and the tongue that You have put in our mouth—they will praise, bless, laud and extol, exalt and adore, sanctify and enthrone Your name, our King. For every mouth will thank You, and every tongue will swear by You, every knee will kneel to You, and all our internal organs will sing praise of Your name, as it is written: "All my bones shall say, '*Adonai,* who is like You? You save the poor from one stronger than he, the poor and needy from his despoiler'" (Ps. 35:10). Who can compare to You, who can equal You, who

בְּרַחֲמִים. וַיי לֹא יָנוּם וְלֹא יִישָׁן – הַמְעוֹרֵר יְשֵׁנִים וְהַמֵּקִיץ נִרְדָּמִים, וְהַמֵּשִׂיחַ אִלְּמִים וְהַמַּתִּיר אֲסוּרִים וְהַסּוֹמֵךְ נוֹפְלִים וְהַזּוֹקֵף כְּפוּפִים. לְךָ לְבַדְּךָ אֲנַחְנוּ מוֹדִים. אִלּוּ פִינוּ מָלֵא שִׁירָה כַּיָּם, וּלְשׁוֹנֵנוּ רִנָּה כַּהֲמוֹן גַּלָּיו, וְשִׂפְתוֹתֵינוּ שֶׁבַח כְּמֶרְחֲבֵי רָקִיעַ, וְעֵינֵינוּ מְאִירוֹת כַּשֶּׁמֶשׁ וְכַיָּרֵחַ, וְיָדֵינוּ פְרוּשׂוֹת כְּנִשְׁרֵי שָׁמָיִם, וְרַגְלֵינוּ קַלּוֹת כָּאַיָּלוֹת – אֵין אֲנַחְנוּ מַסְפִּיקִים לְהוֹדוֹת לְךָ, יי אֱלֹהֵינוּ וֵאלֹהֵי אֲבוֹתֵינוּ, וּלְבָרֵךְ אֶת שְׁמֶךָ עַל אַחַת, מֵאָלֶף אֶלֶף אַלְפֵי אֲלָפִים וְרִבֵּי רְבָבוֹת פְּעָמִים, הַטּוֹבוֹת שֶׁעָשִׂיתָ עִם אֲבוֹתֵינוּ וְעִמָּנוּ. מִמִּצְרַיִם גְּאַלְתָּנוּ, יי אֱלֹהֵינוּ, וּמִבֵּית עֲבָדִים פְּדִיתָנוּ, בְּרָעָב זַנְתָּנוּ וּבְשָׂבָע כִּלְכַּלְתָּנוּ, מֵחֶרֶב הִצַּלְתָּנוּ וּמִדֶּבֶר מִלַּטְתָּנוּ, וּמֵחֳלָיִם רָעִים וְנֶאֱמָנִים דִּלִּיתָנוּ. עַד הֵנָּה עֲזָרוּנוּ רַחֲמֶיךָ וְלֹא עֲזָבוּנוּ חֲסָדֶיךָ, וְאַל תִּטְּשֵׁנוּ, יי אֱלֹהֵינוּ, לָנֶצַח. עַל כֵּן אֵבָרִים שֶׁפִּלַּגְתָּ בָּנוּ וְרוּחַ וּנְשָׁמָה שֶׁנָּפַחְתָּ בְּאַפֵּינוּ וְלָשׁוֹן אֲשֶׁר שַׂמְתָּ בְּפִינוּ – הֵן הֵם יוֹדוּ וִיבָרְכוּ וִישַׁבְּחוּ וִיפָאֲרוּ וִירוֹמְמוּ וְיַעֲרִיצוּ וְיַקְדִּישׁוּ וְיַמְלִיכוּ אֶת שִׁמְךָ מַלְכֵּנוּ. כִּי כָל פֶּה לְךָ יוֹדֶה, וְכָל לָשׁוֹן לְךָ תִשָּׁבַע, וְכָל בֶּרֶךְ לְךָ תִכְרַע, וְכָל קוֹמָה לְפָנֶיךָ תִשְׁתַּחֲוֶה, וְכָל לְבָבוֹת יִירָאוּךָ, וְכָל קֶרֶב וּכְלָיוֹת יְזַמְּרוּ לִשְׁמֶךָ, כַּדָּבָר שֶׁכָּתוּב, כָּל עַצְמֹתַי תֹּאמַרְנָה: יי, מִי כָמוֹךָ! מַצִּיל עָנִי מֵחָזָק מִמֶּנּוּ וְעָנִי וְאֶבְיוֹן מִגֹּזְלוֹ. מִי יִדְמֶה לָּךְ וּמִי

can match You, the LORD, great, mighty, and awesome, supreme LORD, Creator of heaven and earth. We shall praise You, we shall extol You, we shall glorify You, and we shall bless the name of Your holiness, as it is said: "Of David. Bless *Adonai,* O my soul, all my being, His holy name" (Ps. 103:1). "The LORD"—in the might of Your power; "great"—in the glory of Your name; "mighty"—forever; "and awesome"—in Your awe-inspiring acts; the King who sits on a high and exalted throne. He who high aloft forever dwells, whose name is holy (cf. Isa. 57:15). And it says: "Sing forth, O you righteous, to *Adonai,* it is fit that the upright acclaim Him" (Ps. 33:1).

יִשְׁוֶה לָּךְ וּמִי יַעֲרָךְ לָךְ הָאֵל הַגָּדוֹל, הַגִּבּוֹר וְהַנּוֹרָא, אֵל עֶלְיוֹן, קֹנֵה שָׁמַיִם וָאָרֶץ. נְהַלֶּלְךָ וּנְשַׁבֵּחֲךָ וּנְפָאֶרְךָ וּנְבָרֵךְ אֶת שֵׁם קָדְשֶׁךָ, כָּאָמוּר: לְדָוִד, בָּרְכִי נַפְשִׁי אֶת יי וְכָל קְרָבַי אֶת שֵׁם קָדְשׁוֹ. הָאֵל בְּתַעֲצֻמוֹת עֻזֶּךָ, הַגָּדוֹל בִּכְבוֹד שְׁמֶךָ, הַגִּבּוֹר לָנֶצַח וְהַנּוֹרָא בְּנוֹרְאוֹתֶיךָ, הַמֶּלֶךְ הַיּוֹשֵׁב עַל כִּסֵּא רָם וְנִשָּׂא, שׁוֹכֵן עַד מָרוֹם וְקָדוֹשׁ שְׁמוֹ. וְכָתוּב: רַנְּנוּ צַדִּיקִים בַּיי, לַיְשָׁרִים נָאוָה תְהִלָּה.

In the mouths of the upright
You shall be praised;
In the words of the righteous
You shall be blessed;
In the tongue of the pious
You shall be exalted;
Among the holy
You shall be sanctified.

בְּפִי יְשָׁרִים תִּתְהַלָּל,
וּבְדִבְרֵי צַדִּיקִים תִּתְבָּרַךְ,
וּבִלְשׁוֹן חֲסִידִים תִּתְרוֹמָם,
וּבְקֶרֶב קְדוֹשִׁים תִּתְקַדָּשׁ.

In the choirs of the myriads of Your people, the house of Israel, Your name will be glorified in song, our King, in every generation. For it is the obligtion of all creatures to thank, to acclaim, to praise, to laud, to exalt, to extol, to bless, to applaud, to eulogize beyond all the songs and praises of David son of Jesse, Your servant, Your anointed.

וּבְמַקְהֲלוֹת רִבְבוֹת עַמְּךָ בֵּית יִשְׂרָאֵל בְּרִנָּה יִתְפָּאַר שִׁמְךָ, מַלְכֵּנוּ, בְּכָל דּוֹר וָדוֹר, שֶׁכֵּן חוֹבַת כָּל הַיְצוּרִים לְפָנֶיךָ, יי אֱלֹהֵינוּ וֵאלֹהֵי אֲבוֹתֵינוּ, לְהוֹדוֹת לְהַלֵּל לְשַׁבֵּחַ, לְפָאֵר לְרוֹמֵם לְהַדֵּר לְבָרֵךְ, לְעַלֵּה וּלְקַלֵּס עַל כָּל דִּבְרֵי שִׁירוֹת וְתִשְׁבְּחוֹת דָּוִד בֶּן יִשַׁי עַבְדְּךָ, מְשִׁיחֶךָ.

May Your name be praised forever, our King, the LORD, the great and holy King in heaven and earth because for You are all appropriate, our LORD and the LORD of our ancestors, song and praise, psalm and melody, might and government, eternity, greatness, and power, fame and glory,

יִשְׁתַּבַּח שִׁמְךָ לָעַד מַלְכֵּנוּ, הָאֵל הַמֶּלֶךְ הַגָּדוֹל וְהַקָּדוֹשׁ בַּשָּׁמַיִם וּבָאָרֶץ, כִּי לְךָ נָאֶה, יי אֱלֹהֵינוּ וֵאלֹהֵי אֲבוֹתֵינוּ, שִׁיר וּשְׁבָחָה, הַלֵּל וְזִמְרָה, עֹז וּמֶמְשָׁלָה, נֶצַח, גְּדֻלָּה וּגְבוּרָה, תְּהִלָּה וְתִפְאֶרֶת, קְדֻשָּׁה וּמַלְכוּת,

holiness and kingdom, blessings and thanks for ever and ever. Blessed art Thou, *Adonai,* Lord King great in praise, Lord of thanks, Master of wonders, who chooses melodious song, king Lord, life of the universe.

בְּרָכוֹת וְהוֹדָאוֹת מֵעַתָּה וְעַד עוֹלָם. בָּרוּךְ אַתָּה יי, אֵל מֶלֶךְ גָּדוֹל בַּתִּשְׁבָּחוֹת, אֵל הַהוֹדָאוֹת, אֲדוֹן הַנִּפְלָאוֹת, הַבּוֹחֵר בְּשִׁירֵי זִמְרָה, מֶלֶךְ אֵל חֵי הָעוֹלָמִים.

Blessed art Thou, *Adonai* our Lord, King of the universe, creator of the fruit of the vine.

בָּרוּךְ אַתָּה יי אֱלֹהֵינוּ מֶלֶךְ הָעוֹלָם בּוֹרֵא פְּרִי הַגָּפֶן.

One drinks the wine while reclining on the left side. After drinking, one recites the following blessing: grace after partaking of one of the seven varieties of grains and fruits that are the pride of the Land of Israel.

Blessed art Thou, *Adonai* our Lord, King of the universe, for the vine and the fruit of the vine, for the produce of the field and for the lovely, good, and spacious land that You have desired and granted to our ancestors, to eat of its fruits and to be satisfied through its bounty. Please have mercy, *Adonai* our Lord, on Your people Israel, on Your city, Jerusalem, on Zion the abode of Your glory, on Your altar and Your palaces, and build Jerusalem, the Holy City, speedily in our days, and bring us there and make us rejoice in its building and we shall eat of its fruit and be satisfied with its bounty and we shall bless You for it in sanctity and purity, and make us rejoice on the day of the matzah festival for You are *Adonai,* good and beneficial to all, and we shall thank you for the land and the fruits of the vine. Blessed art Thou, *Adonai,* for the vine and the fruit of the vine.

בָּרוּךְ אַתָּה יי אֱלֹהֵינוּ מֶלֶךְ הָעוֹלָם, עַל הַגֶּפֶן וְעַל פְּרִי הַגֶּפֶן, עַל תְּנוּבַת הַשָּׂדֶה וְעַל אֶרֶץ חֶמְדָּה טוֹבָה וּרְחָבָה שֶׁרָצִיתָ וְהִנְחַלְתָּ לַאֲבוֹתֵינוּ לֶאֱכֹל מִפִּרְיָהּ וְלִשְׂבֹּעַ מִטּוּבָהּ. רַחֵם נָא יי אֱלֹהֵינוּ עַל יִשְׂרָאֵל עַמֶּךָ וְעַל יְרוּשָׁלַיִם עִירֶךָ וְעַל צִיּוֹן מִשְׁכַּן כְּבוֹדֶךָ וְעַל מִזְבְּחֶךָ וְעַל הֵיכָלֶךָ וּבְנֵה יְרוּשָׁלַיִם עִיר הַקֹּדֶשׁ בִּמְהֵרָה בְיָמֵינוּ וְהַעֲלֵנוּ לְתוֹכָהּ וְשַׂמְּחֵנוּ בְּבִנְיָנָהּ וְנֹאכַל מִפִּרְיָהּ וְנִשְׂבַּע מִטּוּבָהּ וּנְבָרֶכְךָ עָלֶיהָ בִּקְדֻשָּׁה וּבְטָהֳרָה (וּרְצֵה וְהַחֲלִיצֵנוּ בְּיוֹם הַשַּׁבָּת הַזֶּה) וְשַׂמְּחֵנוּ בְּיוֹם חַג הַמַּצּוֹת הַזֶּה, כִּי אַתָּה יי טוֹב וּמֵטִיב לַכֹּל וְנוֹדֶה לְּךָ עַל הָאָרֶץ וְעַל פְּרִי הַגָּפֶן. בָּרוּךְ אַתָּה יי עַל הָאָרֶץ וְעַל פְּרִי הַגָּפֶן.

נִרְצָה

The completion of the ritual is marked by our confidence that God accepts our worship of Him.

[30]The order of the *Pesach* ritual
has been completed according to law,
in accordance with all its rules
and regulations.
As we have been privileged to
arrange it, so may we be privileged
to perform it.
Pure One, who dwells on high,
[31]restore the community that
cannot be counted.
Soon, [32]lead the planted stock,
redeemed, to Zion with song.
[33]Next year in (rebuilt) Jerusalem.

[30]**חֲסַל** סִדּוּר פֶּסַח כְּהִלְכָתוֹ,
כְּכָל מִשְׁפָּטוֹ וְחֻקָּתוֹ.
כַּאֲשֶׁר זָכִינוּ לְסַדֵּר אוֹתוֹ,
כֵּן נִזְכֶּה לַעֲשׂוֹתוֹ.
זָךְ שׁוֹכֵן מְעוֹנָה,
[31]קוֹמֵם קְהַל עֲדַת מִי מָנָה.
[32]בְּקָרוֹב נַהֵל נִטְעֵי כַנָּה,
פְּדוּיִם לְצִיּוֹן בְּרִנָּה.
[33]לְשָׁנָה הַבָּאָה בִּירוּשָׁלַיִם (הַבְּנוּיָה).

[34]**And so, "it was in the middle of the night"** (Exod. 12:29)
Then You performed many miracles at **night**
At the beginning of the watch of the **night**
[35]A righteous convert You caused to be victorious at the division of the **night**
"it was in the middle of the night" (Exod. 12:29).

[34]**וּבְכֵן וַיְהִי בַּחֲצִי הַלַּיְלָה**
אָז רוֹב נִסִּים הִפְלֵאתָ **בַּלַּיְלָה**,
בְּרֹאשׁ אַשְׁמוֹרֶת זֶה **הַלַּיְלָה**,
[35]גֵּר צֶדֶק נִצַּחְתּוֹ כְּנֶחֱלַק לוֹ **לַיְלָה**,
וַיְהִי בַּחֲצִי הַלַּיְלָה.

30 **The order of the *Pesach* ritual has been completed** See pp. 60–61.
31 **restore the community that cannot be counted** This is a reference to Numbers 23:10 where Bilam said, "Who can count. . . ."
32 **lead the planted stock** This is a reference to Psalms 80:16.
33 **Next year in (rebuilt) Jerusalem** See p. 60.
34 **And so, it was in the middle of the night** This poem was written by Yannai as part of an extensive liturgical composition for *Shabbat,* on which the Torah reading began with Exodus 12:29: "In the middle of the night" (Exod. 12:29). See p. 61.
35 **A righteous convert** This refers to the battle of Abraham against the five kings, with special reference to Genesis 14:15.

[36]You judged the king of Gerar in a dream at **night**
[37]You frightened the Aramean at **night**
[38]Israel struggled with the angel and he defeated him at **night**
"it was in the middle of the night" (Exod. 12:29).

[36]דַּנְתָּ מֶלֶךְ גְּרָר בַּחֲלוֹם **הַלַּיְלָה**,
[37]הִפְחַדְתָּ אֲרַמִּי בְּאֶמֶשׁ **לַיְלָה**,
[38]וַיָּשַׂר יִשְׂרָאֵל לְמַלְאָךְ וַיּוּכַל לוֹ **בַּלַּיְלָה**,
וַיְהִי בַּחֲצִי הַלַּיְלָה.

[39]The seed of the first-born of Pathros you crushed at **midnight**
They did not find their forces when they rose in the **night**
[40]The flight of the prince of Haroshet You crushed with the stars of the **night**
"it was in the middle of the night" (Exod. 12:29).

[39]זֶרַע בְּכוֹרֵי פַתְרוֹס מָחַצְתָּ בַּחֲצִי **הַלַּיְלָה**,
חֵילָם לֹא מָצְאוּ בְּקוּמָם **בַּלַּיְלָה**,
[40]טִיסַת נְגִיד חֲרֹשֶׁת סִלִּיתָ בְּכוֹכְבֵי **לַיְלָה**,
וַיְהִי בַּחֲצִי הַלַּיְלָה.

[41]The blasphemer threatened to stretch his hand over the desired place [Jerusalem], and You dried his corpses at **night**
[42]Bel and his base collapsed at **night**

[41]יָעַץ מְחָרֵף לְנוֹפֵף יָד לְאִוּוּי, והוֹבַשְׁתָּ פְּגָרָיו **בַּלַּיְלָה**,
[42]כָּרַע בֵּל וּמַצָּבוֹ בְּאִישׁוֹן **לַיְלָה**,

36 **You judged the king of Gerar** Avimelech was warned in a dream to return Sarah to Abraham (Gen. 20:6).

37 **You frightened the Aramean** Laban was warned in a dream not to harm Jacob (Gen. 31:24).

38 **Israel struggled with the angel** Genesis 32:26–30.

39 **The seed of the first-born of Pathros** Ezekiel 29:14 refers to Pathros as the homeland of the Egyptians.

40 **The flight of the prince of Haroshet** Sisera's base was *Harosheth-goyim* (Judg. 4:2). The stars in their paths fought against Sisera (Judg. 5:20). The *paytan* (liturgical poet) uses the Hebrew word "paths" (*bimsilotam*) as if it were derived from the root "*s-l-h,*" which means "to treat as worthless, to destroy" (cf. Ps. 119:118; Lam. 1:15).

41 **The blasphemer threatened to stretch his hand** Rabshakeh, the general of Sennacherib, was sent by his master to blaspheme the living God (2 Kings 19:4) by threatening the destruction of Jerusalem. His forces were devastated at night (2 Kings 19:35).

42 **Bel and his base collapsed at night** This is a reference to the apocryphal story of Bel, together with the story of Daniel and the Dragon, which appear in the Septuagint as an appendix to the book of Daniel. The gist of the story is that Daniel sets a trap by which he proves that what are thought to be the actions of Bel are really the nocturnal activities of the priests.

43 לְאִישׁ חֲמוּדוֹת נִגְלָה רָז חֲזוֹת **לַיְלָה,**
וַיְהִי בַּחֲצִי הַלַּיְלָה.

43 To the beloved man was revealed the secret of the vision at **night**
"it was in the middle of the night" (Exod. 12:29).

44 מִשְׁתַּכֵּר בִּכְלֵי קֹדֶשׁ נֶהֱרַג בּוֹ **בַּלַּיְלָה,**
45 נוֹשַׁע מִבּוֹר אֲרָיוֹת פּוֹתֵר בִּעֲתוּתֵי **לַיְלָה,**
46 שִׂנְאָה נָטַר אֲגָגִי וְכָתַב סְפָרִים **בַּלַּיְלָה,**
וַיְהִי בַּחֲצִי הַלַּיְלָה.

44 The one who got drunk from the holy vessels was killed at **night**
45 The one who was saved from the lion's den solves the frights of **night**
46 Agagi bided his hate and wrote letters at **night**
"it was in the middle of the night" (Exod. 12:29).

עוֹרַרְתָּ נִצְחֲךָ עָלָיו בְּנֶדֶד שְׁנַת **לַיְלָה,**
47 פּוּרָה תִדְרוֹךְ לְשׁוֹמֵר מַה **מִּלַּיְלָה,**
צָרַח כַּשּׁוֹמֵר וְשָׂח אָתָא בֹקֶר וְגַם **לַיְלָה,**
וַיְהִי בַּחֲצִי הַלַּיְלָה.

You aroused Your victory over him by disturbing the sleep of the **night**
47 You will trod the vintage for the watchman who calls, "What of the **night**?"
He called like the watchman and said, "Day has come and also **night**"
"it was in the middle of the night" (Exod. 12:29).

43 **To the beloved man was revealed the secret of the vision** This line and the first two lines of the next stanza refer to events in the masoretic text of Daniel. Daniel, the beloved man (Dan. 9:23, 10:11), was granted the secret of Nebuchadnezzar's dream in his own nightly vision (Dan. 2:19).

44 **The one who got drunk from the holy vessels was killed** Belshazzar drank from the vessels of the Jerusalem Temple and was killed that same night (Dan. 5).

45 **The one who was saved from the lion's den** This line refers to Daniel's interpretation of Nebuchadnezzar's dream. However, Nebuchadnezzar had two dreams (Dan. 2:1, 4:2). The first one agitated his spirit, whereas the second one frightened him. The language of the *paytan* seems to show that the *paytan* was thinking of the second one, but this is not conclusive. If this is true, it seems that this interpretation is the same event referred to three lines above. According to some versions, which read "dreams" instead of "frights," Daniel's interpretation could refer to the first dream. In any case, this event took place before the death of Belshazzar mentioned in the line above, and it is not clear why the *paytan* did not follow his usual chronological order.

46 **Agagi bided his hate** This line and the first line of the next stanza refer to the events in the Scroll of Esther. Haman, the Agagite, sent his letters by night and the insomnia of Ahasuerus is considered by many as the turning point of the story, the sign of God's intervention. The sages disagreed whether the sleep of Ahasuerus was disturbed on the first or on the second night of Passover (see Ginzberg, *Legends of the Jews,* CD-ROM ed.).

47 **You will trod the vintage for the watchman** This is a reference to Isaiah 21:11.

The day is coming that will be neither day nor **night**
O High One, announce it for day is Yours and also **night**
Appoint watchmen over Your city all day and all **night**
Light as the light of the day the darkness of the **night**
"it was in the middle of the night" (Exod. 12:29).

קָרֵב יוֹם אֲשֶׁר הוּא לֹא יוֹם וְלֹא **לַיְלָה**,
רָם הוֹדַע כִּי לְךָ הַיּוֹם אַף לְךָ **הַלַּיְלָה**,
שׁוֹמְרִים הַפְקֵד לְעִירְךָ כָּל הַיּוֹם
וְכָל **הַלַּיְלָה**,
תָּאִיר כְּאוֹר יוֹם חֶשְׁכַת **לַיְלָה**,
וַיְהִי בַּחֲצִי הַלַּיְלָה.

And so, [48]"You shall say, 'It is the passover sacrifice'" (Exod. 12:27)
[49]You wondrously showed Your might on **Passover**
[50]First of all festivals You celebrated the **Passover**
[51]You disclosed to the one from the Orient at midnight on **Passover**
You shall say, "It is the passover sacrifice" (Exod. 12:27).

[48]**וּבְכֵן וַאֲמַרְתֶּם זֶבַח פֶּסַח**

[49]אֹמֶץ גְּבוּרוֹתֶיךָ הִפְלֵאתָ **בַּפֶּסַח**,
[50]בְּרֹאשׁ כָּל מוֹעֲדוֹת נִשֵּׂאתָ **פֶּסַח**,
[51]גִּלִּיתָ לְאֶזְרָחִי חֲצוֹת לֵיל **פֶּסַח**,
וַאֲמַרְתֶּם זֶבַח פֶּסַח.

48 **"You shall say, 'It is the passover sacrifice'"** This poem was written by Eleazar Kallir as part of an extensive liturgical composition for the first day of Passover on which, according to mishnaic tradition, the Torah reading began with the verse, "When an ox or a sheep or a goat is born . . ." (Lev. 22:27). See pp. 61–62.

49 **You wondrously showed your might on Passover** This begins a list of events that occurred on Passover.

50 **First of all festivals** Passover was celebrated on the night of the Exodus, becoming the first festival of the Jewish people. It is also the first festival mentioned in the biblical lists of festivals (Num. 29).

51 **You disclosed to the one from the Orient** Usually, the word "*ezrach*" in the Bible is translated as "citizen" or "born in the land." However, the sages identified Eitan ha-Ezrachi, the composer of Psalm 89, with Abraham. This is based on an interpretation of *ezrachi* as one who came from the East (*mizrach*). Most Bible translations leave *ha-ezrachi* untranslated or translate it as *ezrahite.*

The event referred to is the Covenant Between the Pieces (Gen. 15) in which God revealed to Abraham that his children would be slaves in Egypt 430 years and that they would be redeemed from there. This revelation may be dated to Passover because of the idea that the Jews were redeemed on the day that the 430 years came to an end., so the decree must also have been on Passover. Cf. *Mekilta de-Rabbi Ishmael* (ed. Lauterbach), *Pisha* 14, p. 112.

52 You knocked at his door, at the heat of the day, on **Passover**
He fed the shining ones matzah cakes on **Passover**
He ran to the cattle, to commemorate
53 the ox, the passage of **Passover**
You shall say, "It is the passover sacrifice" (Exod. 12:27).

52 דְּלָתָיו דָּפַקְתָּ כְּחֹם הַיּוֹם **בַּפֶּסַח**,
הִסְעִיד נוֹצְצִים עֻגוֹת מַצּוֹת **בַּפֶּסַח**,
53 וְאֶל הַבָּקָר רָץ זֵכֶר לְשׁוֹר עֵרֶךְ **פֶּסַח**,
וַאֲמַרְתֶּם זֶבַח פֶּסַח.

54 The Sodomites were angry and burned with fire on **Passover**
Lot was saved from them and he baked matzah at the time of Passover
55 You swept away the land of Moph and Noph when You passed by on **Passover**
You shall say, "It is the passover sacrifice" (Exod. 12:27).

54 זוֹעֲמוּ סְדוֹמִים וְלוֹהֲטוּ בָּאֵשׁ **בַּפֶּסַח**,
חֻלַּץ לוֹט מֵהֶם וּמַצּוֹת אָפָה בְּקֵץ **פֶּסַח**,
55 טִאטֵאתָ אַדְמַת מֹף וְנֹף בְּעָבְרְךָ **בַּפֶּסַח**,
וַאֲמַרְתֶּם זֶבַח פֶּסַח.

Adonai, the first seed You crushed on the night of watching of **Passover**,
Mighty one, You passed over the first-born son for the blood of **Passover**
To prevent the destroyer from entering my doors on **Passover**
You shall say, "It is the passover sacrifice" (Exod. 12:27).

יָהּ, רֹאשׁ כָּל אוֹן מָחַצְתָּ בְּלֵיל שִׁמּוּר **פֶּסַח**,
כַּבִּיר, עַל בֵּן בְּכוֹר פָּסַחְתָּ בְּדַם **פֶּסַח**,
לְבִלְתִּי תֵּת מַשְׁחִית לָבֹא בִּפְתָחַי **בַּפֶּסַח**,
וַאֲמַרְתֶּם זֶבַח פֶּסַח.

52 **You knocked at his door, at the heat of the day** These three lines all refer to the visit the angels made to Abraham (Genesis 18). This being dated to Passover is based on the fact that, immediately after visiting Abraham, the angels visited Lot, who fed them matzah (Gen. 19:3). The sages also interpreted the "cakes" that Abraham served his guests as matzah cakes (*Bereshit Rabbah* 48:12, p. 490). They must have been unleavened bread since they were speedily baked immediately after kneading the dough.

53 **the ox, the passage of Passover** A reference to the reading of the Torah in the synagogue on Passover that, according to mishnaic tradition, began: "When an ox or a sheep or a goat is born . . ." (Lev. 22:27).

54 **The Sodomites were angry** These two lines refer to the angels' visit to Lot (Genesis 19), which took place immediately after their visit to Abraham.

55 **You swept away the land of Moph and Noph** This line and the first three lines of the next stanza refer to the death of the first-born of Egypt and to the Angel of Death passing over the houses of the first-born of the Israelites because they had smeared sacrificial blood on their doorposts. Moph (Memphis) is mentioned as a major city of Egypt. Noph is apparently a variant for the same place, but the *paytan* considers them both appellations for Egypt.

[56]The besieged one fell at the time of **Passover**
[57]Midian was destroyed by a loaf of barley bread of the *omer* on **Passover**
[58]The fat of Pul and Lud were burned in the burning of the fire on **Passover**
You shall say, "It is the passover sacrifice" (Exod. 12:27).

[56]מְסֻגֶּרֶת סֻגָּרָה בְּעִתּוֹתֵי **פֶּסַח**,
[57]נִשְׁמְדָה מִדְיָן בִּצְלִיל שְׂעוֹרֵי עֹמֶר **פֶּסַח**,
[58]שׂוֹרְפוּ מַשְׁמַנֵּי פוּל וְלוּד בִּיקַד יְקוֹד **פֶּסַח**,
וַאֲמַרְתֶּם זֶבַח פֶּסַח.

[59]This same day at Nob He shall stand (Isa. 10:32) until the arrival of the time of **Passover**
[60]A palm of the hand wrote to destroy Babylon on **Passover**
[61]"Light the candle," "Set the table!" (cf. Isa. 21:5) on Passover
You shall say, "It is the passover sacrifice" (Exod. 12:27).

[59]עוֹד הַיּוֹם בְּנֹב לַעֲמוֹד עַד גָּעָה עוֹנַת **פֶּסַח**,
[60]פַּס יַד כָּתְבָה לְקַעֲקֵעַ צוּל **בַּפֶּסַח**,
[61]צָפֹה הַצָּפִית עָרוֹךְ הַשֻּׁלְחָן **בַּפֶּסַח**,
וַאֲמַרְתֶּם זֶבַח פֶּסַח.

56 **The besieged one fell at the time of Passover** Jericho fell on Passover.
57 **Midian was destroyed by a loaf of barley bread** This refers to Gideon's victory over Midian (Judges 7). The victory was foretold by one of the Midianites who saw a "loaf of barley bread was whirling through the Midianite camp. It came to a tent and struck it, and it fell; it turned it upside down, and the tent collapsed" (Judg. 7:13). Some sages understood the loaf of barley to be a reference to the *omer* sacrifice of barley, which is supposed to occur on the second day of Passover (cf. L. Ginzberg, *Legends of the Jews,* CD-ROM ed.).
58 **The fat of Pul and Lud were burned** Pul was a specific king of Assyria (2 Kings 15:19), but the *paytan* called Assyria by this name. Pul is also the name of another nation. Its exact location is unknown, but it is near a nation known as Lud (Isa. 66:19). The *paytan* uses Pul and Lud as an appellation for Assyria and its king, Sennacherib. This reference is to the destruction of Sennacherib's armies as he camped before the city of Jerusalem (2 Kings 19; Isaiah 37). The *paytan* uses the words of the prophecy of Isaiah (10:16) because the *paytan* understood them to refer to the destruction of Sennacherib's armies. There are conflicting opinions among the sages as to whether Sennacherib's destruction was on the first night of Passover, when Hezekiah sat at the seder, or if it was on the second night, after the *omer* had been harvested (see L. Ginzburg, *Legends of the Jews,* 6, p. 200, n. 100).
59 **This same day at Nob He shall stand** This is a continuation of the last line of the previous stanza. It refers to Sennacherib camping at Nov on the way to Jerusalem. Sennacherib did not realize that it was ordained that he camp there so that he would arrive at Jerusalem on Passover, the time meant for salvation and redemption.
60 **A palm of the hand wrote to destroy Babylon** This was the handwriting on the wall, which was explained by Daniel (5:1–30) to be announcing the destruction of Babylon. *Zul* is a paytanic appellation for Babylon.
61 **"Light the candle," "Set the table!"** The *paytan* has reversed the order of the biblical phrase for the sake of the acrosticon. The modern JPS translation for the first expression is

קָהָל כִּנְּסָה הֲדַסָּה לְשַׁלֵּשׁ צוֹם **בַּפֶּסַח**,
רֹאשׁ מִבֵּית רָשָׁע מָחַצְתָּ בְּעֵץ חֲמִשִּׁים **בַּפֶּסַח**,
62שְׁתֵּי אֵלֶּה רֶגַע תָּבִיא לְעוּצִית **בַּפֶּסַח**,
63תָּעֹז יָדְךָ וְתָרוּם יְמִינְךָ כְּלֵיל הִתְקַדֵּשׁ חַג **פֶּסַח**,
וַאֲמַרְתֶּם זֶבַח פֶּסַח.

Hadassah gathered the community for a three-day fast on **Passover**
The head of the house of evil you destroyed by a fifty-cubit tree on **Passover**
62These two things you shall suddenly bring upon Uzit on **Passover**
63Let your hand be strong; Your right hand, exalted as on the night of the hallowing of the festival of **Passover**
You shall say, "It is the passover sacrifice" (Exod. 12:27).

כִּי לוֹ נָאֶה, כִּי לוֹ יָאֶה.

אַדִּיר בִּמְלוּכָה, בָּחוּר כַּהֲלָכָה, גְּדוּדָיו יֹאמְרוּ לוֹ:
לְךָ וּלְךָ, לְךָ כִּי לְךָ, לְךָ אַף לְךָ, לְךָ יי הַמַּמְלָכָה, כִּי לוֹ נָאֶה, כִּי לוֹ יָאֶה.

דָּגוּל בִּמְלוּכָה, הָדוּר כַּהֲלָכָה, וָתִיקָיו יֹאמְרוּ לוֹ:
לְךָ וּלְךָ, לְךָ כִּי לְךָ, לְךָ אַף לְךָ, לְךָ יי הַמַּמְלָכָה, כִּי לוֹ נָאֶה, כִּי לוֹ יָאֶה.

For to Him is it fitting, for to Him is it suitable

Powerful in kingdom, properly chosen, His legions say to Him:
To You and to You, to You for to You, to You even to You, to You, *Adonai,* is the kingdom, For to Him is it fitting, for to Him is it suitable.

Exalted in kingdom, properly glorified, His faithful say to Him:
To You and to You, to You for to You, to You even to You, to You, *Adonai,* is the kingdom, For to Him is it fitting, for to Him is it suitable.

"Let the watchman watch!" (Isa. 21:5). However, the sages understood it to mean "Light the candle" (*Genesis Rabbah,* 63:14, p. 699). This line is the fulfillment of the prophecy in the prior line about the destruction of Babylon. The verse that begins this passage was understood as showing how the Babylonians sat confidently at the table but then were interrupted by the conquering legions of Persia.

62 **These two things you shall suddenly bring upon Uzit on Passover** Uzit is an appellation for Edom (which is, in turn, an appellation for Rome), based on Lamentations 4:21: "Rejoice and exult, Fair Edom, Who dwell in the land of Uz!"

63 **Let your hand be strong; Your right hand, exalted** Based on Psalms 89:14, this is an appeal to God to show His strong hand and redeem His people, as He did on the first Passover celebration.

Pure in kingdom, properly faithful, His angels say to Him:
To You and to You, to You for to You, to You even to You, to You, *Adonai,* is the kingdom, For to Him is it fitting, for to Him is it suitable.

זַכַּאי בִּמְלוּכָה, חָסִין כַּהֲלָכָה, טַפְסְרָיו יֹאמְרוּ לוֹ:
לְךָ וּלְךָ, לְךָ כִּי לְךָ, לְךָ אַף לְךָ, לְךָ יי הַמַּמְלָכָה, כִּי לוֹ נָאֶה, כִּי לוֹ יָאֶה.

Unique in kingdom, properly mighty, His disciples say to Him:
To You and to You, to You for to You, to You even to You, to You, *Adonai,* is the kingdom, For to Him is it fitting, for to Him is it suitable.

יָחִיד בִּמְלוּכָה, כַּבִּיר כַּהֲלָכָה, לִמּוּדָיו יֹאמְרוּ לוֹ:
לְךָ וּלְךָ, לְךָ כִּי לְךָ, לְךָ אַף לְךָ, לְךָ יי הַמַּמְלָכָה, כִּי לוֹ נָאֶה, כִּי לוֹ יָאֶה.

Governor in kingdom, properly awesome, His environs say to Him:
To You and to You, to You for to You, to You even to You, to You, *Adonai,* is the kingdom, For to Him is it fitting, for to Him is it suitable.

מוֹשֵׁל בִּמְלוּכָה, נוֹרָא כַּהֲלָכָה, סְבִיבָיו יֹאמְרוּ לוֹ:
לְךָ וּלְךָ, לְךָ כִּי לְךָ, לְךָ אַף לְךָ, לְךָ יי הַמַּמְלָכָה, כִּי לוֹ נָאֶה, כִּי לוֹ יָאֶה.

Modest in kingdom, properly redeeming, His righteous say to Him:
To You and to You, to You for to You, to You even to You, to You, *Adonai,* is the kingdom, For to Him is it fitting, for to Him is it suitable.

עָנָיו בִּמְלוּכָה, פּוֹדֶה כַּהֲלָכָה, צַדִּיקָיו יֹאמְרוּ לוֹ:
לְךָ וּלְךָ, לְךָ כִּי לְךָ, לְךָ אַף לְךָ, לְךָ יי הַמַּמְלָכָה, כִּי לוֹ נָאֶה, כִּי לוֹ יָאֶה.

Holy in kingdom, properly compassionate, His hosts say to Him:
To You and to You, to You for to You, to You even to You, to You, *Adonai,* is the kingdom, For to Him is it fitting, for to Him is it suitable.

קָדוֹשׁ בִּמְלוּכָה, רַחוּם כַּהֲלָכָה, שִׁנְאַנָּיו יֹאמְרוּ לוֹ:
לְךָ וּלְךָ, לְךָ כִּי לְךָ, לְךָ אַף לְךָ, לְךָ יי הַמַּמְלָכָה, כִּי לוֹ נָאֶה, כִּי לוֹ יָאֶה.

Powerful in kingdom, properly supportive, His perfect ones say to Him:
To You and to You, to You for to You, to You even to You, to You, *Adonai,* is the kingdom, For to Him is it fitting, for to Him is it suitable.

תַּקִּיף בִּמְלוּכָה, תּוֹמֵךְ כַּהֲלָכָה, תְּמִימָיו יֹאמְרוּ לוֹ:
לְךָ וּלְךָ, לְךָ כִּי לְךָ, לְךָ אַף לְךָ, לְךָ יי הַמַּמְלָכָה, כִּי לוֹ נָאֶה, כִּי לוֹ יָאֶה.

He is powerful, He will build His house soon, speedily, speedily, in our times, soon. LORD, build; LORD, build; build Your house soon.

אַדִּיר הוּא יִבְנֶה בֵּיתוֹ בְּקָרוֹב.
בִּמְהֵרָה, בִּמְהֵרָה, בְּיָמֵינוּ בְּקָרוֹב.
אֵל בְּנֵה, אֵל בְּנֵה, בְּנֵה בֵיתְךָ בְּקָרוֹב.

He is chosen, He is great; He is exalted; He will build His house soon, speedily, speedily, in our times, soon.
LORD, build; LORD, build; build Your house soon.

בָּחוּר הוּא, גָּדוֹל הוּא, דָּגוּל הוּא יִבְנֶה בֵּיתוֹ בְּקָרוֹב.
בִּמְהֵרָה, בִּמְהֵרָה, בְּיָמֵינוּ בְּקָרוֹב.
אֵל בְּנֵה, אֵל בְּנֵה, בְּנֵה בֵיתְךָ בְּקָרוֹב.

He is glorious, He is faithful; He is pure; He will build His house soon, speedily, speedily, in our times, soon.
LORD, build; LORD, build; build Your house soon.

הָדוּר הוּא, וָתִיק הוּא, זַכַּאי הוּא יִבְנֶה בֵּיתוֹ בְּקָרוֹב.
בִּמְהֵרָה, בִּמְהֵרָה, בְּיָמֵינוּ בְּקָרוֹב.
אֵל בְּנֵה, אֵל בְּנֵה, בְּנֵה בֵיתְךָ בְּקָרוֹב.

He is pious, He is pure; He is unique; He will build His house soon, speedily, speedily, in our times, soon.
LORD, build; LORD, build; build Your house soon.

חָסִיד הוּא, טָהוֹר הוּא, יָחִיד הוּא יִבְנֶה בֵּיתוֹ בְּקָרוֹב.
בִּמְהֵרָה, בִּמְהֵרָה, בְּיָמֵינוּ בְּקָרוֹב.
אֵל בְּנֵה, אֵל בְּנֵה, בְּנֵה בֵיתְךָ בְּקָרוֹב.

He is mighty, He is wise; He is king, He is awesome; He is protective; He is strong; He is the redeemer; He is righteous, He is holy, He is compassionate, He is Almighty; He is powerful; He will build His house soon, speedily, speedily, in our times, soon.
LORD, build; LORD, build; build Your house soon.

כַּבִּיר הוּא, לָמוּד הוּא, מֶלֶךְ הוּא, נוֹרָא הוּא, סַגִּיב הוּא, עִזּוּז הוּא, פּוֹדֶה הוּא, צַדִּיק הוּא, קָדוֹשׁ הוּא, רַחוּם הוּא, שַׁדַּי הוּא, תַּקִּיף הוּא יִבְנֶה בֵּיתוֹ בְּקָרוֹב. בִּמְהֵרָה, בִּמְהֵרָה, בְּיָמֵינוּ בְּקָרוֹב.
אֵל בְּנֵה, אֵל בְּנֵה, בְּנֵה בֵיתְךָ בְּקָרוֹב.

Who knows one?

I know one. One is God in heaven and on earth.

אֶחָד מִי יוֹדֵעַ?

אֶחָד אֲנִי יוֹדֵעַ: אֶחָד אֱלֹהֵינוּ שֶׁבַּשָּׁמַיִם וּבָאָרֶץ.

Who knows two?

I know two. Two tables of the law; One is God in heaven and on earth.

שְׁנַיִם מִי יוֹדֵעַ?

שְׁנַיִם אֲנִי יוֹדֵעַ: שְׁנֵי לֻחוֹת הַבְּרִית, אֶחָד אֱלֹהֵינוּ שֶׁבַּשָּׁמַיִם וּבָאָרֶץ.

Who knows three?

I know three. Three fathers; two tables of the law; One is God in heaven and on earth.

שְׁלֹשָׁה מִי יוֹדֵעַ?

שְׁלֹשָׁה אֲנִי יוֹדֵעַ: שְׁלֹשָׁה אָבוֹת, שְׁנֵי לֻחוֹת הַבְּרִית, אֶחָד אֱלֹהֵינוּ שֶׁבַּשָּׁמַיִם וּבָאָרֶץ.

Who knows four?

I know four. Four mothers; three fathers; two tables of the law; One is God in heaven and on earth.

אַרְבַּע מִי יוֹדֵעַ?

אַרְבַּע אֲנִי יוֹדֵעַ: אַרְבַּע אִמָּהוֹת, שְׁלֹשָׁה אָבוֹת, שְׁנֵי לֻחוֹת הַבְּרִית, אֶחָד אֱלֹהֵינוּ שֶׁבַּשָּׁמַיִם וּבָאָרֶץ.

Who knows five?

I know five. Five books of the Torah; four mothers; three fathers; two tables of the law; One is God in heaven and on earth.

חֲמִשָּׁה מִי יוֹדֵעַ?

חֲמִשָּׁה אֲנִי יוֹדֵעַ: חֲמִשָּׁה חוּמְשֵׁי תוֹרָה, אַרְבַּע אִמָּהוֹת, שְׁלֹשָׁה אָבוֹת, שְׁנֵי לֻחוֹת הַבְּרִית, אֶחָד אֱלֹהֵינוּ שֶׁבַּשָּׁמַיִם וּבָאָרֶץ.

Who knows six?

I know six. Six orders of the Mishnah; five books of the Torah; four mothers; three fathers; two tables of the law; One is God in heaven and on earth.

שִׁשָּׁה מִי יוֹדֵעַ?

שִׁשָּׁה אֲנִי יוֹדֵעַ: שִׁשָּׁה סִדְרֵי מִשְׁנָה, חֲמִשָּׁה חוּמְשֵׁי תוֹרָה, אַרְבַּע אִמָּהוֹת, שְׁלֹשָׁה אָבוֹת, שְׁנֵי לֻחוֹת הַבְּרִית, אֶחָד אֱלֹהֵינוּ שֶׁבַּשָּׁמַיִם וּבָאָרֶץ.

Who knows seven?
I know seven. Seven days of the week; six orders of the Mishnah; five books of the Torah; four mothers; three fathers; two tables of the law; One is God in heaven and on earth.

שִׁבְעָה מִי יוֹדֵעַ?
שִׁבְעָה אֲנִי יוֹדֵעַ: שִׁבְעָה יְמֵי שַׁבַּתָּא, שִׁשָּׁה סִדְרֵי מִשְׁנָה, חֲמִשָּׁה חוּמְשֵׁי תוֹרָה, אַרְבַּע אִמָּהוֹת, שְׁלשָׁה אָבוֹת, שְׁנֵי לֻחוֹת הַבְּרִית, אֶחָד אֱלֹהֵינוּ שֶׁבַּשָּׁמַיִם וּבָאָרֶץ.

Who knows eight?
I know eight. Eight days till circumcision; seven days of the week; six orders of the Mishnah; five books of the Torah; four mothers; three fathers; two tables of the law; One is God in heaven and on earth.

שְׁמוֹנָה מִי יוֹדֵעַ?
שְׁמוֹנָה אֲנִי יוֹדֵעַ: שְׁמוֹנָה יְמֵי מִילָה, שִׁבְעָה יְמֵי שַׁבַּתָּא, שִׁשָּׁה סִדְרֵי מִשְׁנָה, חֲמִשָּׁה חוּמְשֵׁי תוֹרָה, אַרְבַּע אִמָּהוֹת, שְׁלשָׁה אָבוֹת, שְׁנֵי לֻחוֹת הַבְּרִית, אֶחָד אֱלֹהֵינוּ שֶׁבַּשָּׁמַיִם וּבָאָרֶץ.

Who knows nine?
I know nine. Nine months of pregnancy; eight days till circumcision; seven days of the week; six orders of the Mishnah; five books of the Torah; four mothers; three fathers; two tables of the law; One is God in heaven and on earth.

תִּשְׁעָה מִי יוֹדֵעַ?
תִּשְׁעָה אֲנִי יוֹדֵעַ: תִּשְׁעָה יַרְחֵי לֵידָה, שְׁמוֹנָה יְמֵי מִילָה, שִׁבְעָה יְמֵי שַׁבַּתָּא, שִׁשָּׁה סִדְרֵי מִשְׁנָה, חֲמִשָּׁה חוּמְשֵׁי תוֹרָה, אַרְבַּע אִמָּהוֹת, שְׁלשָׁה אָבוֹת, שְׁנֵי לֻחוֹת הַבְּרִית, אֶחָד אֱלֹהֵינוּ שֶׁבַּשָּׁמַיִם וּבָאָרֶץ.

Who knows ten?
I know ten. Ten commandments; nine months of pregnancy; eight days till circumcision; seven days of the week; six orders of the Mishnah; five books of the Torah; four mothers; three fathers; two tables of the law; One is God in heaven and on earth.

עֲשָׂרָה מִי יוֹדֵעַ?
עֲשָׂרָה אֲנִי יוֹדֵעַ: עֲשָׂרָה דִבְּרַיָּא, תִּשְׁעָה יַרְחֵי לֵידָה, שְׁמוֹנָה יְמֵי מִילָה, שִׁבְעָה יְמֵי שַׁבַּתָּא, שִׁשָּׁה סִדְרֵי מִשְׁנָה, חֲמִשָּׁה חוּמְשֵׁי תוֹרָה, אַרְבַּע אִמָּהוֹת, שְׁלשָׁה אָבוֹת, שְׁנֵי לֻחוֹת הַבְּרִית, אֶחָד אֱלֹהֵינוּ שֶׁבַּשָּׁמַיִם וּבָאָרֶץ.

Who knows eleven?
I know eleven. Eleven stars; ten commandments; nine months of pregnancy; eight days till circumcision; seven days of the week; six orders of the Mishnah; five books of the Torah; four mothers; three fathers; two tables of the law; One is God in heaven and on earth.

אַחַד עָשָׂר מִי יוֹדֵעַ?
אַחַד עָשָׂר אֲנִי יוֹדֵעַ: אַחַד עָשָׂר כּוֹכְבַיָּא, עֲשָׂרָה דִבְּרַיָּא, תִּשְׁעָה יַרְחֵי לֵידָה, שְׁמוֹנָה יְמֵי מִילָה, שִׁבְעָה יְמֵי שַׁבְּתָא, שִׁשָּׁה סִדְרֵי מִשְׁנָה, חֲמִשָּׁה חוּמְשֵׁי תוֹרָה, אַרְבַּע אִמָּהוֹת, שְׁלֹשָׁה אָבוֹת, שְׁנֵי לֻחוֹת הַבְּרִית, אֶחָד אֱלֹהֵינוּ שֶׁבַּשָּׁמַיִם וּבָאָרֶץ.

Who knows twelve?
I know twelve. Twelve tribes; eleven stars; ten commandments; nine months of pregnancy; eight days till circumcision; seven days of the week; six orders of the Mishnah; five books of the Torah; four mothers; three fathers; two tables of the law; One is God in heaven and on earth.

שְׁנֵים עָשָׂר מִי יודע?
שְׁנֵים עָשָׂר אֲנִי יוֹדֵעַ: שְׁנֵים עָשָׂר שִׁבְטַיָּא, אַחַד עָשָׂר כּוֹכְבַיָּא, עֲשָׂרָה דִבְּרַיָּא, תִּשְׁעָה יַרְחֵי לֵידָה, שְׁמוֹנָה יְמֵי מִילָה, שִׁבְעָה יְמֵי שַׁבְּתָא, שִׁשָּׁה סִדְרֵי מִשְׁנָה, חֲמִשָּׁה חוּמְשֵׁי תוֹרָה, אַרְבַּע אִמָּהוֹת, שְׁלֹשָׁה אָבוֹת, שְׁנֵי לֻחוֹת הַבְּרִית, אֶחָד אֱלֹהֵינוּ שֶׁבַּשָּׁמַיִם וּבָאָרֶץ.

Who knows thirteen?
I know thirteen. Thirteen attributes; twelve tribes; eleven stars; ten commandments; nine months of pregnancy; eight days till circumcision; seven days of the week; six orders of the Mishnah; five books of the Torah; four mothers; three fathers; two tables of the law; One is God in heaven and on earth.

שְׁלֹשָׁה עָשָׂר מִי יוֹדֵעַ?
שְׁלֹשָׁה עָשָׂר אֲנִי יוֹדֵעַ: שְׁלֹשָׁה עָשָׂר מִדַּיָּא. שְׁנֵים עָשָׂר שִׁבְטַיָּא, אַחַד עָשָׂר כּוֹכְבַיָּא, עֲשָׂרָה דִבְּרַיָּא, תִּשְׁעָה יַרְחֵי לֵידָה, שְׁמוֹנָה יְמֵי מִילָה, שִׁבְעָה יְמֵי שַׁבְּתָא, שִׁשָּׁה סִדְרֵי מִשְׁנָה, חֲמִשָּׁה חוּמְשֵׁי תוֹרָה, אַרְבַּע אִמָּהוֹת, שְׁלֹשָׁה אָבוֹת, שְׁנֵי לֻחוֹת הַבְּרִית, אֶחָד אֱלֹהֵינוּ שֶׁבַּשָּׁמַיִם וּבָאָרֶץ.

One kid, one kid, that father bought for two *zuzim*, one kid, one kid.

חַד גַּדְיָא, חַד גַּדְיָא
דִּזְבַן אַבָּא בִּתְרֵי זוּזֵי, חַד גַּדְיָא, חַד גַּדְיָא.

And then came the cat, that ate the kid, that father bought for two *zuzim*, one kid, one kid.

וְאָתָא שׁוּנְרָא וְאָכְלָה לְגַדְיָא, דִּזְבַן אַבָּא בִּתְרֵי זוּזֵי, חַד גַּדְיָא, חַד גַּדְיָא.

And then came the dog, that bit the cat, that ate the kid, that father bought for two *zuzim*, one kid, one kid.

וְאָתָא כַלְבָּא וְנָשַׁךְ לְשׁוּנְרָא, דְּאָכְלָה לְגַדְיָא, דִּזְבַן אַבָּא בִּתְרֵי זוּזֵי, חַד גַּדְיָא, חַד גַּדְיָא.

And then came the stick, that hit the dog, that bit the cat, that ate the kid, that father bought for two *zuzim*, one kid, one kid.

וְאָתָא חוּטְרָא וְהִכָּה לְכַלְבָּא, דְּנָשַׁךְ לְשׁוּנְרָא, דְּאָכְלָה לְגַדְיָא, דִּזְבַן אַבָּא בִּתְרֵי זוּזֵי, חַד גַּדְיָא, חַד גַּדְיָא.

And then came the fire, that burned the stick, that hit the dog, that bit the cat, that ate the kid, that father bought for two *zuzim*, one kid, one kid.

וְאָתָא נוּרָא וְשָׂרַף לְחוּטְרָא, דְּהִכָּה לְכַלְבָּא, דְּנָשַׁךְ לְשׁוּנְרָא, דְּאָכְלָה לְגַדְיָא, דִּזְבַן אַבָּא בִּתְרֵי זוּזֵי, חַד גַּדְיָא, חַד גַּדְיָא.

And then came the water, that extinguished the fire, that burned the stick, that hit the dog, that bit the cat, that ate the kid, that father bought for two *zuzim*, one kid, one kid.

וְאָתָא מַיָּא וְכָבָה לְנוּרָא, דְּשָׂרַף לְחוּטְרָא, דְּהִכָּה לְכַלְבָּא, דְּנָשַׁךְ לְשׁוּנְרָא, דְּאָכְלָה לְגַדְיָא, דִּזְבַן אַבָּא בִּתְרֵי זוּזֵי, חַד גַּדְיָא, חַד גַּדְיָא.

And then came the ox, that drank the water, that extinguished the fire, that burned the stick, that hit the dog, that bit the cat, that ate the kid, that father bought for two *zuzim*, one kid, one kid.

וְאָתָא תוֹרָא וְשָׁתָה לְמַיָּא, דְּכָבָה לְנוּרָא, דְּשָׂרַף לְחוּטְרָא, דְּהִכָּה לְכַלְבָּא, דְּנָשַׁךְ לְשׁוּנְרָא, דְּאָכְלָה לְגַדְיָא, דִּזְבַן אַבָּא בִּתְרֵי זוּזֵי, חַד גַּדְיָא, חַד גַּדְיָא.

And then came the slaughterer, who slaughtered the ox, that drank the water, that extinguished the fire, that burned the stick, that hit the dog, that bit the cat, that ate the kid, that father bought for two *zuzim*, one kid, one kid.

וְאָתָא הַשּׁוֹחֵט וְשָׁחַט לְתוֹרָא, דְּשָׁתָה לְמַיָּא, דְּכָבָה לְנוּרָא, דְּשָׂרַף לְחוּטְרָא, דְּהִכָּה לְכַלְבָּא, דְּנָשַׁךְ לְשׁוּנְרָא, דְּאָכְלָה לְגַדְיָא, דִּזְבַן אַבָּא בִּתְרֵי זוּזֵי, חַד גַּדְיָא, חַד גַּדְיָא.

And then came the Angel of Death, who slaughtered the slaughterer, who slaughtered the ox, that drank the water, that extinguished the fire, that burned the stick, that hit the dog, that bit the cat, that ate the kid, that father bought for two *zuzim*, one kid, one kid.

וְאָתָא מַלְאַךְ הַמָּוֶת וְשָׁחַט לְשׁוֹחֵט, דְּשָׁחַט לְתוֹרָא, דְּשָׁתָה לְמַיָּא, דְּכָבָה לְנוּרָא, דְּשָׂרַף לְחוּטְרָא, דְּהִכָּה לְכַלְבָּא, דְּנָשַׁךְ לְשׁוּנְרָא, דְּאָכְלָה לְגַדְיָא, דִּזְבַן אַבָּא בִּתְרֵי זוּזֵי, חַד גַּדְיָא, חַד גַּדְיָא.

And then came the Holy One, blessed be He, and slaughtered the Angel of Death, who slaughtered the slaughterer, who slaughtered the ox, that drank the water, that extinguished the fire, that burned the stick, that hit the dog, that bit the cat, that ate the kid, that father bought for two *zuzim*, one kid, one kid.

וְאָתָא הַקָּדוֹשׁ בָּרוּךְ הוּא וְשָׁחַט לְמַלְאַךְ הַמָּוֶת, דְּשָׁחַט לְשׁוֹחֵט, דְּשָׁחַט לְתוֹרָא, דְּשָׁתָה לְמַיָּא, דְּכָבָה לְנוּרָא, דְּשָׂרַף לְחוּטְרָא, דְּהִכָּה לְכַלְבָּא, דְּנָשַׁךְ לְשׁוּנְרָא, דְּאָכְלָה לְגַדְיָא, דִּזְבַן אַבָּא בִּתְרֵי זוּזֵי, חַד גַּדְיָא, חַד גַּדְיָא.

Bibliography

Athenaeus. *Deipnosophistae.* Edited by Charles B. Gulick. London and Cambridge, Mass.: Loeb Classical Library, 1927–1941.

Bar Ilan, Meir. *The Mysteries of Jewish Prayer and Hekhalot* [in Hebrew]. Ramat-Gan, Israel: Bar Ilan, 1987.

Beit-Arie, Malachi. *Hebrew Codicology.* Jerusalem: Israel Academy of Sciences and Humanities, 1981.

Ben Jehuda Hazan, Rabbi Jacob of London. *The Etz Hayyim.* Edited by Israel Brodie. Jerusalem: Mosad Harav Kook, 1962.

Ben Menahem, Naphtali. "'*Shfokh Chamatkha' ve-nuscha'otav.*" *Mahanayim* 80 (5723 [1963]): 94–95.

Bloch, Moshe Chayim. *Heichal le-divrei Chazal u-pitgameyhem.* New York: Pardes Publishing and Shoulson Press, 1948.

Bokser, Baruch. *The Origins of the Seder: The Passover Rite and Early Rabbinic Judaism.* Berkeley: University of California Press, 1984.

Breuer, J. "Past Tense and Participle in Portrayals of Ceremonies in the Mishnah" [in Hebrew]. *Tarbiz* 56 (1987): 299–326.

Brumberg-Kraus, Jonathan D. "'Not by Bread Alone...': The Ritualization of Food and Table Talk in the Passover 'Seder' and in the Last Supper." *Semeia* 86 (1999): 165–191.

Buber, S., ed. *Eichah Rabbah.* Vilna, 5659 [1899].

Carmichael, Deborah Bleicher. "David Daube on the Eucharist and the Passover Seder." *Journal for the Study of the New Testament* 42 (June 1991): 45–67.

Charles, R. H., ed. *Pseudepigrapha of the Old Testament.* Bellingham, Wash.: Logos Research Systems, 2004.

Cohen, Naomi G. *Philo Judaeus: His Universe of Discourse.* Frankfurt am Main: Peter Lang, 1995.

Davidson, Israel. *Thesaurus of Medieval Hebrew Poetry.* New York: Jewish Theological Seminary, 1924.

Ehrenreich, H. L., ed. *Sefer Hapardes Le-Rashi Z"l.* Budapest, 1924.

Elazar Vormsensis. *Oratio ad Pascam* [in Hebrew]. Edited by Simcha Emanuel. Jerusalem: Sumptibus Societatis Mekize Nirdamim, 2006.

Ferguson, Everett. "The Disgrace and the Glory: A Jewish Motif in Early Christianity." *Studia Patristica* 21 (1989): 86–94.

Finkelstein, L. "The Oldest Midrash." *Harvard Theological Review* 31 (1938): 291–317.

_____. "Pre-Maccabean Documents in the Passover Haggadah." *Harvard Theological Review* 35 (1942): 291–352; 36 (1943): 1–38.

Fleischer, Ezra. "An Early Siddur of the Erez Israel Rite" [in Hebrew]. In *Me'ah She'arim: Studies in Medieval Jewish Spiritual Life in Memory of Isadore Twersky,* edited by Ezra Fleischer, Gerald Blidstein, Carmi Horowitz, and Bernard Septimus, 21–59. Jerusalem: Magnes, 2001.

Fox, Menachem (Harry). "About the History of the Songs *Ehad Mi Yodea* and *Had Gadya* in Israel and among the Nations" [in Hebrew]. *Asufot: Annual for Jewish Studies* 2 (5748 [1988]): 201–226.

Francis, F. O. "The Baraita of the Four Sons." *Journal of the American Academy of Religion* 42 (1974): 280–297. Previously published in *Proceedings of the Society of Biblical Literature* 1 (1972): 245–283.

Frankel, Yonah. *Machzor lepesach*. Jerusalem: Koren, 1993.

Gavra, Moshe. *Studies in the Yemenite Prayerbook*. Vol. 1, *The Passover Haggadah* [in Hebrew]. Kiryat Ono: Institute for the Research of Yemenite Sages and Their Works, 1988.

Glatzer, Mordechai. "The Ashkenazic and Italian Haggadah and the Haggadot of Joel Ben Simeon." In *The Washington Haggadah,* commentary edited by Myron M. Weinstein. Washington, D.C.: Library of Congress, 1991.

Glatzer, Nahum N. *The Passover Haggadah,* 3d rev. ed. English translation by Jacob Sloan. Introduction and commentary based on the commentaries of E. D. Goldschmidt. Including readings on the Holocaust, illustrated with woodcuts from the first illuminated Haggadah, Prague, 1526. New York: Schocken, n.d., c. 1979.

Goldin, Judah. "Not by Means of an Angel and Not by Means of a Messenger." In *Religions in Antiquity: Essays in Memory of Erwin Ramsdale Goodenough,* edited by Jacob Neusner, 413–424. Studies in the History of Religions XIV. Leiden: Brill, 1968.

———. *Studies in Midrash and Related Literature*. Philadelphia: Jewish Publication Society, 1988.

Goldschmidt, E. D. *The Passover Haggadah: Its Sources and History* [in Hebrew]. Jerusalem: Bialik Institute, 1969.

Gruber Fredman, Ruth. *The Passover Seder: Afikoman in Exile*. Philadelphia: University of Pennsylvania Press, 1981.

Guggenheimer, Heinrich. *The Scholar's Haggadah*. Northvale, N.J.: 1995 (first soft-cover ed., 1998).

Haberman, M. "Had Gadya" [in Hebrew]. *Mahanayim* 55 (Erev Pesach 5721 [1961]): 142.

Ha-Haggadah ha-Meduyeket Ish Mazliach. B'nei Brak, Israel: Machon Harav Mazliah, 5758 (1998).

Hauptman, Judith. "How Old Is the Haggadah?" *Judaism* 51:1 (winter 2002): 5–18.

Henshke, David. "The *Midrash* of the Passover *Haggadah*" [in Hebrew]. *Sidra* 4 (1988): 33–52.

Hoffman, Lawrence A. *The Canonization of the Synagogue Service*. Notre Dame, Ind.: University of Notre Dame, 1979.

Houghton Mifflin eReference Suite. Houghton Mifflin, 2001–2004. CD-ROM.

Ilan, Nahem. "*Midrash al Avraham Avinu Ba-Haggadah Shel Pesach shel Yehudei Jerba.*" *Sefunot* 6:21 (5753 [1993]): 167–196.

Italiener, Bruno. *Die Darmstädter Pessach-Haggadah: Codex Orientalis 8 der Landesbibliothek zu Darmstadt aus dem vierzehnten Jahrhundert*. Leipzig: Karl W. Hiersmann, 1927–1928.

Kahana, Menahem I. *Sifre Zuta on Deuteronomy: Citations from a New Tannaitic Midrash* [in Hebrew]. Jerusalem: Magnes, 2003.

Kasher, Menachem M. *Hagadah Shelemah* [in Hebrew]. Jerusalem: Torah Shelema Institute, 1967.

Kulp, Josh. "The Origins of the Seder and Haggadah." *Currents in Biblical Research* 4:1 (2005): 109–134.

Levi, Doro. *Antioch Mosaic Pavements.* Rome: L'Erma di Bretschneider, 1971.

Machzor Vitri. Edited by Aryeh Goldschmidt. Jerusalem: Ozar Ha-Poskim, 5764 (2004).

Meiri, Menahem. *Bet ha-Behirah al Masechet Pesachim.* Edited by Yosef Hacohen Klein. Jerusalem: Machon Ha-Talmud Ha-Yisraeli Ha-Shalem, 5726 (1966).

Newell, William Wells. "The Passover Song of the Kid and an Equivalent from New England." *Journal of American Folklore* 18 (1905): 33–48.

Rabinovitz, Zvi Meir. *The Liturgical Poems of Rabbi Yannai According to the Triennial Cycle of the Pentateuch and the Holidays* [in Hebrew]. Jerusalem: Bialik Institute, 1985.

Rosenthal, L. "*Über zwei handschriftliche Haggadahs.*" *Magazin für die Wissenschaft des Judenthums* 17 (1890): 312–315.

Rovner, Jay. "An Early Passover Haggadah According to the Palestinian Rite." *Jewish Quarterly Review* 90 (2000): 337–396.

_____. "A New Version of the Eres Israel Haggadah Liturgy and the Evolution of the Eres Israel 'Miqra' Bikkurim' Midrash." *Jewish Quarterly Review* 92 (2002): 421–453.

_____. "Two Early Witnesses to the Formation of the Miqra Bikurim Midrash and Their Implications for the Evolution of the Haggadah Text." *Hebrew Union College Annual* 75 (2004): 75–120.

Safrai, Shmuel and Ze'ev Safrai. *Haggadah of the Sages* [in Hebrew]. Jerusalem: Carta, 1998.

Sefer Haminhagim of Rabbi Eisik Tirna. Edited by Shlomoh J. Spitzer. Jerusalem: Machon Yerushalayim, 1979.

Siddur Avodat Yisrael [in Hebrew]. Edited by Yizchak ben Aryeh Yosef Dov [Isaac Seligman Baer]. Tel Aviv: n.p. 1957 (modified facsimile of Roedelheim, 1868).

Siddur R. Saadja Gaon [in Hebrew]. Edited by I. Davidson, S. Assaf, and B. I. Joel. Jerusalem: Mekize Nirdamim, 1941.

Spitzer, Shlomoh J., ed. *Decisions and Customs of Rabbi Shalom of Neustadt* [in Hebrew]. Jerusalem: Machon Yerushalayim, 1977.

Stein, S. "The Influence of Symposia Literature on the Literary Form of the Pesah Haggadah." *Journal of Jewish Studies* 8 (1957): 13–44.

Szmeruk, C. "The Earliest Aramaic and Yiddish Version of the 'Song of the Kid' (Chad Gadya)." In *The Field of Yiddish: Studies in Language, Folklore and Literature,* edited by Uriel Weinreich, 214–218. New York: Linguistic Circle of New York, 1954.

Tabory, Joseph. "*Haggadat Ha-Pesach Ha-Eretz-yisraelit Ba-Tekufah Ha-Byzantit.*" In *Zechor Davar Le-Avdecha: Asufat Ma'amarim Lezecher Dov Rappel,* edited by Shemuel Glick, 489–508. Jerusalem: Michlelet Lifshitz, 2007.

_____. *The Passover Ritual throughout the Generations* [in Hebrew]. Tel Aviv: Hakkibutz Hameuchad, 1996.

_____. "Towards a History of the Paschal Meal." In *Passover and Easter: Origin and History to Modern Times,* edited by Paul F. Bradshaw and Lawrence A. Hoffman, 62–80. Two Liturgical Traditions 5. Notre Dame, Ind.: University of Notre Dame Press, 1999.

Tigay, Jeffrey H. *JPS Commentary on Deuteronomy.* Philadelphia: Jewish Publication Society, 1996.

Weiss, Moshe. "The Authenticity of the Explicit Discussions in Bet Shammai—Bet Hillel Disputes" [in Hebrew]. *Sidra* 4 (1988): 53–66.

Werner, Eric. "Melito of Sardis, the First Poet of Deicide." *Hebrew Union College Annual* 37 (1966): 191–210.

Wieder, Arnold A., "Ben Sira and the Praises of Wine." *Jewish Quarterly Review* 61 (1970): 155–166.

Winter, P. "*Ou Dia Xeir Presbews oude Dia Xeir Serape oude Dia Angelou: Isa lxiii:9* (Gk) (the Septuagint reading for Isaiah 63:9), and the Passover Haggadah." *Vetus Testamentum* 4 (1954): 439–441.

The Works of Philo: Complete and Unabridged. Translated by C. D. Yonge. Peabody, Mass.: Hendrickson, 1993.

Yudlov, Isaac. *The Haggadah Thesaurus: Bibliography of Passover Haggadot from the Beginning of Hebrew Printing until 1960* [in Hebrew]. Jerusalem: Magnes Press, 1997.

Yuval, Israel J., "Easter and Passover as Early Jewish Christian Dialogue." In *Passover and Easter: Origin and History to Modern Times,* edited by Paul F. Bradshaw and Lawrence A. Hoffman, 106–107. Two Liturgical Traditions 5. Notre Dame, Ind.: University of Notre Dame Press, 1999.

———. *"Two Nations in Your Womb": Perceptions of Jews and Christians* [in Hebrew]. Tel Aviv: Am Oved, 2000.

Zetterholm, Karin. *Portrait of a Villain: Laban the Aramean in Rabbinic Literature.* Leuven, Belgium: Peeters, 2002.

Zion, Mishael and Noam Zion. *Halaila Hazeh Haggadah.* Jerusalem, 2004.

Zucker, Shlomo. *The Moskowitz Mahzor of Joel Ben Simeon.* Jerusalem: Jewish National and University Library, 2005.

Illustrations

אור לארבע עשר
בודקין את
החמץ · ולא
בודקין לאור החמה ולא לאור ה
הלבנה ולא לאור האבוקה · אלא
בנר של שעוה · ובודקין בחורין
ובסדקין ובכל המקומות שדרכו
להשתמש בו שם · ולא יתחיל
שום מלאכה עד שיבדוק ואפילו
בתלמוד תורה · וקודם שיתחיל
לבדוק מברך

ברוך אתה יי אלהינו מלך
העולם אשר קד
קדשנו במצותיו וצונו על ביעור ה
חמץ:

ולא ידבר בין הברכה לתחילת הבדיקה כלל · ואחר
הבדיקה ישמור החמץ בתיבה או יתלנו באויר מקום
שאין עכבר שולט בו שם ויבטלנו ויאמר

כל חמירא וחמיעא דאיכא
ברשותי די לא חמיתיה
ודי לא ביערתיה לבטל ולהוי פ.
כעפרא דארעא:

A page from the 1526 Prague haggadah, which contains the blessings for ridding the home of leaven before Passover. This was the first-ever illustrated haggadah, with all art printed from woodcuts. Though the border here was likely borrowed from a gentile printer, the small woodcut at the top right was made specifically for this haggadah. The picture shows a Jew about to begin the search for leaven in his home, with the aid of a candle, a feather with which to pick up crumbs, and bowl to contain them.

הלילות אנו אוכלין בין
יושבין ובין מסבין הלילה
הזה כלנו מסבין׃

עבדים היינו
לפרעה
במצרים ויוציאנו יי אלהינו
משם ביד חזקה ובזרוע
נטויה ואלו לא הוציא הקב
את אבותינו ממצרים הרי
אנו ובנינו ובני בנינו משעב
דים היינו לפרעה במצרים
ואפילו כלנו חכמים כלנו
נבונים׳ כלנו זקנים׳ כלנו

הזוק לישב בהסיב
דבשאר ימות השנה
אבל או שותה אפילו
מקומר׳ אבל בלילה
הזה אין אפילו עני
שבישרא׳ לא יאכל
עד שישב׳ רוקח

רש בטיט

וחרוסת בל אדמי׳
הם ירקות הרבה ש
שמתתין יחודיו וקם
וקורין אותו חרוסת
וחרוסת שלנו צריך
לעשות עב וכימנן
זכר לטיט׳ ולקחו
תפוחים שבאם תחת
והתפוח עודרתיך׳
לקחו קירה בת יד
החרוסת כענין תבלין זכר לתבן שבחומר
ולקחו אגוזים שנאמר אל
גינת אגוז ירדתי׳
ירדתי זהו יש
ישרא׳׳

וכשהוא יושב לא יטה על גבו ולא
על פניו ולא על ימינו אלא על שמ
שמאלו ודשי פי׳ הטעם שלא
יקדים קנה לוושט לפי זה
אין חילוק בין איטר
לאחר׳
יודעים

A page from the 1526 Prague haggadah highlighting the song "Avadim Hayinu," celebrating that while Jews were once slaves, they are now free and can help make the world a better place. The top woodcut shows a man leaning on his chair, and the text starting above (and continuing on the bottom left) states the obligation for people to recline at the Passover seder. The woodcut on the lower right, of a man hoeing for clay, represents the haroset, a food that symbolizes the clay used by the Jewish slaves in their construction work. The text below it explains the haroset.

The frontispiece of the 1711 Sulzbach haggadah. Above the title, two angels hold a portrait of King David with his harp, with a rendering of the Binding of Isaac below. Moses and Aaron stand on either side of the book's title, their figures copied from the 1695 Amsterdam haggadah. The Amsterdam haggadah was the first to print illustrations from copperplates. It was common for later haggadot to copy the illustrations in the 1695 haggadah because they were so visually stunning, but many people came to feel that the original high quality of these images was diminished by poor-quality reproductions.

הגדה

אַדִּיר הוּא יִבְנֶה בֵיתוֹ בְּקָרוֹב * בִּמְהֵרָה בִּמְהֵרָה בְּיָמֵינוּ בְּקָרוֹב · אֵל בְּנֵה אֵל בְּנֵה בְּנֵה
בֵיתוֹ בְּקָרוֹב : בָּחוּר הוּא יִבְנֶה בֵיתוֹ בְּקָרוֹב * בִּמְהֵרָה בִּמְהֵרָה בְּיָמֵינוּ בְּקָרוֹב *
אֵל בְּנֵה אֵל בְּנֵה בְּנֵה בֵיתוֹ בְּקָרוֹב : גָּדוֹל הוּא : דָּגוּל הוּא : יִבְנֶה בֵיתוֹ בְּקָרוֹב * בִּמְהֵרָה
בִּמְהֵרָה בְּיָמֵינוּ בְּקָרוֹב * אֵל בְּנֵה אֵל בְּנֵה בְּנֵה בֵיתוֹ בְּקָרוֹב : הָדוּר הוּא : וָתִיק הוּא :
זַכַּאי הוּא : חָסִיד הוּא : יִבְנֶה בֵיתוֹ בְּקָרוֹב · בִּמְהֵרָה בִּמְהֵרָה בְּיָמֵינוּ בְּקָרוֹב * אֵל בְּנֵה אֵל
בנה

צורת ב"ה ועיר ירושלים תוב"ב אכי"ר

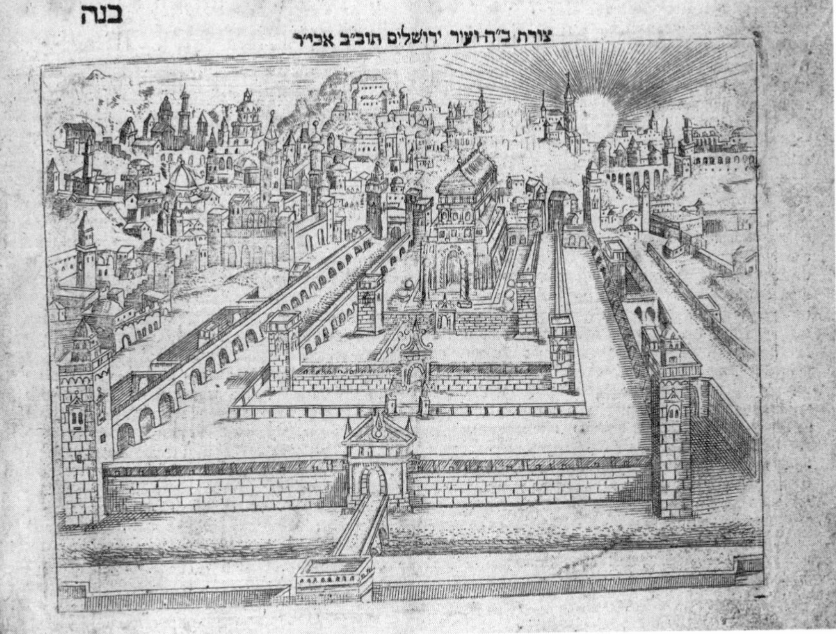

The "Adir Hu" prayer, a hymn that expresses hope for the rebuilding of the Temple, appears over a rendering of Jerusalem and the Temple. This image is from the 1711 Sulzbach haggadah, reproduced from the 1695 Amsterdam haggadah. The unique script on the upper half of the page, Rashi font, frequently used in the design of Jewish commentaries, was first used in one of the earliest printed books, the commentary of Rashi published in 1473; it was meant to look like the handwriting used for copying books at that time.

VISPERA de PESACH

Acoſtumbran amaſſar los ſimurim luego deſpues de baldar el leudo y apartaran la Hala y dira.

BENDICION de HALA

בָּרוּךְ אַתָּה יְיָ אֱלֹהֵינוּ מֶלֶךְ הָעוֹלָם
אֲשֶׁר קִדְּשָׁנוּ בְּמִצְוֹתָיו וְצִוָּנוּ
לְהַפְרִישׁ חַלָּה :

ברוך

A page from the haggadah section of *Sefer ha-Minhagim*, published in Ladino in Amsterdam in approximately 1767. The picture portrays the baking of matzah, illustrating the blessing for separating out the challah, which is done just before the matzah is baked. It was common for Jewish families during this period to own prayer-books that contained the services and rituals for all the holidays of the Jewish year. Thus, the haggadah was often a section of a larger book, not only the stand-alone text with which many contemporary Jews are familiar.

ספר

שבח פסח

פה ליוורנו יע"א

שנת למרבה המשרה לפ"ק

בדפוס המשכיל כמוהר"ר אליעזר סעדון נר"ו

Con Approvazione.

The title page of a 1790 haggadah from Livorno. The text in the upper half on the page appears in Rashi font, a style of type that was commonly used in Jewish commentaries of the time. Toward the bottom, a grandiose design, most likely the publisher's logo, is featured.

סדר
מרבה לספר
והוא
הגדה של פסח.

Vortrag
für die beiden Abende
des
Überschreitungsfestes;
mit Beifügung aller Gebräuche.
Ganz neu in's Déutsche übersetzt
von
M. I. LANDAU.

ויבא משה ואהרן אל פרעה (שמות ז׳ י׳).

PRAG.
Druck und Verlag des M. I. Landau.

1849.

The cover of a haggadah published in Prague in 1849 by Moses Israel Landau, a well-known printer and publisher, and a leader in the Prague Jewish community. Along with the Hebrew and German titles that appear here is an artist's rendering of Moses and Aaron pleading with the Pharaoh to free the Israelite slaves.

חסל סדור פסח כהלכתו • ככל משפטו וחקתו • כאשר
זכינו לסדר אותו • כן נזכה לעשותו : זך שוכן
מעונה • קומם קהל עדת מי מנה • בקרוב נהל נטעי
כנה • פדוים לציון ברנה :

לשנה הבאה בירושלים :

בליל ראשון אומרים זה ובכן ויהי בחצי הלילה :
אז רוב נסים הפלאת בלילה • בראש אשמורת זה הלילה •
גר צדק נצחתו כנחלק לו לילה : ויהי בחצי הלילה :

אברבנאל

אז רוב נסים הפלאת בלילה • שנאמר ליל שמורים הוא לה' וגו' הוא הלילה לה' לילה המשומר הבא מששת ימי בראשית לצורך גאולתם של ישראל והרבה נסים נעשו לאבותינו בזה הלילה ואומר ומונה והולך : בראש אשמורת • קאי על ויהי באשמורת הבוקר : גר צדק • אברהם נקרא גר צדק והיה מנצח את נמרוד שהש"י הצילו מכבשן האש שנאמר אשר הוצאתיך מאור כשדים :

נצחתו • ע"ש לשון המדרש אי אברם נצח מן דאברם אנא וזה נעשה באותו לילה שרדף את המלכים ונחלק לו לילה שנאמר ויחלק עליהם לילה ואמרינן במדרש מאי ויחלק יולדו חלקו אמר הקב"ה אברהם פעל עמי בחצי הלילה אף אני אפעול עם בניו בחצות הלילה ואימתי במצרים שנאמר ויהי בחצי הלילה וגו' וזה היה בליל פסח וכן זה נעשה באותו לילה כי בפסח נולד אברהם ולסוף ג' שנים

A page from a 1878 haggadah published in Vilna. The closing verses of the seder, "*Le-Shanah ha-ba'ah be-Yerushalyim*" (Next year in Jerusalem), are followed by a rendering of the Egyptians being drowned in the Sea of Reeds after the Israelites have safely crossed. Underneath this picture is commentary by Isaac Abravanel, the well-known 15th-century philosopher, commentator, and statesman.

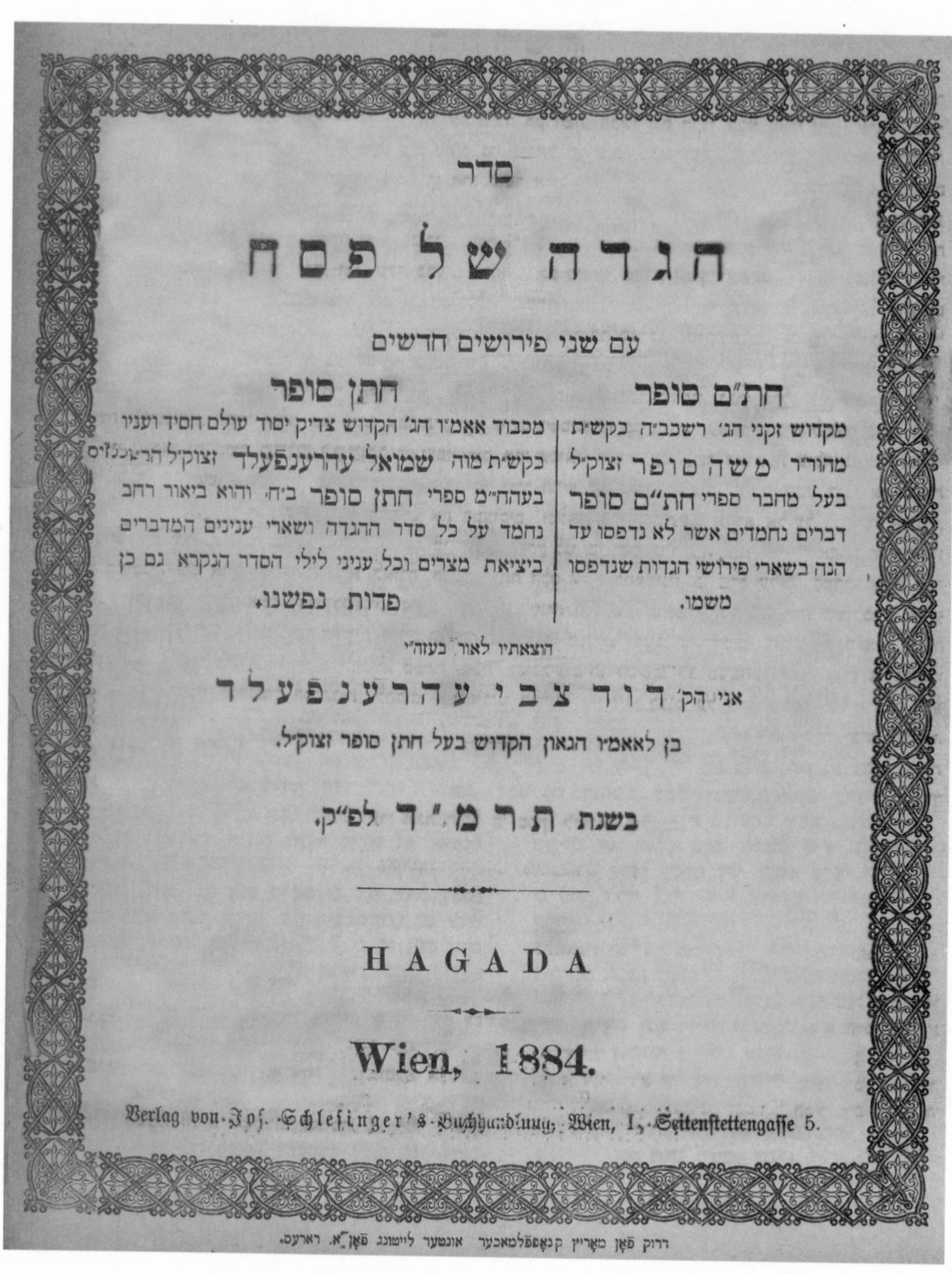

סדר

הגדה של פסח

עם שני פירושים חדשים

חת״ם סופר

מקדוש זקני הג׳ רשכב״ה בקש״ת מהור״ר **משה סופר** זצוק״ל בעל מחבר ספרי **חת״ם סופר** דברים נחמדים אשר לא נדפסו עד הנה בשארי פירושי הגדות שנדפסו משמו.

חתן סופר

מכבוד אאמ״ו הג׳ הקדוש צדיק יסוד עולם חסיד ועניו בקש״ת מוה **שמואל עהרענפעלד** זצוק״ל הר״כ״לז״ס בעהח״מ ספרי **חתן סופר** ב״ח. והוא ביאור רחב נחמד על כל סדר ההגדה ושארי ענינים המדברים ביציאת מצרים וכל עניני לילי הסדר הנקרא גם כן פדות נפשנו.

הוצאתיו לאור בעזה״י

אני הק׳ **דוד צבי עהרענפעלד**

בן לאאמ״ו הגאון הקדוש בעל חתן סופר זצוק״ל.

בשנת **תרמ״ד** לפ״ק.

HAGADA

Wien, 1884.

Verlag von Jos. Schlesinger's Buchhandlung, Wien, I., Seitenstettengasse 5.

דרוק פאָן מאריץ קנאפפלמאכער אונטער לייטונג פאָן א. ראעס.

The title page of a haggadah published in Vienna in 1884 by a grandson of the Hatam Sofer, a leading commentator and Orthodox rabbi of both the late 18th and early 19th centuries. This haggadah contains the commentaries of both the Hatam Sofer, which are in the right-hand column of the page, and those of his son-in-law, the Hatan Sofer, the father of the publisher, in the left-hand column.

Anordnung für den Sedertisch.

Die Sederschüssel wird ähnlich der nebenstehenden Abbildung angeordnet. Sie soll enthalten:

a b c. Die drei Mazzoth in den drei Abteilungen der Sederschüssel. (Wenn keine Sederschüssel vorhanden ist, dann werden die drei Mazzoth, jede für sich verdeckt, übereinander gelegt.)

d. grünes Kraut כַּרְפַּס: Petersilie, Radieschen o. dgl.,

e. ein Näpfchen mit Salzwasser,

f. Bitterkraut מָרוֹר: Meerrettich (Kren), Salat o. dgl.,

g. Latwerge חֲרוֹסֶת: ein Mus aus Äpfeln, Nüssen und Zimmt, mit Wein angerührt.

h. ein Knochen mit ein wenig Fleisch daran זְרוֹעַ, auf Kohlen gebraten,

i. ein Ei בֵּיצָה, in der Schale gebraten.

Der Sedertisch wird noch vor Einbruch der Dämmerung geordnet.

Die Reihenfolge der beim Seder zu befolgenden Handlungen wurde in folgenden hebräischen Sprüchen zusammengefasst:

1 קַדֵּשׁ, Kiddusch-Gebet.

2 וּרְחַץ: Händewaschen des Sedergebenden.

3 כַּרְפַּס, Genuss der Petersilie.

4 יַחַץ: Teilung der mittelsten Mazza zum Aphikoman.

5 מַגִּיד, Erzählung des Auszuges aus Ägypten.

6 רָחְצָה: Händewaschen sämtlicher Tischgenossen.

7 מוֹצִיא מַצָּה: Segenssrüche vor der Mazza.

8 מָרוֹר, Genuss des Bitterkrautes.

9 כּוֹרֵךְ: Ausführung der Vorschrift Hillels.

10 שֻׁלְחָן עוֹרֵךְ: Abend-Mahlzeit.

11 צָפוּן, Essen des Aphikoman.

12 בָּרֵךְ: Tischgebet nach de Mahlzeit.

13 הַלֵּל, Vortrag der Hallel Psalmen.

14 נִרְצָה: Schluss-Gesang.

This page from a 1936 Viennese haggadah shows the order of the seder in German and Hebrew. Tiered seder plates, similar to the one depicted here, have been popular over the years because they allow room on a crowded table for the three matzot.

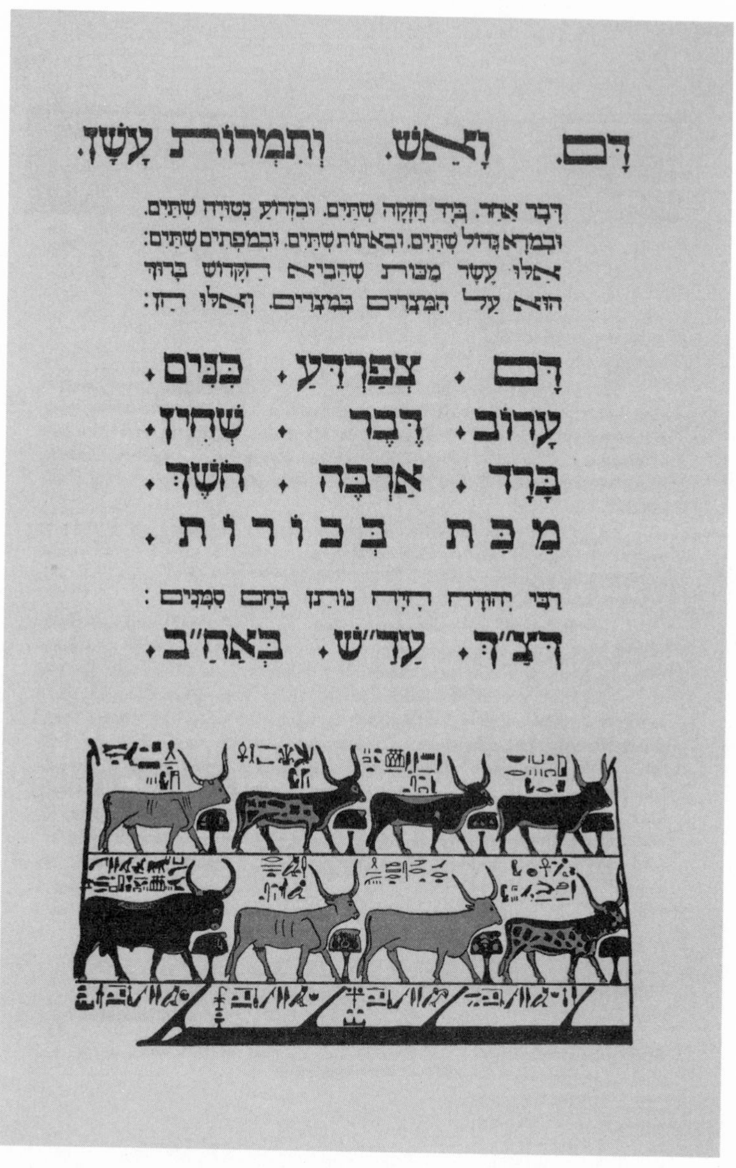

דם. ואש. ותמרות עשן.

דבר אחר. ביד חזקה שתים. ובזרע נטויה שתים.
ובמורא גדול שתים. ובאתות שתים. ובמפתים שתים:
אלו עשר מכות שהביא הקדוש ברוך
הוא על המצרים במצרים. ואלו הן:

דם. צפרדע. כנים.
ערוב. דבר. שחין.
ברד. ארבה. חשך.
מכת בכורות.

רבי יהודה היה נותן בהם סמנים:
דצ״ך. עד״ש. באח״ב.

The Ten Plagues, written in Hebrew (above) and Hungarian (left-hand page), from a 1942 haggadah published in Hungary, most likely in Budapest, by the National Hungarian Jewish Aid Action. By 1942, the Hungarian government had allied with Hitler, passing anti-Semitic legislation, drafting Jewish men into forced labor camps, and deporting thousands of Jews who would ultimately meet their deaths at the hands of the SS. The Egyptian motif was most likely meant to evoke the feeling that Hungary's Jews were linked to the oppressed slaves of ancient Egypt, a feeling that was likely all too real for the Jews who used this haggadah.

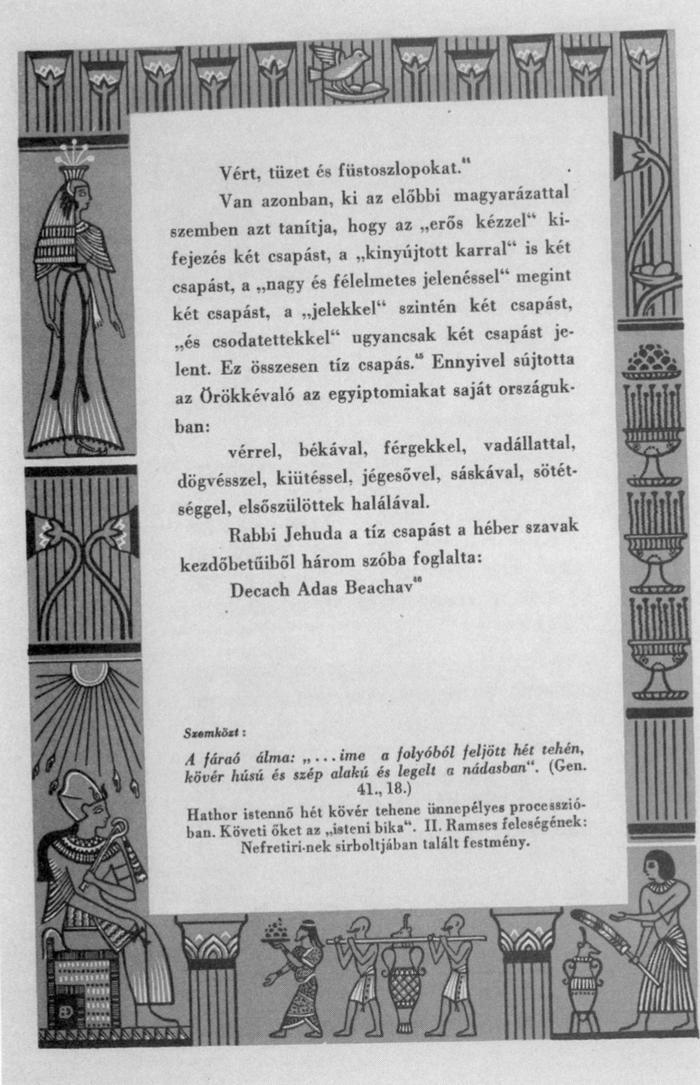

Vért, tüzet és füstoszlopokat."

Van azonban, ki az előbbi magyarázattal szemben azt tanítja, hogy az „erős kézzel" kifejezés két csapást, a „kinyújtott karral" is két csapást, a „nagy és félelmetes jelenéssel" megint két csapást, a „jelekkel" szintén két csapást, „és csodatettekkel" ugyancsak két csapást jelent. Ez összesen tíz csapás.[45] Ennyivel sújtotta az Örökkévaló az egyiptomiakat saját országukban:

vérrel, békával, férgekkel, vadállattal, dögvésszel, kiütéssel, jégesővel, sáskával, sötétséggel, elsőszülöttek halálával.

Rabbi Jehuda a tíz csapást a héber szavak kezdőbetűiből három szóba foglalta:

Decach Adas Beachav[46]

Szemközt:

A fáraó álma: „... ime a folyóból feljött hét tehén, kövér húsú és szép alakú és legelt a nádasban". (Gen. 41., 18.)

Hathor istennő hét kövér tehene ünnepélyes processzióban. Követi őket az „isteni bika". II. Ramses feleségének: Nefretiri-nek sirboltjában talált festmény.

רשב"ם הגדה של פסח רש"י

השתא הכא. לשנה הבאה בארעא דישראל. השתא עבדי לשנה הבאה בני חורין:

מה נשתנה הלילה הזה מכל הלילות. שבכל הלילות אנו אוכלין חמץ ומצה. הלילה הזה כולו מצה: שבכל הלילות אנו אוכלין שאר ירקות. הלילה הזה כולו מרור: שבכל הלילות אין אנו מטבילין אפילו פעם אחת. הלילה הזה שתי פעמים: שבכל הלילות אנו אוכלין בין יושבין ובין מסבין. הלילה הזה כולנו מסבין:

דעת זקנים מבעלי התוספות

של"ה

עוקרין

פיסקא

The Four Questions, as depicted in a page from a 1944 haggadah from Jerusalem. The design is reminiscent of a page of Talmud, with the main text surrounded by various commentaries.